CW00798631

CRIME IN
MEDIEVAL EUROPE

CRIME IN MEDIEVAL EUROPE 1200–1550

TREVOR DEAN

Longman

An imprint of **Pearson Education**

Harlow, England · London · New York · Reading, Massachusetts · San Francisco
Toronto · Don Mills, Ontario · Sydney · Tokyo · Singapore · Hong Kong · Seoul
Taipei · Cape Town · Madrid · Mexico City · Amsterdam · Munich · Paris · Milan

PEARSON EDUCATION LIMITED

Head Office:
Edinburgh Gate
Harlow CM20 2JE
Tel: +44 (0)1279 623623
Fax: +44 (0)1279 431059

London Office:
128 Long Acre
London WC2E 9AN
Tel: +44 (0)20 7447 2000
Fax: +44 (0)20 7240 5771
Website: www.history-minds.com

First published in Great Britain in 2001

© Pearson Education, 2001

The right of Trevor Dean to be identified as Author
of this Work has been asserted by him in accordance
with the Copyright, Designs and Patents Act 1988.

ISBN 0 582 32676 1

British Library Cataloguing in Publication Data
A CIP catalogue record for this book can be obtained from the British Library

10 9 8 7 6 5 4 3 2 1

Set in 10.5/13pt Galliard
Typeset by Graphicraft Limited, Hong Kong
Printed and bound in Great Britain by Biddles Ltd.,
Guildford and King's Lynn

The Publishers' policy is to use paper manufactured from sustainable forests.

Cities and individuals alike, all are by nature disposed to do wrong, and there is no law that will prevent it, as is shown by the fact that men have tried every kind of punishment, constantly adding to the list, in the attempt to find greater security from criminals . . . In the course of time the death penalty became generally introduced. Yet even with this, the laws are still broken.

(Thucydides, History of the Peloponnesian War, *trans. R. Warner, Harmondsworth, 1972, III.45, p. 220)*

CONTENTS

LIST OF ILLUSTRATIONS

PREFACE

The core of this book is the history of England, France and Italy, and there are excursions into Scotland, the Low Countries, Spain, Sweden, Germany and Poland. This balance partly reflects the availability of sources and studies across Europe: the history of crime is much more developed in England and France than in many other countries. Other historians, with different backgrounds, would write a different book with different emphases. This is my version. I have endeavoured, within the scope of this type of book, to draw in as much as possible, and from as far as possible, and to avoid a reliance on the Italian experience. It has to be admitted that more time (ten years?) would have produced a longer book, one that would be very different and probably better. In order to meet the challenge of writing this book, I have resisted drawing very much on my own research into crime and justice in Bologna and Ferrara (although new material from both cities is certainly present). I hope that in doing this I have not disappointed readers looking for Italian material.

I have tried in this book to draw on the benefits of comparative history, while hoping to avoid the dangers. I have certainly not made myself equally expert in the history of all the countries covered in this book, and I hope that local historians, in judging my effort to use material with which they are more familiar, will remember the comparative historian's answer, as once formulated by Marc Bloch: local historians have an advantage of expertise over me, but I have one advantage over them, which is that I have read works on similar matters in other European countries and have tried to draw inspiration from them.[1] I hope also to have avoided the fate of some other Italian historians when they have attempted to extend their coverage to Europe generally. Jacques Heers' books, on family clans and on factions, spring to mind: reviewers variously noted the limitations of applying a model based on Genoa (the site of his Italian research) to the rest of the continent or described his work as 'mostly an essay on Italy, supplemented by samples from other parts of Europe'.[2]

I am very grateful to the following: to the Institute of Historical Research, the Warburg Institute and the British Library, for simply being there; to students past and present on module HISH20.038 'Crime in Britain and Europe 1200–1500', for stimulating discussion of some of the issues dealt with here; and to my colleagues in the History Department, University of Surrey Roehampton, who enabled me to take study leave to complete this book. Professor Paul Brand kindly read and commented on the first chapter. The book has also benefited from the comments of Professor David Bates, the Series Editor, for which I am grateful.

Trevor Dean

Notes

1. 'A contribution towards a comparative history of European societies', in *Land and Work in Mediaeval Europe: Selected Papers by Marc Bloch*, trans. J.E. Anderson (Berkeley and Los Angeles, 1967), p. 51.
2. Philip Jones in *History*, 64 (1979), p. 448.

EDITOR'S PREFACE

Trevor Dean's *Crime in Medieval Europe* is an exceptionally valuable addition to the Medieval World series. Ambitious in its scope, it ranges geographically across most of western Europe, takes into account several distinct national historigraphies which have followed notably different agenda, and adopts a multi-dimensional perspective on the twin themes of crime and punishment. The result is a book which is not just a splendid guide to a host of topics, but also one whose lucid comparative appraisal of historical, anthropological and literary approaches to the subject provides a Europe-wide panorama where one did not previously exist.

Professor Dean persuasively explores what was defined as crime between the thirteenth and fifteenth centuries and how punishment was inflicted according to changing and regionally distinctive ideas and conditions. While the predominant emphasis is on crime and punishment as societally constructed phenomena, much is also said about how both were articulated through law and justice. The book skilfully combines illustrations drawn from primary sources with wider processes of change. Thus, for example, it tackles in an original way that long move away from private remedies and personal or communal revenge towards justice administered through courts of law which characterises the whole medieval and early modern periods. A survey of differences between English jury-based and continental inquisitorial and torture-based procedures and verdicts not only puts another nail in the coffin of the idealism which once characterised the history of English law and emphasises a number of trans-European similarities, it brings together a great deal of discussion of the all-pervasiveness of what we would now call corruption. Complex issues such as the volume of crime, female involvement in crime, crimes against women and the treatment of female victims and offenders, the role of capital punishment, imprisonment and monetary penalties all have their place in the book. The notion of university towns as particularly unruly places is questioned. Above all, there is a consistent attempt to penetrate beyond the limitations of court records to the realities of such matters as the nature of crime, the circumstances of criminals and their victims and the protection which privilege provided. The final chapter provides an important discussion of how literary theory can assist the exploitation of Late Medieval literature, such as Boccaccio's *Decameron* and the Robin Hood ballads, to gain insights into the book's central themes.

A distinguished historian of later medieval Italy, Trevor Dean has here splendidly utilised his familiarity with legal records to write a wide-ranging book which is European in scope. Aware of the technical and conceptual difficulties of the sort of comparative history on which a book of this kind has to be based, he presents arguments with a notable clarity and certainty throughout. On a broad perspective, the book tackles big issues such as state formation, national differences and gender roles. While Foucault's idea that one of the great transforming characteristics in the history of the modern state was the replacement of public ritualised punishment by imprisonment and a concentration on the criminal's mind is shown to be seriously flawed, the importance of penance and ritual as part of punishment in the Later Middle Ages is nonetheless given due emphasis. A concluding comparison between the so-called Late Medieval and Early Modern worlds sets the seal on a book which is notably rich in ideas and material.

DAVID BATES

ABBREVIATIONS

AHDE   *Anuario de historia del derecho español*
ORF   *Ordonnances des rois de France* (23 vols, Paris, 1723–1849)
RHDF *Revue historique de droit français et étranger*
TRG   *Tijdschrift voor rechtsgeschiedenis*

chapter 1

COURTS, CRIMES
AND CAUSES

O n a Saturday night in December 1352, a group of seven men, Gascons and Catalans, were returning from the market in Toulouse, the major city of the Languedoc region of southern France. Some forty miles from Toulouse, they stopped at an inn in the village of Mireval. After dinner, two of the men had an argument about a sum of money that one claimed the other owed him. A dagger was drawn. None of the others present saw the fatal blow, but they heard the victim cry out 'He's killed me, the traitor', and they saw the blood gushing from his belly. The victim survived for a few days, and then died. Physicians were called in from the nearby town of Castelnaudary to certify that he had died of the knife-wound. By this stage legal proceedings were in train. The suspect claimed to have acted in self-defence. Witnesses agreed that the victim had started the quarrel earlier in the day. However, the suspect had previous convictions for murder and theft, and was tortured by the judges. Consequently he confessed to the crime. Though his fate is not recorded, a confession of this sort would have been sufficient to incur the death penalty.[1]

In December 1421, Arnald van Harsill was indicted before the sheriffs and coroner of London for killing John Bene, a London armourer, some six months previously. He had stabbed him with a knife, 'in the left part of the breast . . . the wound being two inches long, one inch wide and in depth to the heart'. John Bene had died immediately. Arnald pleaded not guilty and accepted trial by jury. A jury was summoned, but instead of giving a simple verdict, the jurors declared on oath

that the said Arnald and John were sitting together on a seat in a tavern called 'The Moyses', when abusive words, begun by John, arose between them concerning John's concubine, and that John drew a dagger and attacked Arnald, who did his best to flee, whereupon John pursued him to a wall behind the inn-door, and threw him down and fell on him, repeatedly striking at him with his dagger, and that Arnald, being in great danger of death and unable to escape unless he defended himself, drew a knife and struck John in the left part of the breast, of which John died.

Asked specifically if Arnald could have escaped in any other way, the jurors said not. So Arnald was sent back to prison to await the king's pardon: in effect he had pleaded the excuse of self-defence, and the jury accepted this.[2]

From London we return to the south of France. In 1353 a woman of Mireval and two of her female neighbours were washing their clothes in the stream. She left a cloak to dry on a frame. When she returned to fetch it, it had gone. A few days later a shepherd reported that a vagabond had been seen in a village carrying the cloak. The woman's husband went to the village, entered the tavern and saw a young man with the cloak next to him on a stool. The husband had the youth arrested and summoned to the court in Mireval. The suspect was 15, but this was not, as he admitted, his first time in court for theft. However, he maintained that on this occasion he was innocent. He said that he had bought the cloak on the road from two poor travellers, and he insisted that he had arrived in Mireval on the day after the theft. Asked where he got his boots from, he said that he had won them gambling. The court did not accept his statements, and banished him from Mireval for three months.[3]

Back once more in London, in January 1417 'Edmund ate Chapell' of Finsbury was indicted before the sheriffs and coroner of robbing John Stowe of Norwich at the end of December of a white horse, four bolts of cloth, a knife, a fur and other goods. He pleaded not guilty, and opted for jury trial. A jury was summoned and was sworn in. They said on oath that Edmund was guilty, so he was sentenced to death by hanging.[4]

Rural France is obviously a very different place from urban England: its social, economic, political and administrative structures are entirely dissimilar. A big city that was a port and a capital had a range of activities and functions that was completely alien to the limited world of a village and its peasants. Mireval was in the Lauragais area of the Haut Languedoc in what is now the *département* of Aude. This was a strongly agrarian area, producing wine, grain and, already by the early fifteenth century, the pastel dyestuffs that later attracted merchants from both Toulouse and over the border from Spain. In the mid-fourteenth century, the village population was probably to be numbered in a few hundreds, but today it is too small a place even to warrant a presence on most commercial maps and has been administratively fused with the nearby village of Laurabuc. To judge from the wills made in the Lauragais in the later Middle Ages, it was a poor area: a high proportion of will-makers left bequests to the poor; a very low proportion could afford anniversary masses or funeral meals. Although Mireval was part of the domain of the county of Toulouse, in effect part of the royal domain, criminal justice was administered not by royal officials, but by local 'consuls'.[5] London, by contrast, was 'a vigorous, crowded capital city' of some 40,000 inhabitants, one of the larger cities of northern Europe.[6] Both port and capital, London fused many functions together, with a separate abbey and royal palace at Westminster, with busy wharves lined with ships, with shops and taverns along crowded streets, with dozens of guilds and a strong service economy ranging from wholesale trading to brewing and brothel-keeping, with a population of alien merchants and artisans from Germany, Italy and Flanders, with wide disparities of wealth and status, from the royal court and the houses of the nobility and mercantile elite, to the mass of poor servants and casual workers.

London and Mireval thus offer an extreme contrast of social and institutional context, the one a large, wealthy, successful city, the other a small, obscure village. As we shall also see, the criminal laws and procedures applied were very different. And yet the criminality seems qualitatively very similar. Can this be true? This problem of the possible regional variation in criminality will occupy us later in this chapter (pp. 23–5). Other features of these cases will also recur in this and later chapters: crime as a gendered activity committed predominantly by men, with women more frequently victims than perpetrators (p. 23, and Chapter 4); the common practice of carrying knives (pp. 20, 22); the use of torture (pp. 15–16); and the association of 'vagabonds' with crime (pp. 50–2). This handful of cases also shows some of the typical contexts within which crimes of violence arose: arguments between men over money or women set off confrontations, often in taverns, that led to bloody injury and death. Yet the way that courts in the various parts of Europe dealt with these conflicts varied. In England a jury of local men simply gave a verdict, apparently without much in the way of hearing evidence or witnesses, and the judge issued the sentence which, in the case of felonies such as homicide, could only be death. In many parts of continental Europe, the judge did interrogate the suspect, and question the witnesses. Where the witnesses' statements strongly incriminated the suspect but were inconclusive, as in the first case from Mireval, the judge could use torture to discover the truth. However, an immediate question is whether these different judicial methods led to different outcomes.

Some English contemporaries certainly thought so. In the 1460s, Sir John Fortescue, a former chief justice of England then in exile in France, wrote a short work 'in praise of the laws of England'. In the course of this, he sought to establish the excellence of English trial procedures by contrasting them to those of France. The damning feature of French criminal justice, according to Fortescue, was the ease with which the innocent could be condemned to punishment. On the one hand, what might be called the 'two-witnesses-and-you're-out' rule meant that any two men, motivated by fear, favour or greed, could secure the conviction of innocent people by privately agreeing a story in advance and then by perjuring themselves in court. On the other hand, the use by judges of cruel torture induced the innocent to confess to any crime and led the guilty to make false accusations against others. The first of these features was condemned by Fortescue as 'wicked' and the latter as 'a pathway to hell'.

In contrast, he presents the English system of trial by jury as a guarantor of impartiality and truth. Jurors cannot easily be corrupted, he argues, because they are local property-holders, not greedy paupers. Suspects can object to individual jurors, who will then be replaced, thus ensuring impartiality. The fact that witnesses have to deliver their statements before a jury of twelve neighbours, who know them and their credibility, ensures that false charges cannot easily be sustained. 'Now, is not this procedure for revealing the truth better and more effective?', Fortescue asks: a question that supposes only one answer. The use of neighbours, 'sound in repute and fair-minded', is thus contrasted to the use of suborned witnesses, 'unreliable hirelings, paupers, vagrants'. 'Who then in England can die unjustly for a crime, when he can have so many aids in favour of his life, and none save his neighbours . . . can condemn him?'[7]

Fortescue thus describes English and French trial procedures in terms of opposites: on the one hand, we have the corruption of witnesses and the use of torture; on the other, judgment by fair-minded neighbours. Such conclusions, that English jury trials are 'fair' while foreign judge-led trials are 'unfair', persist in the modern world, surfacing whenever a British citizen is accused of serious crime in a foreign court. Despite the many changes since Fortescue's day, his sense of the innate superiority of this island's institutions remains with us today. In England, we are frequently told, everyone is 'innocent until proven guilty'; on the continent, by contrast, a suspect has to prove his innocence. The adversarial and inquisitorial systems, it has recently been observed, differ in their fundamental assumptions on the best way of going about things. The one puts its faith in 'the dialectical process of persuasion involved in courtroom procedure', while the other trusts the state and its officials to pursue truth 'unprompted by partisan pressures or individual self-interest'.[8] Yet popular participation in justice through the jury and the presumption of innocence are not historically unique to England. In the late medieval kingdom of Mallorca, for example, courts were composed of royal judges accompanied by local 'goodmen' (prohombres) who were present at inquests and participated in sentencing. In some parts of Italy, judges were assisted in framing sentences by groups of local men, elected for the purpose, or chosen at random from prepared lists. In Sweden, too, local juries of twelve free men were the 'dominant form of proof'.[9] The principles of due process, such as the presumption of innocence, were an important part of continental learned law in the later Middle Ages, and the tag 'better to leave one criminal unpunished than to condemn an innocent man' in fact came from classical Roman-law texts and was recycled by medieval Roman lawyers.[10] The presumption of innocence was not a part of the rhetoric of English law before Fortescue. So when he claimed that it was better to free one guilty felon than to hang a hundred innocent men, he was appropriating, as an exclusive feature of English law, a principle of medieval continental law.

However, English law *was* clearly distinct from much continental law in many ways. From the twelfth century onwards, English criminal law and procedure had diverged from much of continental Europe. The resulting common-law system appears to continental lawyers as an 'erratic block, different, unexpected, strange'.[11] The key difference lies in the reception and influence of Roman law: without this as an anchor and inspiration, English law developed its own categories and methods, which vested much more influence in judges and custom, and much less in codified legislation or learned lawyers. However, this divergence, though it made real differences, also conceals a broader convergence of general development. In general terms the late twelfth and thirteenth centuries in Europe saw two movements of change, one relating to trial and proof, the other to punishment. Until that point, crimes had come to court mainly through private accusation, and the parties were adversaries. The right to bring the accusation belonged to the victim or his family, and the trial took the form of a debate: both parties had to be present, the accuser stated his case, and the defendant responded. The court appointed what it regarded as an appropriate method of proof, either compurgation (the defendant and his 'oath-helpers' swore to his innocence) or an ordeal of fire, water or combat. Settlement was in the form of composition, or compensatory payments fixed by a detailed local tariff of injuries. As Mario Sbriccoli has put it, there were essentially three parties to such trials: plaintiff, defendant and judge. The initiative lay with the plaintiff and the defendant; the judge listened, mediated, settled.[12]

In the late twelfth and thirteenth centuries, three general developments disturbed this method of seeking redress for wrongs. First, there was a general retreat from the ordeal, as university-trained lawyers promoted 'a procedure based on evidence and argument', which supplanted the appeal to God by the ordeal. This was made authoritative in 1215 by the 4th Lateran Council of the Catholic Church, which prohibited the participation of clerics in ordeals. This forced secular courts to turn to other means of proof, generally inquest or testimony.[13] Alongside this, the growth of royal power led to the emergence of denunciation as a means of prosecuting criminals: now the victim reported the crime, but the state took over the prosecution. Lastly, inquisitorial procedure was added to the judicial armoury, with its distinctive features of torture and prosecution *ex officio*. The latter allowed judges to prosecute suspects without having received a specific complaint from the victim, and merely on the basis of the notoriety of the crime. The three parties to a trial were thus reduced to two, the accused and the judge; and the judge not only made inquiries but also acted as inquisitor.

England both shares in and stands slightly outside this general trend: even before the late twelfth century, English law had moved away from treating serious crimes as wrongs to be settled by payment of compensation, and was using juries to denounce ('present') serious criminals. Subsequently, it rapidly substituted jury verdicts for the ordeal, extending the role of juries from denunciation to trial, but it stopped short of adopting inquisitorial methods (except in some special courts). In lesser crimes the initiative was left to the injured party to bring a complaint to the royal court in an action for 'trespass'. (Trespass was much broader than the modern 'entering without consent', and encompassed a range of crimes against the person and against property. The Latin term for 'trespass' was *transgressio* or transgression, and this better suggests its scope.) Trespasses were also put to jury trial, except in local courts. In France the mid-thirteenth century sees the appearance of denunciation, torture and proof through inquest, and at the same time proof by combat was banned (by a famous ordinance of King Louis IX in 1260). In northern Italy, denunciation of serious crimes came to be made through elected local officials, while the list of crimes subject to inquisition steadily lengthened. Already in the 1220s in Italy there was complaint about judges' readiness to use torture. The gradual effacement of private accusation has been traced in Bologna: from being the dominant mode of prosecution in the first half of the thirteenth century, it was a minor mode by the end of the century and rare by 1400.[14] In Castile, inquest was already by the thirteenth century prescribed as proof for serious crimes in some municipal laws, and in some towns 'inquirers' (*pesquisidores*) were annually appointed (five or six 'good, well-informed men who fear God'). *Ex officio* prosecutions appear in the mid-thirteenth century, largely as a result of royal legislation (Alfonso X's *Especulo* and *Siete partidas*). The broadly common development was thus towards state prosecution of major crimes, in lists that varied from place to place, but might include homicide, house-breaking, rape and sodomy.[15]

Court structure and criminal trial procedure varied in complexity. The simplest structures are found in the northern Italian city-states. Here, cities tended to centralise jurisdiction in their territories: local judges in small towns and villages would have jurisdiction only in minor cases, for example criminal damage, while the city court of the *podestà* dealt with all serious crimes, including theft. As for trial procedure, there was a distinction between crimes where inquisitorial methods could be used and those where it could not, but this distinction tended to disappear as inquisition came to be applied to most categories of crime. In both England and France, court structure and trial procedure were more complex. In England there was an overlapping structure of local, county and central courts, and an evolving pattern of central supervision and intervention in the shires. At first, in the late twelfth and thirteenth centuries, royal judges were sent out from the central courts on circuits of groups of counties (so-called 'justices in eyre', the word 'eyre' deriving, via Old French, from the Latin *iter*, journey). After this system broke down through overload in the years around 1300, a combination of central and local judges eventually took its place: central judges on circuit and local 'Justices of the Peace' in each county held regular court sessions, with the JPs increasingly receiving powers to try cases without the presence of judges from the central court (though these would still generally be required to try major crimes). Procedure varied according to the manner of initiation of proceedings. In felony trials, the suspect would be arrested and held in custody pending trial, could be outlawed if failing to appear in court, and, if convicted, suffered the uniform penalty of death and confiscation of property. Definition of what constituted felony was not altogether fixed, but by 1300 felonies included treason, homicide, arson, rape, robbery, burglary and grand larceny (that is, theft exceeding 12*d* in value). On the other hand, action for trespass was a form of action for damages: the case was brought into the royal courts because the plaintiff claimed that the injury done to him or his property was done 'in breach of the king's peace'. Under an action for trespass, the defendant would not be arrested at first (though might be later), but was simply summoned to appear, and might be sentenced to 'amercement', that is, put in the king's mercy from which he would have to free himself by payment, or imprisonment pending payment of a fine. The interests of the king in punishing a breach of the peace, and the interests of the injured party in securing damages, were thus combined and satisfied together.

In France, likewise, both structure and procedure were complex. One level of structural differentiation lay in the possession of 'high justice'. Seigneurial lords with this jurisdiction had the power to try the worst crimes and to impose the death penalty. The king was just one 'high justicier' among many, having the same rights on his lands as other lords on theirs. This constitutes an essential point of difference from England, where nearly all courts were royal courts and all officials royal officials. However, the king of France as king also had broader interests and responsibilities than he did as seigneur, and he claimed other categories of crime for his own adjudication, wherever they were committed: attempts on the person or authority of the king (*lèse-majesté*), the counterfeiting of royal coins, the breaking of royal safeguards, armed assembly and crimes on the public highway. In practice, these categories were susceptible to considerable expansion by royal judges. Royal safeguards, for example, covered numerous groups and places: the king's servants and officials, his court and army, travelling merchants, markets and universities, as well as specifically protected individuals. In addition, the king's court in Paris, the Parlement, could receive appeals from lower courts, including those of seigneurs. However a case came to court, whether by accusation, denunciation or notoriety, the judge could proceed in one of two ways: using ordinary procedure, with proceedings in public, allowing the suspect a full defence, and with proof by witnesses and inquest; or using extraordinary procedure, in secret, using torture, and limiting the suspect's defence. In cases initiated by denunciation, the public prosecutor (*procureur du roi*) combined with the injured party (*partie civile*), the one demanding punishment, the other seeking damages.[16]

Within this general picture of transition from accusation to denunciation and inquisition, the pace and extent of change varied considerably. Judicial systems continued to mix new and old elements, as new methods of prosecution and punishment combined with older methods of composition and settlement.[17] Not least as a factor was local and aristocratic resistance to change. In Aragon, torture and inquisition were not accepted into law: it was part of the 'General Privilege' that the king would not hold inquiries in any case nor use torture, though by the early fourteenth century this was apparently subject to numerous exceptions – inquisitions could be held in cases of counterfeiting, sodomy or crimes against officials, while foreigners, vagabonds and men of infamous condition could be tortured. In Catalonia, the Cortes of Barcelona forced the king to retreat from the use of inquisition and to re-establish the principle for all crimes of prosecution by the injured party alone. In Nuremberg accusation remained common in the fourteenth century, with *ex officio* prosecution appearing in 1325, but not for homicide until 1381. Prosecutions for homicide or mutilation in Hainault could be brought only by the victim or his family until as late as 1410, when the count of Hainault allowed his *bailli* to initiate prosecution if the injured party did not. In the nearby city of Ghent, attempts by the *baillis* to introduce torture in the thirteenth century prompted the city government to complain to their ruler, the count of Flanders, who conceded in 1297 that his *bailli* was not to torture any townsman without their consent. In Poland, private prosecution for murder remained the rule until the early sixteenth century, and one writer on Polish law declared 'it is the very foundation of our freedom that the king does not prosecute'. Some kings dealt summarily with such 'freedoms'. Take the example of King Alfonso of Aragon: having conquered the southern Italian kingdom of Naples in the 1440s, he then set about restoring law and order through the use of Spanish police constables endowed with powers to arrest, try and execute suspects; and in 1456 he responded forthrightly to a baronial demand in parliament that the right to prosecute should belong, except in the most serious cases, to the injured party alone. This request Alfonso refused, 'because it is contrary to public good, as many heinous crimes would remain unpunished'. This, as we shall see, became a common argument of rulers seeking to expand their power to punish.[18]

The progress of inquisitorial methods was slowest in the Germanic world. Because of the absence of a central authority of the type developing in France or England, the abolition of the ordeal left only 'a bewildering variety of procedural techniques'.[19] Suspects still had the customary right to defend themselves by swearing an oath, or by presenting oath-helpers to swear to their innocence. Change came through restricting that right, for example by assimilating the suspect to a culprit caught in the act (who was not allowed to swear away his guilt), or by treating the suspect as infamous and therefore liable to summary conviction by the oath of the court officials. In addition, the key inquisition elements of torture, *ex officio* prosecution and proof by rational inquiry, began to appear, in some places in the thirteenth century, but more generally in the fourteenth. Nevertheless, though prosecution was in the hands of officials, it was not professionalised: in cities the investigating panel was still drawn from the civic councillors and did not form a professional magistracy. It was not until the end of the fifteenth century that Emperor Maximilian promoted a strengthening of judicial power, through use of torture and reducing the role of local juries. In the Tirol, for example, inquisition was being used in the late fifteenth century, but it generated protest, especially regarding torture, custody, secrecy and the rapidity of trials.[20]

In France, too, inquisitorial procedure was seen as an erosion of privileges by both towns and nobility. In 1347 the city of Lyon complained that the royal officials there were inquiring into all crimes, without an accusation or denunciation, whereas it was local custom to limit inquisition to cases of theft, homicide and treason. Nobles too saw denunciation and proof by witnesses as an attack on their 'freedoms', which in their case meant accusation, judgment by peers and proof by combat. In a *cause célèbre* of about 1260, Louis IX tried to proceed by inquest against a nobleman, Enguerran de Coucy, for having summarily hanged three children who had been seized shooting arrows at rabbits in Enguerran's forest. Enguerran, supported by an array of prominent barons, argued that he should not be subject to inquest and offered combat instead, but in a lively exchange the king argued that in such cases, involving the poor and defenceless, combat was inappropriate and unequal, and he declared adamantly that he was not going to let Enguerran's noble status or the power of his friends stop him doing full justice. Alarm bells began to ring among the French aristocracy at such claims, and these are echoed in a contemporary poem addressed to the feudal nobility:

> You're no longer free, you've been put right out of your freedoms, for you're being judged by inquest. You've all been cruelly deceived and betrayed, as no defence can any longer come to your aid. *Douce France*: we can't call you that any more: you're a land of subjects, enserfed and defenceless, exposed to countless acts of violence.

Aristocratic resistance also led the nobles of Burgundy and Champagne to demand, in a general movement of reaction against royal power in 1314–15, assurances that they would not be prosecuted by denunciation nor judged by inquest. As part of the same adherence to separate means of proof, combat, far from dying out following its prohibition in 1260, continued. And everywhere in fact, private accusation remained one way for injured parties to prosecute offenders: the numbers of accusations remained small, but they showed little sign of disappearing – indeed in late fifteenth-century England they seem to have increased.[21]

But what difference did these changes make to the prosecution of crime? At first sight, modern quantitative research might seem to confirm Fortescue's argument that Roman-law procedures led to the conviction of the innocent. There are two ways to examine these figures: to look either at conviction rates or at acquittal rates. Conviction rates in some continental courts appear to be high, and in English courts low. However, we have to beware of procedural differences in registering what counts as a 'conviction'. A major difference is the readiness of Roman-law courts to convict in absence: where the suspect absconded and failed to appear in court, his flight was taken as a confession of guilt and the judge proceeded to give sentence. Thus, in Milan between 1385 and 1429 nearly 3,000 suspects were tried in the court of the *podestà*, or chief judge, and of these over 2,000 were convicted in absence.[22] The English equivalent was the outlawry of fugitive offenders, but this is not counted as 'conviction'. The picture from conviction rates is therefore unclear; much clearer is the picture from acquittal rates. In Milan 20 per cent of suspects were acquitted (600). Contrast the very high rates of acquittal in English courts. In the Midlands counties studied by Edward Powell for the years 1400–29 acquittals occurred in over 70 per cent of cases; and similar figures have been produced for jury trials in Yorkshire in the 1360s and in other counties in the first half of the fourteenth century.[23] The English jury had a strong tendency to acquit. This tendency, however, was selective, not indiscriminate, and did not extend to thieves and 'notorious' criminals, whom juries more readily declared guilty.

It is unclear, and unlikely, that this preference for acquittal was related to impartiality and a desire for the truth. Fortescue's vision of the security and soundness of juries has been wiped out by historical studies that have revealed either the corruption of juries or their selective attitudes. What we know of the influence that could be brought to bear on jurors and the ways that they reached their decisions together destroy any faith in Fortescue's idealistic picture.

Historians have easily found all manner of complaints against corrupt jurors: they took money for giving favourable verdicts or for ensuring that indictments were not made, while local officials are often criticised for packing juries, receiving false indictments or concealing crimes. In addition, jurors could be pressured – intimidated, threatened, terrorised – by the local gentry or by criminal gangs.

It is instructive to listen to complaints and legislation regarding jurors in civil litigation. Legislation in 1285 (the second Statute of Westminster) attempted to remedy the oppression of the people by sheriffs who put on jury panels 'men who are ailing, decrepit, permanently or temporarily incapacitated and even men not living in the district'. Fifteen years later a further enactment stipulated that sheriffs were to put on juries 'the nearest, the most suitable and the least suspect', suggesting that there were still abuses in the empanelling of jurors. The offence of assaulting jurors for telling the truth was sufficiently serious in the early fourteenth century to be added to special commissions of inquiry appointed to investigate 'enormous' crimes; and Parliament in 1315 complained of 'conspirators' in every city and district who were bound together by oaths, and drew jurors into their conspiracy so as to ensure that they gave the verdicts they wanted. In Yorkshire it was alleged that juries were made up of poor people 'who do not dare to tell the truth for fear of the great'.[24] Were similar problems present in the practice of criminal juries?

Even if they were not subject to such extreme pressure, criminal jurors still worked within a framework of local social expectations and influence.

Although there was a difference in function and personnel between juries of 'presentment' and juries of trial, these social attitudes affected the work of both, albeit in different ways. When asked to name those suspected of felony, presenting jurors engaged in a sort of social calculus, screening out those who had committed only one theft, for example, or focusing on 'habitual petty offenders', or discriminating by gender. When trial jurors came to make their verdicts, their own idea of fairness rather than the law's idea of justice seems to have prevailed: 'repeated theft or burglary (which caught the victim off-guard) was unfair; unexpected killing in a fair fight was not'. Juries convicted accordingly: as we have seen, Arnald's version of his fight with John Bene was endorsed by the London jurors. Social status, local standing, gender and fairness all came into play as juries named suspects and found verdicts: 'indictment was more a question of influence and access than of objective reporting of crime'.[25]

Three problems have especially exercised historians of the English jury. When asked to present those suspected or reputed of felonies, how did jurors know who these were? When asked to decide the guilt of suspects, how did trial jurors find out? And why did they acquit so many felons?

Powell's answer to the first problem is that jurors relied on a mixture of information from victims, complainants and local officials, especially as any of these might themselves be jurors. However, not all information was treated equally: a gentleman would be taken at his word in alleging a felony committed by a commoner, but stronger evidence would be needed to support allegations by commoners against gentlemen. It has been said that indictments give us only a 'gentleman's-eye view' of crime. Answers to the second and third problems, of verdicts and acquittals, have to be taken together. In his influential work on the jury, Greene answers these problems by reference to the penalty for felony and to community standards of behaviour. The penalty for felony was death: the distinction in law between excusable and inexcusable killing was narrow; and the definition of felonious theft was rigid (anything above one shilling in value). Excusable homicide required a royal pardon; and all thefts above one shilling in value had to incur the death penalty. However, juries' view of what was excusable was more generous than the law's. While acknowledging the guilt of some suspects, jurors did not believe that they deserved to die for their offence: as a result they would either acquit or would find some way of re-grading the offence, by valuing goods stolen at one shilling or less, or by declaring that a killing had been done in self-defence. Community values were thus asserted against the values of royal law, or, in Greene's formulation, juries 'nullified' the law of felony.

However, this image of juries acquitting in the face of the evidence has been challenged. It has been pointed out that juries often acquitted because of a *lack* of evidence: though they were supposed to know the facts of the case, as residents near the scene of the crime, it turns out that they rarely lived in the village where the crime was committed. The jury was thus not local, and jurors were not neighbours in a strict sense of the term. Studies of jury composition have revealed that, although some jurors came from the hundred where the crime was committed, there was increasingly little correlation between jurors' residence and location of the crime. So how did trial juries decide guilt or innocence? Two further elements of courtroom practice point to an answer: the hearing of evidence and the length of trials. The presentation of evidence and the hearing of testimony in court seem not to be common until the late fifteenth century. Although one late thirteenth-century text suggests that suspects were directly and aggressively questioned by judges, we have to wait until the fifteenth century for the presentation and examination of evidence to become common in English criminal trials. The implication is that criminal trials in the later Middle Ages were generally conducted at 'breakneck speed'. Jury trials were over quickly, and were not drawn out by the lengthy examination of witnesses; nor did juries withdraw for long deliberations of their verdicts. What this means instead is that they decided cases on the reputation and demeanour of suspects. 'Juries decided cases as much on the basis of the prisoner's general reputation as on that of the specific charges against him' says McLane, echoing Maitland ('Trial by jury must have been in the main trial by general repute'). Indeed, from the very beginning of their history in the 1220s, it has been said that juries' verdicts were 'assertive and non-evidentiary', in other words were based not on evidence or testimony, but on assertion and reputation.[26]

Juries, far from naturally disclosing the truth, could thus act as obstacles in the search. Two examples, one from a chronicle, one from a court record, illustrate the problem. In 1249 some merchants of Brabant complained to King Henry III of being robbed of a large sum of money in Hampshire, which was a county busy with traders owing to the presence of the port at Southampton and the royal palace at Winchester. The suspects were arrested and tried, but were acquitted by the jury. When the merchants persisted in their complaint, the king took advice from his counsellors and was surprised to learn that attacks on travellers were rife in Hampshire, that the visiting royal justices had failed to 'cleanse' the county, that there was a conspiracy to conceal crimes from justice and that even jurors were the 'partners and accomplices' of the robbers. The king summoned the sheriff and freemen of the county, and sternly told them that no county in England was so contaminated with criminality and that the stench of it was disgusting and shaming. Under threats of severe action, twelve jurors were chosen to reveal the names of the thieves. They refused to do so. This threw the king into a fury of rage: he ordered them to be bound tightly and thrown into a dungeon. Another jury was chosen. This second group, fearing the worst, finally yielded up some names. Among the thirty or so subsequently arrested and hanged were men of apparently good reputation and considerable wealth, even some chaplains and archers of the king's own household.[27]

The second example takes us to London in 1379. The coroner and sheriff of London were holding an inquest into the death of a Genoese man, one Janus Imperial. At first, all that the jurors would say was that he had been killed on the night of 26 August by unknown malefactors. They were given the weekend to find out who these were and how it had happened. They returned on the Monday still claiming to know nothing, so were given another month to try again. When they reappeared they were able to give a detailed account: Janus had been sitting outside his house chatting to his servants, when two men, John Kirkby and John Algor, passed by and one of them 'unwittingly' trod on Janus's feet; an argument ensued, in which Algor drew a knife and attacked Janus's servants; when Janus tried to calm the situation down, Kirkby dealt him several blows to his head and face with a sword, including two fatal wounds, each seven inches long and deep into his brain. However, though the jury acknowledged that Kirkby killed Janus, they claimed that it was not with malice aforethought, and they tried to reduce his culpability by making the initial contact an accident ('trod unwittingly'). When Kirkby and Algor were brought for trial in March 1380, the trial jury declared that Algor was not guilty and that Kirkby had killed in self-defence. But when questioned by the judges how this was self-defence, they said they did not know! This verdict seems to have been overruled, as the order was given for Kirkby to be hanged. Such a case seems to show the jury as an obstacle to royal justice: the inquest jury wanted to pass the killing off as homicide by unknown hands, but only the insistence of the sheriff and coroner got them to discover or concoct a satisfactory narrative; the subsequent trial jury wanted to exonerate the killer by transforming what looked like an overheated reaction to a street quarrel into a killing in self-defence.[28]

Two cases, separated by over a century in time, do not of course prove that this sort of behaviour was either widespread or frequent. Moreover, both cases involve crimes against foreign merchants, and this might be thought to limit their significance. They can, however, be connected to more general complaints of 'conspiracies' to conceal crimes or to influence juries, and they do reveal something of the mechanisms and prejudices of local opinion, which could operate just as discriminately against other social groups. Though exceptional, these two cases illustrate the general tension between the values of royal justice and those of local communities, as reflected by juries. Juries wanted to protect local men of standing against complaints from outsiders; royal justice wanted to ensure that all crimes were punished. In both cases the findings of juries had to be overridden in the interests of justice. The jury was thus not necessarily an agent of truth at all. It remains to consider whether French and other continental procedures were any different.

The first 'damnable' element of French procedure was its use of torture. Judicial torture is indefensible in the modern world, although violence in the course of interrogation was not unknown even in the twentieth-century West. Historians of medieval Europe are often at pains to dispel the assumption that torture was used indiscriminately and carelessly. It is quite common to point out that torture was subject to strict regulation. There had to be strong suspicion, circumstantial evidence close to proof or some eye-witness testimony before a suspect could be 'put to the question' (the usual formulaic phrase, meaning 'tortured'). Torture had to be applied moderately and on one occasion only. The interrogation had to relate to offences already known about (interrogators could not go on 'fishing expeditions' for as yet unsuspected crimes). The use of torture had to be authorised beforehand by judicial authorities. Any confession made under torture was not legally valid until ratified by the suspect outside the torture room. These rules constituted guarantees against the capricious use of torture. Everything, it has been said, was fixed: who could be tortured, the types of crimes, the place and time of torture, the need for witnesses, the status of the confession. Some legislation even specified how questions under torture should be posed:

> 'You, so-and-so, do you know anything of the death of so-and-so? Now, say what you know, and don't fear that they will do anything to you, except what is legal.' And the judge should not ask if he killed him, nor mention anyone else by name . . . as such a question would not be good, as it could give him the opportunity to tell lies.[29]

Legal reform in Germany in the 1490s included instructions on 'How to conduct examination under torture': 'the law officers are instructed not to torture if there is an easier way to get at the truth; to use reason and restraint lest the investigation be worse than the crime'.[30] Lawyers and judges recognised the perils of leading questions posed to a suspect in pain. Further in defence of torture, we might use the comparative argument expressed by Samuel Johnson: faced with an ingratiating Dutchman, who was eager to praise justice in England and to condemn that in Holland for its inhuman use of torture, Johnson replied:

> The torture in Holland is considered as a favour to an accused person; for no man is put to the torture there, unless there is as much evidence against him as would amount to conviction in England.[31]

None of this, it might be countered, was enough. It was not only in cases of exceptional crimes, such as witchcraft in the sixteenth and seventeenth centuries, that these strict rules were laid aside. Leading questions and the hunt for previous offences were routine. In a study of theft trials in Venice, it was found that torture was normal in such cases, that the prior suspicions were merely generic and unspecific, that torture was repeated or excessive, breaking bones or distorting limbs, and that deaths did result from its use. Some suspects clearly confessed to anything in order to end the pain.[32] In fourteenth–fifteenth century Paris, too, torture seems to have been much used in the trials of thieves and robbers. Contemporaries were very much aware of the danger that torture might pervert justice. The notaries' guild of Florence, for example, petitioned the government in 1346 about the use of torture 'contrary to the dictates of law and equity', and complained that as a result the truth is not discovered and 'many each year are unjustly condemned to death, who can more properly be said to be killed than judged'.[33] Historians have also focused on the psychological drama of the torture room, and on the isolation of the suspect in his experience of pain, in the trials of brigands in Provence in the 1430s and of Jews in Trent in 1475.[34]

However, it remains to be shown how far torture was a routine part of late medieval criminal trials. Claude Gauvard has argued against seeing torture as systematic in late medieval France. The Parlement of Paris intervened in lower courts to end abusive torture, while the records of the main civic court (the Châtelet) in Paris in 1488 show that only a tiny proportion of prisoners were tortured (20 out of 600), and those mostly for theft. It has been said that 'only a thorough examination of actual courtroom practice will give us some idea of whether [the theoretical] limitations were respected in practice'.[35] The problem is that trial records often omit any mention of torture, even when its use alone can explain a sudden change in a suspect's readiness to talk. For example, in a murder case examined by the Parlement of Paris in 1332, a suspect produced the names of his accomplices only after a break in the trial record, suggesting an interval in the torture room.[36] In theft trials in Bologna, suspects sometimes confessed, apparently spontaneously, to a long string of offences, yet torture is never mentioned.

Fortescue's other charge against French criminal trials related to the use of witnesses: he claimed that this endangered the innocent by allowing conviction on the say-so of just two witnesses, who could easily be put up to this by an accuser. But the Roman-law requirement for two witnesses was intended as a safeguard for suspects. In Bolognese trials, the witnesses were closely questioned on what they knew, and if both had not actually seen the injury or offence take place, then the suspect was acquitted: hearsay was not enough. There were also regulations governing who could give testimony. Witnesses had to be irreproachable eye-witnesses. For Baldus, the celebrated Italian jurist, proofs in criminal cases had to be 'clearer than the light of day'. Suspect testimony was generally ruled out of court, and, as one historian has put it, rigour of proof was preferred to rigour of repression.[37] In learned legal theory, children, the poor and the infamous (those with criminal convictions or in degrading occupations such as prostitution) were absolutely excluded. Servants could testify against their master, but not in his favour; a suspect's mortal enemies could not testify against him. Most of these exclusions seem to have been followed in practice, at least until the mid-fifteenth century. However, it was from this point that something of Fortescue's criticism might have begun to ring true. 'Faced with exceptional crimes that were very serious but also very difficult to prove' – crimes committed secretly or at night – Roman-law jurists began to accept that some previously excluded categories of witness could be admitted, when other testimony was lacking. From this point on, rigour of repression began to prevail over rigour of proof, with the list of crimes in which such testimony was admissible lengthening from the late fifteenth century onwards. Fortescue's 'unreliable rogues, paupers, vagrants' were now allowed to testify.

This shift in attitudes to witnesses was indicative of broader trends of thought in the later Middle Ages, which were towards severity and rigour. The banner under which all such trends marched was the concern that crimes should not go unpunished. In the Italian city of Ferrara, for example, it was declared in 1330 that statutory restrictions on the use of inquisition procedure were allowing many crimes to remain unprosecuted, and the criminal judge was therefore licensed to use inquisition in cases where local districts were negligent in reporting crimes or arresting criminals.[38] Subsidiary to this was a rejection of old, fixed, monetary penalties. Such penalties had become devalued over the course of time by debasement of local coinages, and now appeared too slight. These twin objectives – ensuring that more crimes were punished, and that punishments were appropriate – were the ostensible arguments veiling an expansion of the arbitrary or discretionary powers of judges. Finding the right language to describe this development is difficult: if we talk of repression and arbitrary penalty, we create a picture of tyranny and harsh rule; but if we talk of discretion and fitting the punishment to the crime, the picture becomes one of modernisation and rationality. As Schnapper has shown, royal ordinances in France from the late thirteenth century carried forward a campaign not only against customary fixed penalties, but also against private settlements and compositions, especially for homicide. In 1356 the king forbad all judges, royal and seigneurial, from receiving compositions in criminal cases.[39] Ordinances increasingly threatened arbitrary penalties, 'according to the type of crime and criminal, and such that it be an example to all'.

This expansion of judicial discretion in French royal ordinances was mirrored by similar development in jurisprudence in fourteenth-century Italy. The ideas became established that fixed penalties could be 'corrected' by reference to mitigating or aggravating circumstances, while arbitrary penalties should take account of the type and timing of the crime and the status and motives of the criminal. It emerged that more importance should be given in principle to discretionary than to fixed penalties. Central to these changes in thinking were debates on the meaning of a text from Roman law (Digest, 48.19.13, 'Hodie'): 'Nowadays, a judge who is hearing a criminal case according to extraordinary procedure may lawfully pass what sentence he wishes, whether heavier or lighter . . .'. This was extended to apply not only to extraordinary prosecutions, but to ordinary ones too.

Discussions of Roman law by academic lawyers and the growth of royal and princely power in the fifteenth century went hand in hand in expanding the arbitrary powers of judges against the fixed penalties of customary or statute law. In Italy we can find in the first half of the fifteenth century the Duke of Milan authorising torture and trial outside statutory limits, and in the second half the Duke of Ferrara overriding statute law through the use of special commissioners.[40] Nor was England outside this general development, though here it took the form of summary process rather than discretionary sentencing. In the later fourteenth and fifteenth centuries, local justices were empowered to imprison 'without waiting for indictments' or to convict 'by their own record' armed crowds who occupied farms, abducted women and ransomed men.[41] Later statutes subjected a variety of minor offences to such summary powers: vagrancy, riot, permitting illegal gambling, hunting in disguise, and so on. Although the early statutes granting these powers were sometimes obscurely worded or restricted in their scope, the fifteenth century saw the gradual extension of summary procedures, either through 'conviction by record' or through simple 'examination' of suspects under oath.[42] In English political crimes the same process occurred with the development of 'attainder' from the 1390s. This allowed the simple pronouncement in Parliament of a penalty for notorious traitors, with no preceding trial.[43]

In a very different way, the progress of judicial discretion is also evident in republican Florence. Here in the fifteenth century the ordinary judges (the *podestà* and *capitano*) were gradually displaced by a citizen committee, the Otto di guardia, which had full discretionary powers. Hitherto Florence had followed the general practice of north Italian cities to employ outsiders as judges. These judges would be trained lawyers, hired on six-month contracts, and would circulate among the cities from one semester to the next. On entry into office they would take an oath to observe and enforce the local statutes. The emergence of the Otto di guardia therefore signified a manifold transformation of judicial action: trained lawyers were replaced by untrained citizens, outsiders were replaced by members of the local elite, and a commitment to observe statute law was replaced by release from its constraints. It is no coincidence that this change took place in a period of strengthening oligarchic rule in Florence: it is the period of the Medici regime.[44]

Crimes and causes

Paradoxically, this increasing severity of procedure was not matched by increasing capital or corporal punishment, as we shall see in Chapter 6. This was at least partly because increasing judicial scope to act was only one method of government response to crime. The forceful impact of exemplary punishment in deterring crime was certainly one of these methods. However, governments and public opinion also addressed criminality in other ways. They believed that crime was like a stream that could be diverted or stanched by government intervention. This is most apparent in policies towards theft, the carrying of weapons, and pardon. For example, the apparent ease with which stolen goods could be disposed of through Jewish pawnbrokers or second-hand clothes dealers led some governments to impose restrictions on either or both of these commercial groups. In Paris repeated prohibitions were issued on the purchase or sale of stolen goods, among both the established and itinerant traders. In Bologna in 1454, in an attempt to stem the number of thefts and robberies committed after dusk, second-hand clothes dealers and pawnbrokers were ordered to shut up shop earlier and leave their premises promptly. In 1369 the city of Cracow made a series of complaints to the King of Poland about the damage being caused to the city by Jews. Included in this anti-Semitic tirade was the claim that the city was full of thieves who were found to be taking their booty to Jewish houses, pawning it and then absconding. This hostility to Jewish presence, seen as encouraging theft, could also be reflected in penalties: in Sardinia in the mid-fourteenth century, a Jew who had traded in stolen goods was fined at the level of other offenders who had committed homicides.[45]

As we shall see in Chapter 3, governments also tried to curtail and restrict gambling, as a major source of fighting. In the same vein, the carrying of bladed weapons was addressed: prohibitions on carrying arms are among the most common pieces of late medieval legislation. The problem was, however, that the same governments, while they might seek to restrain arms carrying for the sake of public order, were ready to make exceptions for vulnerable groups who might need protection, or were keen to encourage able-bodied men to train in using weapons of war for the purposes of state security.

Lastly, public opinion, as expressed at parliaments and assemblies, often criticised rulers for too freely granting pardons to convicted criminals. In the modern world, it is the wrongly convicted who are pardoned; in the Middle Ages, it was the excusable convicts, those who confessed to the crime but presented persuasive arguments for lessening their responsibility. It also became common at various times for kings to grant pardons to criminals who had no excuse but were prepared to enrol in royal armies. To public opinion, and to judges too, excessive clemency was dangerous and encouraged crime. In Spain in 1462, for example, the Cortes asserted in a petition to the king that crime had increased because criminals knew how easy it was to obtain pardon. 'It is notorious', the petition argues, 'with what audacity many people, fearless of God, king and justice, commit crimes, killings, robberies . . . etc, which they do with the hope that they will soon obtain pardon, and they are pardoned for all their misdeeds, whether great or small, without restoring stolen property, without being forgiven by their enemies.' Kings bowed to such pressure to restrict their exercise of mercy: in England, in 1389 Parliament petitioned regarding the pardons for murder, treason and rape which, it claimed, had been 'too lightly' granted in the past, 'to the great comfort of malefactors', and some restrictions were then enacted.[46]

Easy access to outlets for stolen goods, to weapons and to pardon could all be made more difficult, so it was thought, by legislation. These were practical ways of trying to reduce criminality. There was also some awareness of the origins of the criminal instinct. Theologians recognised that food shortage and hunger could impel poor people to theft. This was reflected in some secular law. For example, in a town in the Dauphiné in southern France, it was accepted that if anyone stole bread, meat or other food, 'out of necessity of hunger', then he or she was to be condoned 'up to the level of one meal'.[47] One exemplary tale, designed for use in sermons to encourage such charitable attitudes, told of a cellarer in a rich abbey who turned a blind eye to pilfering of food by the abbey's servants and wage workers: they were poor and needy, the cellarer reasoned, and the abbey was not lacking in wealth.[48]

Ineffective parenting, specifically fatherhood, was also identified as an original cause of some men's slide into criminality. Sometimes this took the form of over-stern fatherhood. For example, in Bologna in 1389 a bigamous arsonist, who had once been a priest, wrote from prison to his brother, appealing for help to save his life, and instructing him, 'Tell my father that if he had taken me into his mercy, I would never have come to this pass.'[49] More often, however, the paternal deficiency lay in a lack of sternness. Gilles de Rais, a French nobleman of the fifteenth century, blamed his upbringing and early diet for his later descent into the horrible crimes of child murder. He is reported as saying that his own degeneracy was an example to fathers to bring children up strictly, not too delicately dressed or accustomed to idleness. In Ferrara a few decades later, a convicted thief, before he was hanged, spoke from the scaffold, recommending all the boys present to obey their parents and avoid bad company, as it was because of such company that he was to be executed.[50] According to these voices, ineffective parenting led to crime, but before we accept their reasoning, we have to remember the ideological function of such stories: they are part of a medieval discourse about criminality, a Christian ideology of discipline, not evidence for a modern explanation of crime. We should not take words from the scaffold at their face value. Confessed and convicted criminals were expected to play a role in a didactic drama of punishment in which Christian ideology was forcefully restated. Honour thy father and thy mother, said one of the Christian commandments. Equally important, the idea of order maintained through physical punishment was strongly propagated. We find in several collections of thirteenth-century *exempla* the story of the thief who, being led to the gallows, saw his weeping father, and called to him to kiss him. As the father did so, the thief bit him on the lips till they bled, saying, 'All these evils you have done to me, for when I was a boy and began to steal, you never beat me or chastised me.'[51] This example reveals the notion that obedience to social norms was to be enforced through patriarchal violence: the exact opposite of some modern criminology, which holds that exposure to violence in childhood increases the likelihood of violent offending in adulthood.

Conversely, some of the responses to crime that we have surveyed bear striking similarity to some trends in modern criminology. The title of an article in a recent issue of the *British Journal of Criminology*, for example, asked the question 'Does the market for second-hand goods play a role in keeping crime figures high?'. One trend in modern criminology (New Administrative Criminology) argues that most crime is opportunistic and can therefore be deterred by restricting opportunity through better security and surveillance. Medieval governments too sought to restrict opportunity and to strengthen security. Despite these clear parallels between modern, 'neo-classical' criminology and medieval government responses, historians have pursued rather different paths in explaining medieval criminality. Only rarely – as in the case of weapons or poverty – do these intersect with contemporary responses. Most historians make much of the fact that 'everyone' carried a knife in the Middle Ages. In his study of homicide in England, for example, Given cites the 'ubiquitous presence of knives' as one factor explaining the high level of violence. There is an obvious fallacy to this argument. If everyone carried knives, why did so few women kill or inflict bloody injury? Even if 'everyone' is construed as 'every man', we are still faced with the fact that most murders did not involve knives: only a third of homicides in thirteenth-century England were committed with a knife. So maybe it is not true that every man carried a knife. Given too sees this problem, although his answer is a different one. He argues that the presence of knives takes us only to an initial level of explanation because 'the availability of weapons does not guarantee their use'. This sounds rather like the argument used by the gun lobby in the USA to resist statutory controls on gun ownership: people, not guns, kill, it asserts. This argument is highly controversial and it can be countered that the availability of weapons does facilitate the infliction of greater injury than might otherwise occur. Either way, we have to look further than the presence of knives, ubiquitous or not. Given points to three other powerful factors: alcohol, culture and social structure. Consumption of large amounts of alcohol had powerful effects on self-restraint, and explains the clustering of assaults and homicides in or outside taverns. From the general culture, men learned to respond violently to affronts or challenges: the use of violence to discipline children, wives and servants was legally tolerated; public whippings were imposed as penances by the Church courts; and many popular games consisted of fighting. Lastly, the social structure could at various times inhibit or engender violence as a means of resolving conflicts, depending on the strength of local mechanisms to settle disputes by other means and on the cohesiveness of the local community.[52]

These arguments have been disputed by other historians. The role of alcohol seems to be more easily assumed than proved. Schüssler did not find it to be frequently mentioned in judicial sources in Nuremberg. Gauvard found that it was used as an excuse by French petitioners for pardon, but much less than one might expect and much less than the excuse of anger. Under 15 per cent of homicides, she concludes, were attributed to drunkenness.[53] More of a consensus exists regarding what Huizinga called 'the violent tenor of the age', the emotional volatility that led to fights breaking out without warning. The orthodox view among historians is that medieval man's first response to any challenge or obstacle was a violent one. The path was easy and quick from verbal provocation to physical assault: 'emotional self-control was minimal', and it was 'a world of thin skins, short fuses and physical violence'.[54] Despite this weight of opinion, some challenges have been made to the ortho- doxy. Given's own third factor is a limitation here: friends and colleagues did step in to pull brawlers apart before serious injury was inflicted, and forms of collective responsibility were widely used to ensure individual good behaviour. If violence was a learned response, then so too was the prevention of violence. Gauvard has drawn a much more nuanced picture of assaults and homicides, distinguishing various phases that marked the progression from words to blows. Violence, she insists, was not spontan- eous, but was the final phase in a sequence, which might start in some pushing or rudeness, progress to insult and punching, and finally result in bloodshed. Some individuals, some groups (specifically men in their twenties) might miss out the middle elements in the sequence, but most would not. Pythian-Adams has presented a similar analysis of the 'rituals of confrontation', arguing that physical violence was sequenced precisely to allow or encourage intervention by possible conciliators: the first blows were of a sort actively to invite intervention, for example, glancing blows with the flat of a blade.[55]

One element of Given's explanation of violence that has been much built on in recent years is masculinity. It was men, not women, who committed the bulk of crimes. Female criminality, as we shall see in Chapter 4, had its own pattern, which avoided homicide and preferred petty theft. Medieval ideas of masculinity are therefore of great relevance to the problem of violence. It comes as no surprise to find that the dominant and enduring ideal of masculine conduct was violent confron- tation. The man who faced his enemy and fought, rather than turning his back and running away, was considered 'manly' or 'virile'.[56] This applied whether the enemy was real and physical or imagined and spiritual. The tavern and the gaming house were prime locations where masculinity was asserted and tested.

This chapter started by perhaps giving the impression that, while criminality was uniform across Europe, the judicial response to it varied. This might be broadly true in the sense that similar patterns of crime – a prevalence of violence over theft – have been found in much of pre-industrial, *ancien régime* Europe. Trial statistics often show assault accounting for around half of prosecutions and theft in all its forms for between a fifth and a quarter. Other crimes, in varying proportions, make up the total: homicide, arson, rape, and so on. The pattern in England is more difficult to examine, because assault was not a felony, yet some historians have limited themselves to investigating felonies alone. Thus Hanawalt's study of eight English counties in the first half of the fourteenth century shows theft, in all its varieties, accounting for over three-quarters of felony prosecutions, while homicide accounted for most of the rest.[57] 'Larceny was the most prevalent crime in medieval society', she proclaims, and her preceding references to French and German medieval literature lend her text a spurious authority as generalisation. Her point continued to hold true in England: when judges came to East Anglia in the fifteenth century to try suspects held in gaol, 86 per cent of charges were for non-violent crime, mainly larceny, and only 7 per cent for homicide and 5 per cent for assault.[58] In the early modern period, theft again predominated among serious crimes.[59] In England, theft was the one felony most often prosecuted; but in many other places, assault accounts for the lion's share of prosecutions. We have to assume, surely, that this divergence is the result of different judicial systems, not different criminal behaviour.

Such figures can never reveal the whole truth, of course. Prosecuted crime is not the same thing as criminality. Prosecution of the numerically rarer crimes was liable to oscillate according to panics and purges. Moreover, even the patterns of common crimes could vary according to local circumstances. Take the example of late medieval Cumberland, a poor, sparsely populated part of England, exposed to harsh weather and hostile Scottish raiding. Here, according to Summerson, crime adapted to the local conditions. 'The pastoral economy dictated the nature and timing of crime.' Theft took the form mostly of cattle-rustling. This was most conveniently done in the autumn, and by men wealthy enough to own horses. Scottish raiding had already cleared most valuables out of churches, leaving nothing there for the natives to steal. A sparse population with low levels of social contact produced a low homicide rate. On the other hand, the harsh conditions bred 'cruelty and hardheartedness' on those occasions when physical violence was used, as in the case of the burglars who tortured their female victims by forcing them to sit on red-hot trivets.[60]

This notion of crime adapting to its environment finds echoes in the work of other historians. Sam Cohn has recently found differences in prosecuted crime between the mountains and the plains of Florentine territory in Tuscany. In England once more, Barbara Hanawalt famously found that the pattern of violence in a university town (in this case

Oxford) followed the course of the academic year, while in the country-side it followed the agricultural calendar. Homicides happened in term time in Oxford, in harvest time in Northamptonshire.[61]

If these pictures are persuasive, then it means that patterns of pros-ecuted crime varied according to the local economy, local demography and the proximity of hostile borders. Such conclusions, however, face a challenge in the work of Claude Gauvard, whose study of royal pardons in France in the reign of King Charles VI comes to some very opposite judgments. She notes how historians' search for the sensational has led to some very impressionistic uses of judicial material (*touché*: Summerson's burglars and trivets). Her more rigorous statistical analysis of pardons reveals a distribution of crime that registers only minor fluctuations across the various regions of the kingdom. Overall, pardons for homicide constitute 57 per cent of the total, for theft 16 per cent, and for moral offences 4 per cent. She is thus able to reject supposed differences in criminality between centre and periphery, between city and country, and between north and south. Everywhere she finds the same types of crime and the same types of criminal: she calls this the 'ordinary world' of crime, as opposed to the 'exotic' world constructed by historians' liking for the sensational. She minimises the differences of frontier zones, and sees 'frontier lawlessness' as a stereotype, as discourse divorced from reality.[62]

This is an unresolved problem. It may be that it can be made to disappear by considering the nature of the sources used by these his-torians. Hanawalt used a combination of coroners' rolls and gaol delivery records (made when judges arrived to 'deliver', that is try, the prisoners in a given gaol). Gauvard used petitions for pardon. Both have been criticised. Coroners' rolls, it has been shown, are an unreliable guide to dating crimes, as coroners wrote them at a distance of anything up to several weeks after the event. Petitions, it is often argued, are socially skewed towards those social groups who had easier access to the king and sufficient money to afford the incidental fees; they were, in any case, restricted during the fifteenth century to cases of homicide. Gauvard, in acknowledging these biases, urges a modest assessment of their effect on the usefulness of petitions as a source.[63]

This difference clearly throws up one of the major difficulties facing the historian of crime: that it is much easier to write about criminal justice than about criminality. Given everything that has been said in this chap-ter, it should become obvious that judicial records tell us much more directly about judges and court practice than about criminals and their victims, while other sources, for example chronicles and *exempla*, become ideological in their selection and description of individual cases. Yet historians are used to using documents for purposes beyond those for which they were created, for example using tax records for demography. So the chapters that follow will attempt to recover the history of criminals and victims, while also investigating further both the courtroom and the medieval discourse about crime.

Notes

1. M. Sherwood, 'Un registre de la cour criminelle de Mireval–Lauragais au quatorzième siècle', *Annales du Midi* 53 (1941), pp. 170–2.
2. *Calendar of Plea and Memoranda Rolls . . . of the City of London AD 1413–1437*, ed. A.H. Thomas (Cambridge, 1943), p. 114.
3. Sherwood, 'Un registre', pp. 176–7.
4. *Calendar of Plea Rolls of London*, pp. 54–5.
5. J. Ramière de Fontanier, *Recueil de documents relatifs à l'histoire du droit municipal en France des origines à la Révolution: Chartes de franchises du Lauragais* (Paris, 1939), pp. 11–16, 77, 107–11, 495; M-C. Marandet, *Le souci de l'au-delà: la pratique testamentaire dans la région toulousaine (1300–1450)* (Perpignan, 1998), pp. 96, 197, 226, 235, 465.
6. For the quotation and for what follows: M. Keen, *English Society in the later Middle Ages, 1348–1500* (Harmondsworth, 1990), ch. 5.
7. Sir John Fortescue, *On the Laws and Governance of England*, ed. S. Lockwood (Cambridge, 1997), pp. 30–47.
8. N. Jörg, S. Field and C. Brants, 'Are inquisitorial and adversarial systems converging?', in *Criminal Justice in Europe: A Comparative Study*, ed. P. Fennell *et al.* (Oxford, 1995), pp. 42–3.
9. A. Planas Rosselló, 'La participación popular en la administración de justicia del reino de Mallorca', *AHDE* 66 (1996); G. Fasoli, 'Un comune veneto nel Duecento, Bassano', *Archivio veneto* 5th ser., 15 (1934), pp. 26–7; T. Lindkvist, 'Law and the making of the state in medieval Sweden: kingship and communities', in *The Origins of the Modern State in Europe, 13th to 18th Centuries: Legislation and Justice*, ed. A. Padoa-Schioppa (Oxford, 1997), p. 224.
10. K. Pennington, *The Prince and the Law: Sovereignty and Rights in the Western Legal Tradition* (Berkeley, 1993), pp. 155–7.
11. R.C. Van Caenegem, 'The English Common Law: A divergence from the European pattern', *TRG* 47 (1979), p. 1.
12. M. Sbriccoli, 'Legislation, justice and political power in Italian cities, 1200–1400', in *Legislation and Justice*, ed. Padoa-Schioppa, pp. 51–2.
13. Pennington, *The Prince and the Law*, pp. 132–5.
14. S. Blanshei, 'Crime and law enforcement in medieval Bologna', *Journal of Social History* 16:1 (1982), p. 122; T. Dean, 'Criminal justice in mid-fifteenth century Bologna', in *Crime, Society and the Law in Renaissance Italy*, ed. T. Dean and K.J.P. Lowe (Cambridge, 1994), p. 17.
15. J. Cerdà Ruiz-Funes, 'En torno a la pesquisa y procedimiento inquisitivo en el derecho castellano-leones de la Edad Media', *AHDE* 32 (1962); A. Esmein, *Histoire de la procédure criminelle en France* (Paris, 1882), pp. 43–132.

16. Ibid.; E. Perrot, *Les cas royaux: origine et développement de la théorie aux XIIIe et XIVe siècles* (Paris, 1910); F. Pollock and F.W. Maitland, *The History of English Law before the Time of Edward I*, 2nd edn (Cambridge, 1968), II, pp. 462–70, 488–518, 558–73.

17. H. Zaremska, *Les bannis au Moyen Age* (Paris, 1996), pp. 66–74.

18. A. Lopez-Amo Marin, 'El derecho penal español de la baja edad media', *AHDE* 26 (1956), p. 358; M.K. Schüssler, 'German crime in the later Middle Ages: A statistical analysis of the Nuremberg Outlawry Books, 1285–1400', *Criminal Justice History* 13 (1992), pp. 26–7; F. Cattier, 'Evolution du droit pénal germanique en Hainaut jusqu'au XVe siècle', *Mémoires et publications de la Société des sciences, des arts et des lettres du Hainaut* 5th ser., 7 (1894), pp. 179–85; A. Ryder, *The Kingdom of Naples under Alfonso the Magnanimous* (Oxford, 1976), pp. 162–3; D.M. Nicholas, 'Crime and punishment in fourteenth-century Ghent', *Revue belge de philologie et d'histoire* 48 (1970), p. 321; W. Uruszczak, 'Constitutional devices implementing state power in Poland, 1300–1700', in *Legislation and Justice*, ed. Padoa-Schioppa, p. 193.

19. J.H. Langbein, *Prosecuting Crime in the Renaissance: England, Germany, France* (Cambridge, Mass., 1974), p. 145, and generally pp. 131–57.

20. M. Bellabarba, *Giustizia ai confini: il principato vescovile di Trento agli inizi dell'età moderna* (Bologna, 1996), pp. 275–7, 282–306.

21. *ORF*, II, pp. 256–7; E. Faral, 'Le procès d'Enguerran IV de Coucy', *RHDF*, 4th ser., 26 (1948); Le Roux de Lincy, 'Chansons historiques des XIIIe, XIVe et XV siècles', *Bibliothèque de l'Ecole des chartes* 1 (1839–40), p. 372; C. Whittick, 'The role of the criminal appeal in the fifteenth century', in *Law and Social Change in British History*, ed. J.A. Guy and H.G. Beale (London, 1984).

22. E. Verga, 'Le sentenze criminali dei podestà milanesi, 1385–1429', *Archivio storico lombardo* 3rd ser., 16 (1901), p. 130.

23. E. Powell, 'Jury trial at gaol delivery in the late Middle Ages: the Midland circuit, 1400–1429', in *Twelve Good Men and True: The Criminal Trial Jury in England, 1200–1800*, ed. J.S. Cockburn and T.A. Green (Princeton, 1988), p. 100; *Yorkshire Sessions of the Peace, 1361–1364*, ed. B.H. Putnam (Yorkshire Archaeological Society, Records Series, vol. 100, 1939), xxxiv–vii; B. Hanawalt, *Crime and Conflict in English Communities, 1300–1348* (Cambridge, Mass., 1979), p. 58.

24. *Statutes of the Realm* (9 vols, London, 1810–22), I, pp. 89, 139; *Rotuli parliamentorum* (6 vols, London, 1767–77), I, p. 289; R. Kaeuper, 'An historian's reading of *The Tale of Gamelyn*', *Medium Aevum* 52 (1983), pp. 55–6.

25. B.W. McLane, 'Juror attitudes toward local disorder: the evidence of the 1328 Lincolnshire Trailbaston proceedings', in *Twelve Good Men and True*, pp. 58–60.

26. J.B. Post, 'Jury lists and juries in the late fourteenth century', in *Twelve Good Men and True*; Powell, 'Jury trial at gaol delivery', ibid.; R.D. Groot, 'The early thirteenth-century criminal jury', ibid. (pp. 18–19 for the quotation); McLane, 'Juror attitudes', ibid. (p. 57 for the quotation); Pollock and Maitland, *History of English Law*, II, p. 655.

27. *Matthaei Parisiensis monachi sancti Albani chronica majora*, ed. H. Richards Luard (7 vols, London, 1872–83), V, pp. 56–60; J.B. Given, *Society and Homicide in Thirteenth-century England* (Stanford, 1977), p. 113.

28. *Select Cases in the Court of King's Bench under Richard II, Henry IV and Henry V*, ed. G.O. Sayles (London, 1971), pp. 14–21. See also P. Strohm, 'Trade, treason and the murder of Janus Imperial', *Journal of British Studies* 35 (1996).

29. G. Martinez Diez, 'La tortura judicial en la legislación histórica española', *AHDE* 32 (1962), p. 258. See also A.T. Sheedy, *Bartolus on Social Conditions in the Fourteenth Century* (New York, 1942), pp. 100–1.

30. Langbein, *Prosecuting Crime*, p. 160.

31. Boswell, *Life of Johnson*, ed. R.W. Chapman, 3rd edn (Oxford, 1976), p. 330.

32. S. Piasentini, *'Alla luce della luna': I furti a Venezia 1270–1403* (Venice, 1992), pp. 34–6.

33. C. Caduff, 'I "publici latrones" nella città e nel contado di Firenze a metà Trecento', *Ricerche storiche* 18 (1988), p. 517.

34. F. Gasparri, *Un crime en Provence au XVe siècle* (Paris, 1991); R. Po-Chia Hsia, *Trent 1475: Stories of a Ritual Murder Trial* (New Haven, 1992).

35. Pennington, *The Prince and the Law*, p. 158.

36. Ibid.; C. Gauvard, *'De grace especial': Crime, état et société en France à la fin du Moyen Age* (Paris, 1991), pp. 157–62; M. Vincent-Cassy, 'Comment obtenir un aveu? Etude des confessions des auteurs d'un meurtre commis à Paris en 1332', in *L'aveu: antiquité et moyen âge* (Rome, 1986).

37. B. Schnapper, *'Testes inhabiles*: les témoins reprochables dans l'ancien droit pénal', *TRG* 33 (1965), p. 576.

38. Archivio di stato, Ferrara, Archivio storico del commune, Libro di statuti e provvigioni, fol. 62v.

39. *ORF*, III, p. 130; B. Schnapper, 'Les peines arbitraires du XIIIe au XVIIIe siècle', *TRG* 41 (1973).

40. *Inventari e regesti dell'Archivio di Stato in Milano*, vol. II, *Atti cancellereschi viscontei*, ed. G. Vittani (Milan, 1920), p. 221; and vol. III, *I registri dell'ufficio degli statuti di Milano*, ed. N. Ferorelli (Milan, 1920), p. 32; D.S. Chambers and T. Dean, *Clean Hands and Rough Justice: An Investigating Magistrate in Renaissance Italy* (Ann Arbor, 1997), pp. 180, 182.

41. *Statutes of the Realm*, II, pp. 9–10, 78.

42. J.G. Bellamy, *Criminal Law and Society in Late Medieval and Tudor England* (Gloucester and New York, 1984), pp. 8–19.

43. J.G. Bellamy, *The Law of Treason in England in the Later Middle Ages* (Cambridge, 1970), p. 177.

44. G. Antonelli, 'La magistratura degli Otto di Guardia a Firenze', *Archivio storico italiano* 112 (1954), pp. 21–4; A. Zorzi, 'The judicial system in Florence in the fourteenth and fifteenth centuries', in *Crime, Society and the Law in Renaissance Italy*, pp. 47–51, 56–7; idem, *L'amministrazione della giustizia penale nella repubblica fiorentina: aspetti e problemi* (Florence, 1988), pp. 87–92.

45. B. Geremek, *The Margins of Society in Late Medieval Paris* (Cambridge, 1987), pp. 263–9; Dean, 'Criminal justice in Bologna', p. 32; *Najstarsze Księgii i rachunki miasta Krakowa od r. 1300 do 1400*, ed. F. Piekosinski and J. Szujski (Cracow, 1878), pp. 23–4; P. Roqué Ferrer, 'L'infrazione della legge a Cagliari dal 1340 al 1380', *Quaderni sardi di storia* 5 (1985–6), pp. 13–15, 18.

46. M.I. Rodriguez Flores, *El perdono real en Castilla (siglos XIII–XVIII)* (Salamanca, 1971), pp. 52, 71, 117; *Cortes de los antiguos reinos de Leon y de Castilla*

(5 vols, Madrid, 1883–1903), III, pp. 732–4; *Rotuli parliamentorum*, III, p. 268.

47. *ORF*, XX, p. 133.

48. *Caesarii Heisterbacensis monachi ordinis Cisterciensis Dialogus Miraculorum*, ed. J. Strange (2 vols, Cologne, 1851), I, p. 359–60.

49. J. Heers, *Gilles de Rais* (Paris, 1997), p. 193; A. Palmieri, 'Un processo importante nel capitanato di Casio', *Atti e memorie della Deputazione di storia patria per la Romagna* 4th ser., 15 (1924–5), pp. 109–14.

50. Bernardino Zambotti, *Diario ferrarese dall'anno 1476 sino al 1504*, ed. G. Pardi, *Rerum italicarum scriptores*, vol. 24, pt 7 (Bologna, 1934–7), p. 92.

51. *The Exempla or Illustrative Stories from the Sermones Vulgares of Jacques de Vitry*, ed. T.F. Crane (London, 1890), no. 287, p. 121.

52. Given, *Society and Homicide*, pp. 188–212.

53. Schüssler, 'Nuremberg Outlawry Books', p. 20; Gauvard, *Crime, état et société*, pp. 430–6.

54. T. Dean and K. Lowe, 'Introduction' in *Crime, Society and the Law*, pp. 4–5 for references; V.I. Comparato, 'Il controllo del contado a Perugia nella prima metà del Quattrocento: Capitani, vicari e contadini tra 1428 e 1450', in *Forme e tecniche del potere nella città (secoli XIV–XVII)* (Perugia, 1980).

55. Gauvard, *Crime, état et société*, pp. 707–45; C. Pythian-Adams, 'Rituals of personal confrontation in late-medieval England', *Bulletin of the John Rylands Library* 73 (1991).

56. This interpretation runs counter to the historiographical trend, which is to find multiple masculinities, diverse according to class or age. However, even in *Medieval Masculinities: Regarding Men in the Middle Ages*, ed. C.A. Lees (Minneapolis and London, 1994), the pull of aggression–competition–dominance is evident (see pp. xxi, 22, 40).

57. Hanawalt, *Crime and Conflict*, pp. 7, 65–6, 75.

58. P.C. Maddern, *Violence and Social Order: East Anglia, 1422–1442* (Oxford, 1992), pp. 27–8, 33, 48–50.

59. J.A. Sharpe, *Crime in Early Modern England, 1550–1750* (London, 1984), pp. 49, 54.

60. H. Summerson, 'Crime and society in medieval Cumberland', *Transactions of the Cumberland and Westmorland Antiquarian and Archaeological Society* 82 (1982).

61. S.K. Cohn, *Creating the Florentine State: Peasants and Rebellion, 1348–1434* (Cambridge, 1999), pp. 29–31; B.A. Hanawalt, 'Violent death in fourteenth and early fifteenth-century England', *Comparative Studies in Society and History* 18 (1976), p. 304.

62. Gauvard, *Crime, état et société*, pp. 2–3, 241–70. Cf. Sharpe, *Crime in Early Modern England*, pp. 56–7.

63. Gauvard, *Crime, état et société*, pp. 64–76.

chapter 2

JUDICIAL CORRUPTION

The ancient biographer Plutarch, in his 'Life of Solon', the Athenian law-giver of the sixth century BC, has a foreign visitor to Athens mock Solon's legislation in the following terms: ' "These decrees of yours are no different from spiders' webs . . . They'll restrain anyone weak and insignificant who gets caught in them, but they'll be torn to shreds by people with power and wealth." '[1] This image of the spider and the flies entered the repertory of late medieval poets and writers as a characteristic indictment of criminal justice. The French poet Eustache Deschamps, writing in the early fifteenth century, compares justice to the spider's web: it catches and destroys small flies, but it breaks if a big fly comes along, and the spider hides. Drawing out the analogy, and carelessly changing the metaphor, the poet continues: so it is that justice cripples poor people for petty offences, but when 'disloyal dogs' appear who have ravished, killed and wounded, they are not arrested and justice flees at their approach.[2] The contemporary English writer Thomas Hoccleve made exactly the same use of this analogy in his 'Regiment of Princes' of 1411: little comfort is had of our laws these days, he says, for if one of the great swells does something against the law, he is not punished at all. The law operates just like a cobweb ('right as lop-webbys'), which takes small flies and gnats, but lets big flies go. When a 'rich and mighty man' commits an offence, no one says a word ('no man sayeth once that black is his eye'), whereas the poor man is snubbed and tormented: he is caught in the web and may not escape.[3]

Such observations were not confined to secular writers. The popular religious reformer of the 1490s in Florence, Girolamo Savonarola, also used this analogy in a sermon. The figure of the spider's web connects with other indictments of secular justice in religious sources. Collections of *exempla* for use in preaching often contain the story of an observer who laughed as he saw a judge leading a petty thief to the gallows: 'There's a great thief leading a little one', he remarked. As one author explained, 'officials are thieves', 'the real thieves are not hanged'.[4]

Medieval justice suffered from these two interlocking defects: the ability of noblemen to commit crimes with impunity, and the extortion/ bribery of judges. The social power of the nobility and the attachment to it of judges were but two of the complaints that historians have directed against late medieval justice. There are many others. It was difficult, first of all, to bring suspects to court: those who absconded were rarely caught and brought to trial, and the court system could be seen as a machine for producing outlaws and bandits, rather than for repressing crime. In a world of fragmented and competing jurisdictions, there were many means of avoiding prosecution: flight into an adjacent jurisdiction or sanctuary in a nearby church are the two most obvious. Claiming clerical status, and thus immunity from prosecution in the secular courts, was another. Even when suspects were detained, the arrangements for holding them securely were often inadequate. Prison break-outs were frequent. Only a small proportion of cases travelled the whole judicial distance from denunciation to implemented sentence. At each stage social pressures could be applied to prevent or mitigate the rigour of the law: friends and kinsmen would influence those with duties to denounce crimes, or they and their noble protectors could press or persuade judges to lenience. After conviction there was a fair chance that they would succeed in obtaining pardon for the crime: the ease with which pardons were granted was often criticised. Wherever we look, one or more of these elements can be found at any time. The purpose of this chapter is to take a closer look at these many faults, but also to examine the various revisionist approaches that help us to understand them in a new way.

Noble impunity

Studies from various places and periods confirm the contemporary observations. In Romagna, Italy, there was no punishment of nobles for their crimes in the fifteenth century. In Brescia the middling and privileged classes are absent from lists of convictions, and the courts dealt mainly with the violence and unruliness of the poor and rootless. In Venice, the court records throw up only one conviction of a nobleman for theft. In thirteenth-century England, not a single knight or lord has been found among 3,500 prosecuted killers. In Nuremberg the city patriciate feature rarely as offenders in the Outlawry Books.[5] However, narrative sources give more frequent reference to noble crimes. So the absence of noblemen from the records of trial and punishment does not mean that they committed no crime. Noblemen were more likely to request and obtain pardon for their misdeeds. This explains the disproportionate numbers of noblemen who petitioned for pardons. In Guyenne in south-west France, for example, in the later fifteenth century, they accounted for 21 per cent of petitioners.[6] In addition, noble crime as presented in pardon petitions had very specific features. As Gauvard puts it, noblemen were quicker on the draw and did not kill their own class. A far greater proportion of noble pardons are for assault and homicide than was the case with the whole class of pardons. Noblemen attacked local people, especially labourers and craftsmen. The insolence of inferiors (as noblemen saw it) was a frequent trigger unleashing noble violence. This insolence was often conveyed in the form of insult, asserting that X was not a gentleman, that Y deserved no more honour than a dog or a Jew and so on.[7]

A major reason that noblemen were not prosecuted was their social power over the levers of the judicial system. Local people were afraid to denounce them or to give evidence against them. This is all too evident in the histories of gentlemen gangsters in the fourteenth and fifteenth centuries. These noblemen fall into two types: those who wilfully terrorise the locality in order to seize property and exploit the weak; and those who turn to local brigandage in the course of a property dispute or because of some disturbance in the local balance of power. Two examples of the first type would be Jean de Belloy, active in and around Amiens in the 1390s, and Sir John Molyns in Buckinghamshire in the 1330s.[8] A variant on these cases would be the attacks by the Folville gang in mid-fourteenth-century England on unofficial 'public enemies' in the locality, including an extortionate judge who sold the law 'like cows'.[9] Examples of the second type would be Sir Thomas Malory and William Tailboys in England, Gilles de Rais in France, and Ghino di Tacco in Italy.[10]

Of the first kind of robber baron, Jean de Belloy seems to have responded with exaggerated violence to any refusal of his outrageous requests: an innkeeper who asked for repayment of a loan was chased out of his inn, a man who failed to deliver up his maidservant was seized and beaten, an abbot who refused to open his abbey door was hit and insulted in his church soon afterwards, a man who declined to sell Jean his house had all his doors and windows broken and all his doves slaughtered. Nor were Jean's actions mere bluster: he was also accused of rape, of pushing people off bridges at night in Amiens, and of conducting a private war over a property boundary. The same excessive violence marks the actions of John Molyns. He had thrived in the political and military service of King Edward III in the 1330s, receiving posts of honour and responsibility, as well as grants and concessions that allowed him to build up his landed wealth and local power in Buckinghamshire. However, when the king conducted an angry inquiry into official corruption in 1340, charges against Molyns were made by local men. He had repeatedly used gangs to assault and kill his prey, including the sheriff of the county. He had oppressed the local inhabitants, by appropriating land and felling trees. He had used an ally on the king's bench of judges to manipulate the law and to procure acquittals for himself and convictions of his enemies.

Of the second type, Malory's brief criminal career, in which he tried to kill the Duke of Buckingham and committed a series of thefts in Essex, was triggered by the disturbance caused to an established magnate affinity by deaths in the dominant family of the county. According to Christine Carpenter, Malory was not a bandit, but was simply an incompetent loser in the game of local politics. Tailboys' murderous behaviour in Lincolnshire and London has also been traced to local property disputes and the state of local power in Lincolnshire: too many gentry and too many great lords looking for their service. Conditions of competition and patronage allowed Tailboys to get away with murder. Like Malory, Gilles de Rais had lost out in politics, though in his case national rather than local. Gilles de Rais had deserted his first master, Richemont, in order to enter the service of a court leader, Georges de la Trémoille, thanks to whom he was promoted to the distinction of marshal of France. The fall of his patron in 1433, supplanted by none other than Richemont, necessarily brought de Rais's fall too. Now without a patron and no longer serving in the royal armies, his resources dwindling, he retreated into a life of brigandage around his castles, pursuing property disputes with his neighbours, raiding and ransoming.

In these examples, shifts in the balance of power appear as arbitrary events in the political 'game', caused by death, demography or disgrace. However, that such shifts could also have an objective cause is made clear in Italian examples of robber barons. Cherubini has suggested that there were two sides to the actions of such barons in the Appennine hills. Viewed from the city, they appear as relics of an older, lawless, 'feudal' aristocracy, conducting raids from their hill forts and plundering merchants and travellers on the roads. What city observers overlooked, however, was the role of the city itself in producing these conditions: urban expansion and conquest of territory had reduced noble territories and cut into their revenues.[11] Just such an aristocratic victim of urban expansion became a legendary bandit, transformed in later literature into the figure of the generous bandit, the Italian Robin Hood (see Chapter 6). This was Ghino di Tacco, of the della Fratta family of the Val di Chiana in Tuscany. As the city of Siena attempted to expand its control of this territory in the 1270s, it encountered the lively resistance of this family, who were engaged in their own internal struggle over a castle. The overlapping of these forces led to Ghino, his father and his uncle fighting and killing Sienese officers, robbing merchants on the roads and terrorising the region through stealing and barn-burning. The city of Siena saw these actions as rebellion, such that Ghino's father was captured and executed in 1285 and five years later Ghino himself was condemned to death for rebellion and highway robbery. However, it is suggested that Ghino saw his actions as 'a legitimate form of war against the city that had dispossessed his family, killed his father and condemned him to death'.[12]

All of these examples of gentry violence share two features. The first is the role of protection, the second is private war (which will be dealt with in Chapter 5). Tailboys and Molyns got away with their crimes partly because of the protection afforded them by powerful magnates. Malory and Gilles de Rais ended their lives, the one in prison, the other on the scaffold, because they lost the protection of their patrons. Ghino di Tacco's protectors, in Siena and outside, were not powerful enough. It was this protection of criminal gentlemen by greater lords that was attacked by some late medieval governments. The protection often took the form of issuing followers with 'liveries' to wear on their garments, to display their allegiance to a powerful aristocratic affinity. The dukes of Burgundy addressed several ordinances to this problem. One in 1459 expounded the problem: 'many great lords endeavour to have a great number of followers wearing their liveries and devices, such that, on account of their great number and riotousness, these followers . . . may beat and cut people; and no one dares speak of it out of fear of their masters'.[13] Those with liveries regarded them as licences to carry weapons and armour, and to behave in a lawless fashion: 'they are rough and disobedient' complained another ordinance. Ordinances attempted to restrict the wearing of such signs to those actually in a lord's service. In England the 'maintenance' of quarrels was already the subject of numerous enactments before an ordinance was issued in 1389 forbidding lords from giving 'liveries of company' to any men who were not either their household servants or their retainers engaged for life. The declared aim was to prevent 'outrageous oppressions and maintenances' that were encouraged by less permanent membership of noble retinues.[14] The intent and effects of this law are much debated.

Judicial misbehaviour

In line with contemporary comment, the perversions of justice by the rich and powerful have been a favourite theme of historians. Maddicott examined the ways that thirteenth- and early fourteenth-century judges in England were retained by noblemen and great landowners, paying them 'fees and robes' in return for their expertise and influence as and when required. At one level such practice was innocuous and unobjectionable:

the legal profession worked for all clients on a fees-and-costs basis, and it viewed requests from abbeys and earls in this light; also, in an increasingly litigious age, landlords needed the best legal advice they could get. Besides, judges were themselves, or had become, members of the gentry and shared the class interests of other landowners in defending lordship against the claims of tenants. On the other hand, this neutral provision of technical expertise was accompanied by a more worrying exercise of influence. When judges' areas of responsibility overlapped with the lord-ships that retained them, when they heard cases involving their patrons, public opinion was likely to smell corruption. Royal officials, it was felt, should not have such close friendship with local noble power. From the late thirteenth century complaints about such attachments and alliances did lead to royal action. There were periodic purges that cleared out whole benches of judges (1290, 1340–1, 1388), and at other times the dismissal of egregious individuals (in 1350 William Thorp, Chief Justice of the King's Bench, was condemned to death for taking bribes). An ordinance in 1346 prohibited judges from taking fees and robes except from the king. Increases in judges' salaries made some attempt to com-pensate them for lost income. Yet none of this cut through the stitching holding judges and great landlords together: fees continued to be paid, attachments were maintained by other means ('less palpable ties of entertainment, fellow-feeling and favours') and the dismissed judges were soon reappointed. Thorp, though convicted, was pardoned. It is little surprise that popular complaint against judicial malpractice there-fore continued: year after year in the 1380s petitions in Parliament complained of judges taking fees and gifts, or of judges appointed to hear cases in their home districts; and at either end of the decade two Chief Judges of the King's Bench were murdered. The intensity of these popular reactions does seem to have forced some division between landed power and the judiciary: noblemen stopped retaining judges, although they continued to retain lawyers, and developed other forms of connec-tion with judges.[15]

Against judicial malpractice, rulers were active in ordering inquiries into the misdeeds of officials. If we compare the 1274 (Hundred) inquiry held by King Edward I in England with the 1247 inquiry ordered by King Louis IX of France we cannot avoid being struck by the great similarities in the allegations laid against local judicial officials, the sheriffs and bailiffs in England, and the *prévôts* and *sergents* in France. The 1274 inquiry offers 'countless instances of [sheriffs] taking gifts to conceal felonies by not making arrests', and reveals sheriffs extorting large sums from the wealthy to secure bail, while letting the poor rot in jail until the judges visited, or arresting people who were not the subject of an accusation or indictment. In their role of selecting men to serve on juries, sheriffs had 'unlimited opportunities to harass ordinary freemen and to influence verdicts'. And they 'flayed' the countryside by imposing on litigants and jurors fees for permissions and fines for irregularities in procedure. Meanwhile, bailiffs, who had the task of implementing court orders and collecting debts and fines if necessary through seizure of property (distraint), took fees, bribes and levies, sometimes in the form of weekly or annual payments in cash or food. The business of bailiffs brought them into 'close contact and conflict' with local people, and they were subject to violence, being assaulted, even killed. A 'Song against sheriffs' reflected popular resentments: 'Who can tell truly how cruel sheriffs are? Of their hardness to poor people no tale can go too far.' The song lists the gifts that had to be offered ('the best of meat, the best of drink') not only to the sheriff, but also to his wife ('a gown of rainbow hue') and his staff ('their teeth grow long, their heads grow high'). Rapacity and harshness thus seemed the hallmarks of local officials in late thirteenth-century England.[16]

The French inquiry only confirms this. *Prévôts* bought their offices and recouped the outlay by taking gifts. One such had encouraged the right attitude by reminding listeners that, as *prévôt*, he could either help people or harm them; another said 'Pay up, or I'll seize your livestock.' Some took annual payments in cash or food, indeed in Languedoc it was customary to give a share of the harvest to the *bailli*. Officials demanded respectful treatment, and imposed fines for refusals of hospitality, or for not giving officials full, immediate and personal attention when they appeared. Most local hatred, however, was reserved for the *sergents*, who were the executive arms of judicial authority, pursuing criminals, making arrests and enforcing payment of fines. One study of the 1247 inquiry, focusing on the fifty complaints from just one remote village, concluded that what royal government amounted to for these villagers was the apparently arbitrary seizure by *sergents* of men, horses and goods: 'royal government made its impact in these upland villages in the form of the seizure of property and the imprisonment of the inhabitants', displaying the character of 'a gangsterish machine running the countryside'. Royal justice was a violent intrusion of outsiders seeking personal gain.[17]

An episode from Joinville's biography of King Louis IX illustrates the reputation of *sergents* and the heat of local reaction. Joinville was travelling to Paris when he came across a cart carrying three dead men who had been killed by a cleric and were being taken to the king. When they arrived, the king asked the *prévôt* of Paris what had happened.

The provost . . . told him that the dead men were three of his *sergents* from the Châtelet who had been going round unfrequented streets and robbing people.

'And', said he to the king, 'they met this clerk whom you see here, and stripped him of all his clothes. The clerk, with nothing on but his shirt, went back to his lodgings, snatched up his crossbow, and got a child to carry his sword. As soon as he caught sight of the thieves, he shouted after them, saying he would kill them. He got his crossbow ready and shot at them, piercing one of them through the heart. The two others took to their heels, but the clerk seized hold of the sword the child was carrying and followed after them in the moonlight . . .

'One of them,' added the provost, 'tried to get through a hedge into a garden, but the clerk struck at him with his sword, cutting right through his leg, so that it only holds to the boot, as you may see here. He then went after the other man, who tried to get into a . . . house where the people were still awake; but the clerk struck him a blow with his sword right through the middle of his head, and split it open down to the teeth, as your Majesty can also see.'[18]

Despite the ferocity of these killings, the king, who was about to depart on crusade, pardoned the cleric and, 'because of his courage', took him into his crusading army. This transformation of *sergents* into thieves in dark Parisian alleys, and of the killer into a crusader, has multiple meanings, not least of which is the scope and power of royal pardon, to which we shall return. Also important is the belief, illustrated by this story, that victims and bystanders had a right to attack thieves or burglars caught in the act: this led to near-lynchings. Criminals seized *in flagrante delicto* were liable to immediate punishment: flagrancy was thought to convict of itself, without need for further judicial process. As we shall see (below, pp. 137–8), such notions remained especially attached to the adulterous lover discovered by the husband. What is most important, however, is that this tale from Joinville depicts in sinister tones the figure of the dissolute *sergent*. Popular opinion of *sergents* was uniformly negative: the whole lexicon of ill-doing was applied to them. They were formulaically known as 'eaters and wasters' (*mangeurs et gasteurs*), a reputation earned from their habit of occupying the properties and consuming the goods of arrested suspects on the pretext of preserving them for the payment of eventual fines. More importantly, evidence suggests that this reputation was not undeserved. *Sergents* were often badly paid men of few means, reduced to extorting money from those they arrested, or tempted to use their authority to settle personal scores. Numerous studies have shown that *sergents* were often recruited from the very criminal milieux they were expected to police. An organised criminal gang in Provence in the 1430s contained a number of current or former *sergents*, prompting the comment by one historian that the line was porous between the propertied and criminal classes. The records of the Parlement of Paris throw up the example of a *sergent* at Sucy-en-Brie who did not denounce local thieves because they were all his favourite drinking companions. In Avignon, it has been argued, the job of *sergent* positively required brutality. Their small numbers meant that their only means of maintaining order was through fear of indiscriminate violence. As Chiffoleau presents them, the *sergents* of Avignon attacked the weak and innocent, hired themselves out to the powerful for dirty work, and oppressed the inhabitants of villages.[19]

In the long catalogue of corrupt officials some stand out for the range and intensity of their criminal conduct. In 1334 a former *prévôt* of Bourges, Jean Brunet, was pardoned for a long list of serious abuses of office.[20] In forty-three separate incidents (all of which he admitted), he committed not only extortion and wrongful imprisonment, but also excessive torture, theft and homicide. The least serious charges involved appropriating goods from houses, or arresting people, taking their money and valuables, and holding them until their families paid a ransom. He also concealed crimes in return for gifts: the friends of a woman suspected of poisoning her husband persuaded him to tear up a royal instruction to prosecute her, in return for two tuns of wine and a certain amount of cloth. In investigating crimes he might pretend to torture suspects in order to give an appearance of rigour, but at subsequent court sessions he would claim to find no truth in the charges. Brunet also had a sister and a brother, both of whom were involved in stealing: he managed not only to conceal their involvement, but charged others with the crimes and pocketed some of the loot. He raped a servant girl, threatening to imprison her, and abducted a wife, having his men assault and rob the husband when he tracked her down. He threatened those who came before him: one was told that if Brunet did not receive 20 *livres*, he would make his feet rot in prison; another man was indeed kept in irons so long that he lost a foot. Most serious of all was his lustful and brutal treatment of women, in three dreadful cases. In one, he arrested a woman on suspicion of theft from a guest at an inn: though he knew her to be pregnant, he tortured her so much that the foetus died and was stillborn. In a second case, he went armed at night to the house of another pregnant woman, seizing her with such force that she miscarried, and when her servant tried to rouse the neighbours, he grabbed her by the throat and stopped her. When he heard that this woman intended to complain, he threatened to kill her, 'and because he was used to hitting people, she did not dare complain'. In the third case, Brunet held out the promise to a suspect's young wife that he could ensure his release, provided she let him have his way with her, which she did.

Such a case is hardly unique in later medieval Europe: Gene Brucker has given us the Florentine examples of one judge who sexually assaulted the daughter of an exile, another who misbehaved at markets, railed against preachers and went around town eating, drinking, gambling and shouting with a 'gang of armed hoodlums', and of a third who had to be reminded by the government that officials are appointed 'to maintain justice among our subjects, and to conserve them in peace and unity, and not to engage in violence and extortion under cover of the offices and dignities which they hold'.[21] Complaint arose not just against judges, but against all those involved in public justice, from district officials and court notaries to gaolers. In Florence there was complaint about district officials who concealed crimes or denounced the innocent in return for payment. In Milan in 1425 it was the court notaries who were accused of inventing brawls and blasphemies, and of taking payments from suspects in return for promises to cut off prosecutions. In England complaints made against prison-keepers raise the figures of gaolers who refused to take prisoners into custody, or released them without authority, or who abused the vulnerability of prisoners, damaging their health and physical integrity: cell floors full of water that rotted prisoners' feet, prisoners stripped of their clothes and starved of food, injuries caused by chains and shackles too heavy or too tightly bound, physical assault and rape. In 1355 and again in 1376 it was alleged in Parliament that sheriffs and gaolers were getting themselves appointed to judicial commissions in order to indict and imprison innocent people who could then be induced to offer bribes for their release.[22]

However, the strong colours of Brunet's case should not allow us to think it was typical: we hear of bad judges because they were themselves the object of inquiry; and the fact that they were prosecuted might foster our belief in the integrity of the system as a whole. Moreover, Brunet's alleged misdeeds conform so closely to the image of the evil judge that they would seem to constitute an exemplary prosecution. The charges against Brunet invert the ideal of the good judge: he was supposed to protect women, not prey on them; he was supposed to condemn the guilty, not release them; he was supposed to refuse gifts, not demand them. Above all, the ideal judge would condemn even his own son or brother if he committed a crime, not conceal and profit from such misdoing. A judge who reportedly embodied the ideal was Etienne Boileau, whom Louis IX had employed to rid Paris of thieves and murderers: he is recorded to have hanged his own godson when he could not be stopped from thieving.[23] Moreover, many of the charges against Brunet are partial versions of legitimate actions: when the *prévôt* is accused of entering houses and 'stealing', he is probably taking goods in lieu of money, in order to pay fines or debts; when he releases suspects in return for payment, he is probably collecting legitimate fees and costs. Exactly the same sort of complaint was made against Italian judges, and their actions can be defended in exactly the same way. Peasants in particular refused to accept the legitimacy of the actions of judges and their officers: they tended to view the levying of court fees as robbery, and believed that judicial action against them was instigated by their enemies.[24]

Cases such as Brunet's were exceptional and called forth exceptional royal action. According to the fifteenth-century chronicler Jan Dlugosz, King Casimir of Poland reacted with ferocity to complaints about the protection of thieves by one of his governors in the 1350s. Maczko Borkowycz, *voivode* (governor) of Poznan, instead of arresting thieves and highway robbers, had started to be their chief harbourer in secret, and then the chief author of their robberies. King Casimir tried persuasion and threats, but could not halt the wayward governor's conduct. As Dlugosz tells it, the tale is one of the confrontation between the governor's confidence in his noble birth and the king's great abhorrence of theft and robbery. When the governor at last came before the king, he was at once condemned to death, put in a dungeon and starved to death: at the king's order, he was given only a handful of straw and a goblet of water, but he survived for forty days by eating the flesh on his own hands. The king's reputation as a great, reforming law-giver, already established by his numerous statutes, was thus extended into action.[25]

Despite these reservations, late medieval literature abounds in false accusations, forced confessions and corrupt judges. Boccaccio gathers a series of such stories in Day IV of his *Decameron*, a collection of one hundred tales told over ten days by a group of young Florentines taking refuge from the Black Death. Thus, a wife arrested for poisoning her husband is released after her friend offers to sleep with the local ruler (IV.3). In the same story, two innocent people confess under duress to a murder but bribe their guards to let them escape. In other tales, judges attempt to extract sexual favours from vulnerable women who come before them (IV.6, 10) and torture is used to extract untrue confessions (IV.10). Such themes recur in other parts of the *Decameron* too. When an innocent man is convicted of a murder, another character reflects upon 'the blind severity of the law and its administrators, who in order to convey the impression that they are zealously seeking the truth, often have recourse to cruelty and cause falsehood to be accepted as proven fact' (III.7). In the first story of Day II, such a judge is so convinced by a (false) report of theft that he tortures the suspect and refuses to listen to proofs of his innocence. Such themes also appear in the literature of other countries. In the mid-fourteenth-century English poem *The Tale of Gamelyn*, the figures of the corrupt judge and sheriff and the bribed jury appear: Gamelyn's wicked brother, who has deprived him of his inheritance, becomes sheriff, arrests Gamelyn and packs the jury that is to try him.[26]

The issue of bribes and gifts to judges is humorously taken up by the poet Eustache Deschamps, himself a sometime *bailli* of Senlis. The poem is written in the form of a mock letter of instruction issued on 24 December 1388, 'after midnight', by the 'conservator-general of the privileges and customs of *baillis*'. There have been complaints, the conservator records, in the matter of gifts of wine, meat, venison, rabbit, partridge, pheasant, capons, cheese, fruit, fish, apples, pears, nuts, and other such morsels traditionally given to royal judges. A number of badly advised people have taken to presenting very small quantities of wine, 'such that there isn't enough wine to say mass', and have ceased making gifts of food altogether, thus unjustly depriving the judges and their court officers of their dues. The conservator therefore orders that convention should be reinstated, that all small wine-jugs should be broken and replaced by large, round pots, and that gifts of food should be resumed.[27] As this ironic poem suggests, justice was normally accompanied by gift-giving. An informal rule promoted gifts, while the formal rule aimed to suppress them. What might seem like corruption to us was part of everyday social exchange.

Corruption: function or dysfunction?

Recently, some historians have tried to put some anthropological or sociological distance between modern morality and medieval 'corruption', seeing rather the positive functions of gift-giving.[28] It is too easy to smile at amusing instances of corruption in the past, comfortably tut-tutting from our historical armchairs. As Waquet has argued, corruption has been treated anecdotally rather than systematically by historians: 'nobody takes the subject seriously enough'. Wim Blockmans, for one, has attempted to remedy this deficiency in his study of the Burgundian state in the fifteenth century. He has argued that the centralisation and bureaucratic expansion that accompanied state formation so pressed and injured vested interests at the local and regional level as to create the need for mediating systems of brokerage and corruption. Arguments such as this show us how corruption was not just a matter of personal insufficiency. Since corruption survived both condemnation by governments and changes of regime, Waquet asks 'could it not be said that what appears to be a "dysfunction" is in fact a latent function?' Corruption should thus be considered not as a disturbance of social order, but an essential part of it, and should be redefined as part of the gift economy.

In similar vein, Natalie Zemon Davis has recently conducted a survey of gift-giving in sixteenth-century France. She sees gift exchange as 'a register with its own rules, language, etiquette and gestures'. Practising anthropological 'thick description', she distinguishes the different functions of gifts, for example the benign gifts that knotted friendship or confirmed status, and the troublesome gifts that engendered rivalry and violence. 'Gifts were everywhere', she says, in politics, justice and appointments to office. On the other hand, gift-giving was also strongly condemned. The biblical injunctions were graphic: bribes blind judges. The law forbad judges from accepting gifts, except for food and wine (see Deschamps's satire). Kings had an interest in eliminating gifts to judges, as this would tighten 'judges' ties to the monarch as against their competing ties to local aristocracies'. What Davis describes is a clash of politico-religious cultures. On the one hand, the monarchy, with support from the Old Testament, sought to control its own officials according to its own rules; on the other hand, wider social practice, supported by Christian injunction to love one's neighbour and to practise charity, sought to create links of friendship with local officials. The border between these two worlds was easily crossed: 'In a world of gifts that created "friendships" and grateful obligations, where did bribery begin?'[29]

This is an important corrective. It is joined by others in the area of the defects and incapacities of medieval justice. One attractive but deluding metaphor for understanding criminal justice was to see it as a machine: accusations and indictments are fed in at one end, and physical punishments come out at the other. The efficiency of the machine can be simply measured by calculating the numerical difference between input and output. Maitland, in his great history of English law, had something of this approach, evaluating criminal law by the number of hangings it inflicted. His text is punctuated with laments at the lack of severity in late medieval punishment. He himself produced some figures from thirteenth-century eyres: for example, in Gloucestershire in 1221, 330 homicide cases were heard, but only fourteen resulted in hangings. 'Crimes of violence were common', but 'the criminal law was exceedingly inefficient.' Later historians have only confirmed this statistical picture. In his study of homicide in the thirteenth century, Given found that of 3,500 accused, only 247 were executed (most of the rest being either outlawed or acquitted). The passing of centuries brought little change: when King Henry V held a special session of the central criminal court in some Midlands counties in 1414, it received over 2,000 indictments, but managed only three executions.[30] In Italy, where courts could convict in the absence of the suspect, such convictions always outnumbered convictions where the suspect was present. For example, of eighty-one people charged with theft in Florence in the mid-1340s, two were acquitted, thirty-three were hanged, but forty-six were condemned in absence.[31]

However, since the 1970s this simple reckoning of judicial efficiency has been criticised and superseded by more sophisticated approaches. Against the temptation to see the few hangings and the many outlawries in England as signs of failure, Henry Summerson has turned the criticism on its head and argued that, for the thirteenth century at least, outlawry and even abjuring the realm were signs of success. These were 'effective means of punishing felons who could not be captured'. They were effective because the overlapping system of local courts – hundred, sheriff, county – ensured the broadcasting of the names of outlaws such that they could effectively be excluded from their communities and 'hunted and harassed at every turn'.[32]

Moreover, a focus on failures and incapacity overlooks the successes and competency of medieval criminal justice. One common observation among historians is that coordination was lacking, between either overlapping levels or adjacent territories of jurisdiction. However, courts could cooperate as well as compete. Extradition treaties existed from an early date and were used. Judges in adjacent jurisdictions shared information and coordinated action.[33] Moreover, it can be argued that the evidence for judges' disinterest and benevolence far outweighs that for their greed: they could adhere to ideals of incorruptibility and resist the social pressures they faced.[34]

In a famous article in 1975, Hanawalt tackled precisely the problem that medieval justice did not touch the wealthy and powerful for their crimes. Statistically, she finds this to be startlingly true: of 10,000 felony indictments from fourteenth-century England, she found only fourteen that involved noblemen. One part of her analysis is to ask why this was: possible explanations include the use of social power to avoid prosecution (the intimidation of jurors and judges) or the use of servants and retainers to do any dirty business. More important, however, is her examination of the royal response, and the conclusion she draws from that: despite concern at noble criminality expressed in parliaments, petitions and statutes, the kings sought 'only to regulate, not to eradicate, noble crime'. Typically, kings imposed light penalties on noble criminals, or recruited gentry troublemakers into royal armies or royal officialdom. The important conclusion drawn is that 'both king and barons assumed that a certain amount of criminal activity was involved in being a noble and would be tolerated'.[35]

Revisions of this sort have been joined by more radical reinterpretations of the social relations between the parties to a criminal trial. The innovation lies in replacing a rule-centred analysis, from the viewpoint of the law, by a processual analysis, from the viewpoint of the parties in conflict. What this means is that events in trial records are seen not as breaches of the criminal law but as episodes in disputes that were often resolved by other means. The law courts thus did not intervene in social relations to punish behaviour because it broke a law, but bringing a case to court was a tactic in a larger dispute. And that larger dispute was often settled out of court through mediation or arbitration.[36] Drawing on such arguments, as well as on much broader anthropological literature, Claude Gauvard has recently advanced an even more powerful revision of this type. Gauvard sees two parallel systems of conflict resolution: the formal structure of trial and punishment, and the informal structure of vengeance, pacification and reparation. Whether a conflict entered the formal structure or not depended on the local community and on the identity and reputation of those involved. Criminals, she argues, were of two types: those who committed crimes in their own locality and who remained within the unspoken rules of informal conflict resolution; and those whom the community decided to deliver up to formal justice. 'The community is thus free to keep quiet or to denounce, according to its interests.' The community delivered up those it did not know, or those of whom it did not know the truth. Where it knew the truth, informal mechanisms could be set in motion to pacify and compensate. State justice thus dealt with only a part, and an unrepresentative part, of criminality.[37]

All of these approaches offer us new ways forward in writing the history of late medieval justice. Instead of looking from the top down and seeing a heroic judicial system frustrated by villains among the aristocracy or judiciary, they enable us to look from the bottom up and see local communities bravely resisting the predatory visitations of official justice or trying, through the common practice of gift-giving, to forge bonds of reciprocity with the holders of official power. It must always be remembered, however, that the rising trajectory of monarchical or state power placed such relations between officials and communities under increasing strain.

Notes

1. Plutarch, *Greek Lives*, trans. R. Waterfield (Oxford, 1998), pp. 49–50.
2. *Oeuvres complètes de Eustache Deschamps* (11 vols, Paris, 1878–1903), III, pp. 161–3.
3. *Hoccleve's Works*, ed. F.J. Furnivall, vol. III, *The Regiment of Princes* (London, 1897: EETS, Extra Series, 72), p. 102.
4. H. Oesterley, *Gesta Romanorum* (2 vols, Berlin, 1872), II, p. 502; T.F. Dunn, 'The *facetiae* of the *Mensa philosophica*', *Washington University Studies* new ser., 5 (1934), p. 35.
5. J. Larner, 'Order and disorder in Romagna, 1450–1500', in *Violence and Civil Disorder in Italian Cities*, ed. L. Martines (Berkeley and London, 1972), p. 50; G. Bonfiglio Dosio, 'Criminalità ed emarginazione a Brescia nel primo

Quattrocento', *Archivio storico italiano* 136 (1978), pp. 163–4; S. Piasentini, *'Alla luce della luna': I furti a Venezia, 1270–1403* (Venice, 1992), pp. 107–12; J.B. Given, *Society and Homicide in Thirteenth-century England* (Stanford, 1977), pp. 71–81; M.K. Schüssler, 'German crime in the later Middle Ages: A statistical analysis of the Nuremberg Outlawry Books, 1285–1400', *Criminal Justice History* 13 (1992), p. 11.

6. C. Gauvard, *'De grace especial': Crime, état et société en France à la fin du Moyen Age* (Paris, 1991), pp. 423–7; R. Harris, *Valois Guyenne: A Study of Politics, Government and Society in Late Medieval France* (Woodbridge, 1994), pp. 137–8.

7. Gauvard, *Crime, état et société*, pp. 423–7; D. Potter, ' "Rigueur de justice": Crime, murder and the law in Picardy, fifteenth to sixteenth centuries', *French History* 11 (1997), p. 298.

8. *Documents inédits concernant la ville et le siège du bailliage d'Amiens*, ed. E. Maugis (2 vols, Amiens and Paris, 1914), II, pp. 43–8; N. Fryde, 'A medieval robber baron: Sir John Molyns of Stoke Poges, Buckinghamshire', in *Medieval Legal Records*, ed. R.F. Hunnisett and J.B. Post (London, 1978).

9. E.L.G. Stones, 'The Folvilles of Ashby-Folville, Leicestershire, and their associates in crime', *Transactions of the Royal Historical Society* 5th ser., 7 (1957).

10. C. Carpenter, 'Sir Thomas Malory and fifteenth-century local politics', *Historical Research* 53 (1980); R.V. Virgoe, 'William Tailboys and Lord Cromwell: Crime and politics in Lancastrian England', *Bulletin of the John Rylands Library* 55 (1972–3); J. Heers, *Gilles de Rais* (Paris, 1997); G. Cecchini, 'Ghino di Tacco', *Archivio storico italiano* 115 (1957).

11. G. Cherubini, 'Appunti sul brigantaggio in Italia alla fine del Medioevo', in *Studi di storia medievale e moderna per Ernesto Sestan* (Florence, 1980), I, pp. 119, 128–9.

12. Cecchini, 'Ghino di Tacco', p. 281.

13. J-M. Cauchies, *La législation princière pour le comté de Hainaut: Ducs de Bourgogne et premiers Habsbourg (1427–1506)* (Brussels, 1982), pp. 496–503.

14. *Statutes of the Realm* (9 vols, London, 1810–22), II, p. 74.

15. J.R. Maddicott, 'Law and lordship: royal justices as retainers in thirteenth and fourteenth century England', *Past & Present* Supplement 4 (1978).

16. H. Cam, *The Hundred and the Hundred Rolls* (London, 1930), *passim*; pp. 69–70, 78, 106 for quoted material.

17. C-V. Langlois, 'Doléances recueillies par les enquêteurs de Saint Louis', *Revue historique* 92 (1906), esp. pp. 17–19, 26; R. Bartlett, 'The impact of royal government in the French Ardennes: the evidence of the 1247 enquête', *Journal of Medieval History* 7 (1981), pp. 89–90.

18. Joinville and Villehardouin, *Chronicles of the Crusades*, trans. M.R.B. Shaw (Harmondsworth, 1963), p. 153.

19. J. Chiffoleau, *Les justices du Pape: délinquance et criminalité dans la région d'Avignon au quatorzième siècle* (Paris, 1984), pp. 66–7; *Confessions et jugements de criminels au Parlement de Paris (1319–1350)*, ed. M. Langlois and Y. Lanhers (Paris, 1971), p. 36; N. Coulet, 'Une enquête criminelle au XVe siècle', *Provence historique* 39 (1989), pp. 568–9; N. Gonthier, *Cris de haine et rites d'unité: La violence dans les villes, XIIIe–XVIe siècle* (n.p., 1992), pp. 154–8.

20. Douët-D'Arcq, 'Lettres de rémission pour Jean Brunet, prévôt de Bourges, 1334', *Bibliothèque de l'Ecole des chartes* 4th ser., 2 (1886).

21. G. Brucker, *The Society of Renaissance Florence* (New York, 1971), pp. 130–6 (examples dated respectively 1382, 1418 and 1461).

22. H. Manikowska, ' "Accorr'uomo": il "popolo" nell'amministrazione della giustizia a Firenze durante il XIV secolo', *Ricerche storiche* 18 (1988), pp. 542–3; E. Verga, 'La giurisdizione del podestà di Milano e i capitani dei contadi rurali, 1381–1429', *Rendiconti dell'Istituto lombardo di scienze e lettere* 2nd ser., 34 (1901), p. 1254; R.B. Pugh, *Imprisonment in Medieval England* (Cambridge, 1970), pp. 180–2.

23. *Histoire littéraire de la France*, vol. XIX (Paris, 1838), p. 108.

24. D.S. Chambers and T. Dean, *Clean Hands and Rough Justice: An Investigating Magistrate in Renaissance Italy* (Ann Arbor, 1997), pp. 52–3; V.I. Comparato, 'Il controllo del contado a Perugia nella prima metà del Quattrocento: Capitani, vicari e contadini tra 1428 e 1450', in *Forme e tecniche del potere nella città (secoli XIV–XVII)* (Perugia, 1980), p. 169.

25. *Joannis Dlugossii . . . Historiae Polonicae libri XII*, in *Joannis Dlugosz senioris canonici cracoviensis opera omnia*, ed. A. Przezdziecki (14 vols, Cracow, 1867–87), vol. XII, pp. 269–70.

26. R. Kaeuper, 'An historian's reading of *The Tale of Gamelyn*', *Medium Aevum* 52 (1983), pp. 55–6.

27. *Oeuvres complètes de Eustache Deschamps*, VIII, pp. 3–11.

28. J-C. Waquet, *Corruption: Ethics and Power in Florence, 1660–1770* (Cambridge, 1991), pp. 2–14; W. Blockmans, 'Patronage, brokerage and corruption as symptoms of incipient state formation in the Burgundian-Habsburg Netherlands', in *Klientelsysteme im Europa der Frühen Neuzeit*, ed. A. Maczak (Munich, 1988).

29. N.Z. Davis, *The Gift in Sixteenth-century France* (Oxford, 2000), pp. 4, 15, 142–51.

30. F. Pollock and F.W. Maitland, *The History of English Law before the Time of Edward I*, 2nd edn (Cambridge, 1968), II, p. 557; Given, *Society and Homicide in Thirteenth-century England*, pp. 92–3; E. Powell, *Kingship, Law and Society: Criminal Justice in the Reign of Henry V* (Oxford, 1989), pp. 178–87.

31. C. Caduff, 'I "publici latrones" nella città e nel contado di Firenze a metà Trecento', *Ricerche storiche* 18 (1998), p. 502.

32. H.R.T. Summerson, 'The structure of law enforcement in thirteenth-century England', *American Journal of Legal History* 23 (1979).

33. For Italy, see material in Chambers and Dean, *Clean Hands and Rough Justice*.

34. H. Zaremska, *Les bannis au Moyen Age* (Paris, 1996), pp. 163–4; L.T. Maes, 'L'humanité de la magistrature du déclin du Moyen Age', *TRG* 19 (1951).

35. B.A. Hanawalt, 'Fur-collar crime: the pattern of crime among the fourteenth-century English nobility', *Journal of Social History* 8 (1975).

36. Powell, *Kingship, Law and Society*, pp. 91–2.

37. C. Gauvard, 'Les sources judiciaries de la fin du Moyen Age peuvent-elles permettre une approche statistique du crime?', in *Commerce, finances et société (XIe–XVIe siècles): recueil de travaux d'histoire médiéval offert à H. Dubois*, ed. P. Contamine, T. Dutour and B. Schnerb (Paris, 1993), pp. 478–80; Gauvard, *Crime, état et société*, pp. 164–71.

chapter 3

LATE MEDIEVAL
CRIME WAVES?

A strong tradition associates the later fourteenth and fifteenth centuries with greater lawlessness. It is generally argued that this resulted from the social and economic crisis brought about by repeated epidemics of bubonic plague from 1348 onwards and by extensive international warfare. Plague and warfare together are said to have generated three new social problems: rural misery, urban unemployment and predatory vagabondage.[1] The destructive effects of plague on rural communities led to migration into the towns, but towns sought to encourage the immigration only of skilled workers and were unable to absorb large numbers of unskilled newcomers, either because of guild regulations or because of lack of economic demand. Contemporary comment and action supports the suggestion that crime flourished in these conditions. The chronicler Jean de Venette claimed that 'brawls and disputes' increased after the Black Death of 1348, and he was not alone in noting greater greed and insolence as features of post-plague society. In 1350 the Sienese government lamented the great increase in violent crimes in the city and 'the ever-growing impunity of criminals', and it consequently went on to create a new police official in 1352. A Venetian chronicler noted that 'in this plague arose countless robbers, who thieved and looted houses', and to combat them the government doubled the night-watch.[2] Venice also passed new legislation in 1349 to facilitate the prosecution of those who fornicated with nuns.[3]

It might be thought that these were exaggerated responses and perceptions. An expectation that plague would be accompanied by other social ills, particularly a rupture of normal social bonds, was encouraged by biblical and historical examples. A little looting perhaps of abandoned homes during the plague confirmed this in the eyes of observers. However, the statistics of prosecutions (unless these are simply a function of increased fear of crime) speak clearly enough. In Florence between the mid-1340s and mid-1350s there was a rise in prosecuted crime, while in

Venice the number of theft trials remained high, and included some cases of looting during plague emergencies. In Cagliari (Sardinia) a lower population seems to have committed more offences, and in Susa (Savoy) fines for adultery and sexual violence continued their long-term rise, uninterrupted by the fall in population.[4] As for the connection of economic crisis, vagabondage and theft, Pinto has presented the case of a 'typical' vagabond-thief, Sandro, also known as 'Big Fish' ('Pescione'), who was captured and executed by Florence in 1375. He was convicted on twenty-eight counts of theft and deception: he stole from churches, and pretended to be a collector of debts, fines or charitable donations. He was, says Pinto, the victim, like many others, of an economic crisis that swelled the numbers of vagabonds while also creating spaces for them to live at the geographical margins of ordinary society.[5]

The form of insolence that was especially condemned was that of labourers and artisans demanding higher wages or moving from place to place in search of better wages or conditions. This social disobedience among the labouring classes affected the criminal law in two broad ways. First, it prompted legislation to curtail excessive wages and to restore subservience; second, it eroded traditional local mechanisms for maintaining order and reporting crimes. R.C. Palmer has argued that concern to re-establish the social equilibrium disturbed by the plague became the driving force in the development of English law in the later fourteenth century. This is a controversial thesis which has met considerable criticism.[6] Although Palmer concentrates on trends in civil law (contract and obligation), a parallel to his thesis can be found in the criminal law. As Bellamy has shown, the labour legislation introduced summary procedures into English law that were then gradually extended to other offences, all of which shared a connection to the master–servant relationship.[7] Moreover, greater mobility among the labouring classes affected the self-policing mechanisms of local communities in both town and country. In England the system of frankpledge declined: under this system, the male inhabitants of every locality had been arranged into groups, notionally of ten, which were duty-bound to denounce, arrest, guard and bring to court any one of their number who offended; but this depended on a level of stable residence that no longer obtained in the more fluid social conditions of the fourteenth century. In Florence, for the same reason, the system of denunciation of crimes by local communities also ceased to function.[8] Despite these ways in which Palmer's thesis might be supplemented and developed, doubts remain about it, especially for its exclusion of other forces driving legal change, for example warfare or practical and legal problems. The decline of English frankpledge, for example, has been related, rather, to developments in the judicial structure and in policing. In Italy, Florence was perhaps unique in losing its system of local denunciation: many other cities kept theirs.

Meanwhile, it is clear that warfare also stimulated violence in many ways. In England, kings recruited convicted criminals into their armies in return for pardons, while in France veterans with good service records found it easier to obtain pardons for their later, peacetime offences. Armies took young men and taught them 'the habits of hardened soldiers at war with society'. When peace came, they refused to return to their former occupations or to reintegrate into society. Once military campaigning ceased or truces were concluded, demobbed soldiers were released onto the highways of France and Italy, living by a combination of brigandage, extortion and mercenary fighting. In France in the late fourteenth and early fifteenth centuries, soldiers formed perhaps 1 per cent of the total population, but received 2.5 per cent of pardons for crimes. More generally among French petitioners for pardons, when explanations are offered for their crimes, warfare is mentioned as often as anger or alcohol. Moreover, it is said that, just as the king's presence had a restraining effect on disorders, so too his absence on campaign allowed wrongdoing to flourish, creating a flood of complaint. Warfare also created frontiers and this added further to the problem of maintaining order: enemy raiding could wreak destruction deep into home territory, but protective garrisons could be equally disruptive, as soldiers confronted local populations over food, lodgings and women.[9]

However, this picture has to be tempered. No quantitative study of crime has yet shown that the fourteenth-century crisis brought with it sustained increases in crime levels. The long-term trend in violent crime in Florence seems to have been downward. On the manors of Spalding Priory in Lincolnshire, where the Priory had the right to execute thieves caught red-handed, eleven men were hanged in the first half of the fourteenth century, none in the second half: 'in this little corner of the Fens, the traditional picture of increased disorder in the late Middle Ages is not evident'.[10] What does seem to have increased is fear of crime, which is of course a variable independent of crime levels. Gauvard has argued that it was fear of crime that established the image of greater lawlessness, with stereotypical connections to plague and warfare. Because both crime and disease threatened society as a whole, the presence of the one called forth fear of the other. The image of horrible crimes committed by soldiers was also a stereotype, amplified by sensitised opinion fed by fear of war and distrust of soldiery. It was facilitated by the fact that soldiers were instantly recognisable but individually unknown, and were distinct by age and group behaviour. Although in late fourteenth- and early fifteenth-century France the majority of soldier crimes do seem to have been committed against civilians, this does not seem to be the case at other times, in other theatres of war. For example, in Picardy in the later fifteenth century, most violence was among the soldiers themselves, who apparently lived in a world of their own when it came to the exchange of violence. Moreover, the effect of the king's absence on levels of crime has been challenged, and almost the reverse has been argued for: that war promoted responsible behaviour among noblemen, and that temporary arrangements for ensuring public order in the king's absence could be effective.[11]

Criminalisation of vagrancy

Greater fear of crime also made stereotypical associations of lawlessness with travelling foreigners, whether soldiers or vagabonds. This can be seen clearly in the developing criminalisation of vagabondage. Vagabondage had for centuries been viewed by the civil and ecclesiastical authorities as reprehensible, but it had not been criminalised: vagrants might be presumed to be involved in crime and could therefore be arrested and questioned, but being a vagabond was not in itself a crime. This changed in the mid-fourteenth century, it is claimed. After the Black Death, governments in many parts of Europe quickly issued laws to control the 'insolence', as they saw it, of labourers and artisans demanding higher wages, who thus forced up the price of labour and of manufactured goods. These concerns with the labour market also led governments to tackle vagrancy and voluntary unemployment. With the numbers of unemployed vagrants and able-bodied beggars multiplying in towns, governments took measures to direct this surplus labour to the shortages that existed. Deservedly famous is the Parisian ordinance of 1351 which complained of the wilfully unemployed who frequented taverns and brothels. This ordinance proceeded to create a range of penalties, from imprisonment to branding and banishment, for refusing to earn a living or to leave town. In 1367 the able-bodied in Paris were directed to work on the town ditches (on pain of a flogging) and in 1382 to find work in the countryside. So far the chief concern of this sort of legislation was the state of the labour market, but according to Geremek a key change came from the second decade of the fifteenth century as public order replaced such concerns. Thus, in ordinances of King Charles VII (1422–61) we find vagabonds treated as robbers and brawlers, and beggars seen as fakers; and they were not only compelled to work, but subject to heavier penalties.

However, this development is disputed for France: Cohen points to an ordinance of 1395 which painted the unemployed as responsible for all crimes and disorders, and a regulation of similar date from the city of

Toulouse laments the great ills that result from the 'ribaldry' of vagabonds. At roughly this time too, Eustache Deschamps's vitriolic poems
against 'false' beggars – who cause a stinking, noisy, pestering crowd
during mass – ask for them to be chased out of churches, put in the
pillory or hanged as thieves of God.[12] Nor can Geremek's construction be
translated to other areas. Already in 1379 the Cortes of Castile enacted
measures to compel the unemployed into work and associated the
begging of vagabonds with thefts and robberies. Even earlier, in the
mid-fourteenth century statutes of King Casimir of Poland, penalties are
decreed against vagrants who 'do not fear seizing other people's property',
thus clearly associating vagrancy with robbery. In England, a new statute
of 1383, 'to restrain the malice of vagrants', said to be travelling from place
to place more than in the past, ordered Justices of the Peace and sheriffs
to interrogate such vagabonds and compel them to provide guarantors of
good behaviour, or to imprison them if they could not do so.[13]

Conversely, one country where Geremek's schema does seem to work
is Scotland. Here labour-market concerns seem uppermost still in 1424:
a statute of that year ordained that the local authorities would give a
token to genuine beggars, to distinguish them from the idlers, who 'shall
be charged to labour and to pass to crafts for winning of their living'.
Twenty-five years later the attitude to beggars had been transformed. A
statute was enacted in 1449 'for the away putting of sornares, over-lyars
and maisterfull beggars'. Officials in town and country were to inquire at
every court session, and if any such beggars were found, they were to be
put in custody, to await the king's will, and any goods they had were to
be confiscated. Moreover, any 'fuiles . . . bairdes or uthers sik like rinnares-
about' (fools, strolling rhymers or other such-like vagabonds), if they had
any goods, were to be put in irons in prison, and if not, 'their eares be
nailed to the trone [pillory] or till [to] ane uther tree, and their eare
cutted off', and then they were to be banished.[14]

There is a further difficulty with the overall thesis of post-plague
criminalisation of vagrancy. Vagrancy did not suddenly appear with the
first outbreaks of plague. Already in the late thirteenth century the
frequency of crimes committed by vagabonds was causing problems for
the local mechanisms of crime prevention. Similarly in Italy some sources
make it clear that vagabondage was a problem already before 1348. In
the theft trials studied by Piasentini, for example, vagabonds are first
mentioned in the 1320s, with numbers rising in the following decades.
The city of Lucca was trying to clear the town and environs of vagabonds
in 1346. Nevertheless, these same sources do show an intensification of
the problem after the Black Death. Thieving vagabonds in Venice carry
on growing in numbers. In the 1350s Lucca saw the need to appoint an

official specifically to round up and punish vagabonds and other criminals in its territory.[15]

There could be still other motives for hostility to beggars. This is well illustrated in a story told of Vlad the Impaler, lord of Valachia in the mid-fifteenth century. On one occasion, he allegedly summoned all the old, the sick, the poor, the blind and the lame to appear before him. When they had assembled, he had them lodged in a large house, where he gave them as much food and drink as they wanted. He then asked them if they would like him to relieve them of all their cares in this world and to stop them being a burden on others. They said 'Yes'. So Vlad had all the doors and windows locked and set the house ablaze. Explaining his actions to the nobles, he said that he had done this to stop such people being a burden, as he wanted no more paupers in his lands, and to liberate them from poverty and disease.[16] Such feelings, of the intolerable burden placed on ordinary society by those who could not or would not work for a living, perhaps lies behind all the legislation that we have examined.

Prostitution, gambling and blasphemy

The same sentiment of menace to respectable society informed government attitudes to other perceived sources of disorder. As causes of crime, governments often targeted three offensive behaviours: prostitution, gambling and blasphemy. Repression of one of these was often associated with repression of one or both of the others. In Milan, for example, a proclamation on 4 August 1416 ordered that prostitutes wear cloaks and that no one play dice in the new government building on the Broletto; a proclamation on 18 May 1417 ordered that no one blaspheme and that all prostitutes return to the brothel.[17]

At first it might be thought that there was little evolution in such edicts: this trio of offences was a constant concern of governments. Let us compare a thirteenth-century French ordinance with a fifteenth-century Italian one, King Louis IX's famous ordinance of 1254 with the Duke of Ferrara's proclamation of 1496. Though chiefly concerned with the conduct in office of royal judges and their subordinates, Louis IX's ordinance concludes with five clauses aimed at perceived social dangers. It ordered that previous ordinances on Jewish usury and 'blasphemous books' were to be enforced; that prostitutes were to be expelled from towns and their belongings seized, 'even down to their tunic and fur-coat'; that games of dice, 'tables' and chess were banned, as were gaming houses ('dice schools') and dice-making; and that inns were to give lodging only to travellers lacking a local dwelling. In a later ordinance of 1268–9, Louis IX also dealt with blasphemy, setting a sliding scale of monetary or corporal penalties according to the gravity of the offence.[18] The Ferrarese decree of two and a half centuries later, after a long preamble announcing the Christian purposes of a campaign against vice – 'to put a sword to the root of the crimes that greatly provoke God' – contains a succession of clauses regarding Jews, prostitutes, gambling, blasphemy and sodomy. Jews are to wear an 'O' sign, 'so that they can be recognised . . . and distinguished from Christians'; all pimps are to leave the city, and all women 'living indecently in districts where decent people live' are to move to the brothel, so that 'neither the ears, nor the eyes, nor the reputations of honest women are offended'; and arbitrary penalties are announced for blasphemy and for playing prohibited games, 'as from them arise blasphemies, thefts, woundings, homicides and many other disorders'.[19] There are clear differences between these two enactments, apart from the lengthier rationales of the later decree. Where the saintly King Louis wants prostitutes expelled, the pious duke wants them confined; where the one simply prohibits specific activities, the other imposes discretionary penalties; where the one interferes in Jewish business and religion, the other wants Jews only to be marked in public. Inns are absent from Duke Ercole's decree, sodomy from King Louis's. Nevertheless, the same targets are chosen to bear the cost of Christian purification: the prostitutes who pollute respectable areas, the gamblers who cause public disorder, the blasphemers who invite divine retribution, and the Jews who mix too easily in Christian society. A stress on similarities would in the end, however, be deceptive: first, because Louis IX's abolitionism was exceptional, and second, because each of these criminogenic social practices in fact followed a different evolution.

Of these various activities, the link to violence was strongest in games and gambling. Mehl has dissected the violence that gambling engendered, classifying it into five types. Some violence was accidental, as when children wandered into the path of arrows or boules, or when men or boys, falling on each other in rough play, wounded themselves on protruding knives. Verbal violence was more common, as players responded with insults to an opponent's success or bad play, seeing these as a form of aggressive challenge. A refusal to play could also draw forth verbal or physical violence: in 1477 one player who wanted to withdraw from a game of 'knives' was confronted by his opponent threatening to 'make his head softer than a rotten apple'. There was a social expectation that members of groups would play and would not leave a game unilaterally. The fourth type of violence came when a game was disturbed by a non-player, who either commented on the course of the game, or tried to end or move it. 'Game time was sacred', comments Mehl, 'and breaking it was sacrilege.' Last, the game might itself be a pretext for pursuing an existing quarrel or reviving an old grudge, in which case violence was the desired outcome rather than a sudden disruption of play.[20]

Although the attention of governments focused most on dice games, it is worth putting them into the broader context of other games. Historians have divided games into various categories: games of chance (dice, some card games), games of skill (chess, boules) and sports (archery, ball games). Prohibitions might include games from any of these categories, because the evils of gambling could be associated with them all: the English ban of 1388, for example, covered football, tennis, quoits and dice. Board games were, however, broadly tolerated, while games of chance were condemned. The reasons for this condemnation were essentially twofold: gambling led directly to other crimes; and it brought about consequential damage to families, society and local economies. Nothing is more frequent in the preambles to bans of dice games than the assertion that they led to theft, brawling and even homicide; and to these disturbances of social order was added disturbance of divine order through blasphemy. Among the indirect damage caused by gambling, we find claims that gambling impoverished players and their families, leaving wives and children destitute, that games distracted workers from productive activities, and that merchants visiting town wasted at dice games the money they might have spent on merchandise. Gambling was thus an attack on all the normal means of sustenance and sociability: production, commerce, the family. These concerns were shared across Europe: King Casimir of Poland attempted to regulate gambling in the mid-fourteenth century, focusing on the impoverishment of parents by the gambling debts of their sons, and on the exploitation of drunk or angry gamblers by their opponents, who stripped them of money, horses and inheritances.[21] Chaucer reflects them too in his depiction of the world of the tavern in *The Pardoner's Tale*: gambling is 'the very mother of lying, of deceit and cursed swearing, of blasphemy and manslaughter', and a waster of time and money.

In governments' attitudes to gambling, a general development is evident from tolerant licensing to prohibition and penalisation. In the cities of Tuscany, gambling was legally permitted at specified places and at specified times, but banned in others. These legal sites might be the main square or the marketplace, and the legal times might include feast days, fairs and the twelve days of Christmas. The legal prohibitions covered private houses, taverns and brothels, churches and cemeteries, workshops and market stalls. In some cities (though not in Florence) licensed gaming houses were organised as a public monopoly, and were farmed out to contractors, thus producing revenue for the city. Penalties for gambling outside these tolerated times and places were monetary, although insolvent and fraudulent gamblers might incur a shaming dip in the River

Arno (ironically dubbed 'baptism'). During the fifteenth century, however, the influence of the great reform preachers, combined with changes
in the nature of government, led to greater repression of gambling and
the decline of private contracting.[22] In Florence, more intensive activity
by police patrols and a shift in government approach, from episodic
repression to more constant control and containment, brought more
frequent punishment of gambling, through fines and corporal punishment. In one year alone in the early fifteenth century, the police patrols
netted over 400 gamblers caught *in flagrante*.[23]

In Flanders there was a somewhat similar progression. Here the Count
of Flanders had a monopoly on granting gaming concessions, and these
proliferated in the later fourteenth century as they spread from the towns
to the countryside. Gaming outside the count's licensed premises, for
example in taverns, was an offence. However, though the count granted
licences, the towns sought to regulate gambling. Ypres attempted a
general ban on gambling in 1285; other towns banned particular games,
for example cards or boules, or games at particular times. Penalties were,
again, mainly monetary, though at Ghent in 1365 banishment of three
years was ordained for hosts of unlicensed gambling. Repression, which
had begun in the late thirteenth century, does seem to have gathered
pace after the mid-fourteenth century, with urban ordinances at Ghent,
for example, in 1365, 1377, 1486 and 1491. Finally, in 1495, the
count's gaming houses were closed.[24] In nearby Hainault in the mid-
fifteenth century, we also find general decrees, this time issued by the
duke, one of them forbidding all dice games, the others closing gaming
houses in specific towns.[25] Confirming the quickening of repression in
the fifteenth century is the experience of England: although games had
been prohibited in 1388, it was only in the course of the following
century that this order was enforced at the local level.[26] In France and
Scotland the military needs of the war with England led kings to order
that all existing games be replaced by archery contests: King Charles V of
France prohibited dice, board games and various ball games, 'which do
not serve to exercise or prepare our subjects in the use of weapons for the
defense of our realm'; in Scotland, King James I 'forbids that na man play
at the fute-ball' in 1424, and James II ordered 'that the fute-ball and
golfe be utterly cryed downe and not to be used' in 1457.[27] In both cases
transgressors were to be fined.

In place of such evolution, however, Mehl's study of games in France
proposes constant oscillation in government intervention, between prohibition and toleration. As in Flanders, princely legislation was modest
(only a dozen royal ordinances on games between 1254 and 1537), com-
pared to urban (the small town of Amiens alone issued twenty prohibitions

between 1417 and 1539). Some French bans were global, naming long lists of prohibited games, and adding 'all other illicit games' as a catch-all. Other bans prohibited gaming at night, or on certain feast days, or in taverns, stews (brothels), cemeteries and hospitals. Alternatively, they might focus on the organisers of games or the makers of dice. Penalties, once more, were mainly monetary, although examples of the pillory or corporal punishment are known in the fifteenth century. Mehl contrasts this with the more drastic physical punishment of gamblers, especially cheats, in Germany (burned in Berlin, beheaded in Breslau, drowned in Frankfurt).[28] This oscillating intervention may also characterise Italian cities outside Tuscany, where government action falls outside the schema of increasing repression in the fifteenth century. Already in 1327 the Lord of Verona terminated licensed gambling at one site in the city, and prohibited it in private houses and inns. Fifty years later the Lord of Milan ended all licensed gambling, as part of a campaign to 'cut out the root' of the social evil of blasphemies in word and deed.[29]

Gambling was also strongly associated with another, even greater evil, which was blasphemy. At the Estates of Provence in 1472 it was declared that God had grown angry at the great blasphemies of dice and card players, and had punished the region with epidemics and other afflictions. In the book of Breton customary law there was a warning that evils, wars and pestilence would ensue from the God-denying swearing that was common-place. In Florence denunciations of public gambling were motivated by desires to protect 'our wives and daughters' from hearing such indecent words, and to save the city from the pestilence that divine anger was expected to despatch.[30] The great seriousness of blasphemy can be gauged by the nature of the penalties imposed, corporal rather than monetary. In fourteenth-century France, the kings ordained that for a first offence blasphemers should be punished with a session in the pillory, from dawn till the afternoon, and with a month in prison on bread and water. For a second offence, the pillorying should be on a market day, and be accompanied with the slitting of the upper lip. A third offence should incur slitting of the lower lip. For a fourth, all the lower lip would be cut off. Finally for a fifth offence – it is significant of the incorrigibility of blasphemers that there needed to be penalty for a fifth offence – the tongue was to be cut out. The threat of these penalties was not enough, however, and in 1397 the king instituted a further penalty, for denying Christ or uttering other oaths, of imprisonment at the judge's discretion. Moreover, this ordinance made the denunciation of blasphemers an obligation on bystanders.[31]

Nearly a century later, the king was still lamenting the detestable blasphemies of his subjects, and the scale of penalties he now ordained included a greater discretionary element.[32] The Castillian Cortes in 1462 complained of the bold and fearless blaspheming both in and outside the royal court, and asked for the imposition of supplementary penalties including amputation of the tongue and a hundred lashes.[33] The frequent issue of such ordinances is testimony to the sense of Christian duty incumbent on rulers and governments: accepting the Christian interpretation of misfortune as God's punishment of sin, they shouldered the hopeless task of restraining the verbal pollution that was bound to anger God and to bring disaster down on the whole community. Moreover it was not only rulers who took on the task of eradicating blasphemy: in Florence in 1501, a gambler was hanged for the sacrilegious act of defacing an image of the Virgin Mary with horsedung, and this was but one of a number of similar cases in those years in which popular reaction led to the death by lynching or stoning of men who maliciously damaged images of the Virgin Mary or Christ.[34]

A concern for religious purity and divine approval most clearly motivated government repression of blasphemy. While rulers such as the duke of Ferrara or the king of France might also associate blasphemy with gambling and prostitution in their campaigns against vice, more social motives seem to explain the growing regulation and changing penalisation of these other activities: concern for the honour of respectable women, easily besmirched by proximity to prostitution; concern for production, commerce and the economic well-being of families; concern for the military preparedness of national manpower.

Sexual deviancy

Such trends in law and social response perhaps received reinforcement from the changed moral climate following outbreaks of plague from 1348 onwards. In those circumstances there was a heightened sense of sinfulness, of disease as God's punishment for sin, and of the need to purge cities and nations of elements that imperilled the community. The Old Testament (Deuteronomy 28) threatened communities that did not observe God's commandments with misfortune and sterility in all their deeds: crop failures and loss of livestock, indebtedness, defeat and enslavement in war, and above all disease ('the botch of Egypt . . . the scab and the itch', 'great plagues'). Fear of divine anger thus mobilised governments against crime, but this operated selectively: especially feared were those crimes that touched God directly (blasphemy) or that evoked biblical precedents (sodomy, identified as the sin that had provoked destruction of the biblical city of Sodom).

Alternatively, the increased anxiety regarding sodomy has been seen as a response to the heavy population losses of the mid–late fourteenth century: 'lawmakers in the generation after 1348 suddenly perceived sodomy as a grave threat to society', because it jeopardised social re-production.[35] The problems, as we shall see, with these links between sodomy and plague are ones of chronology and geographical spread: in some parts of Europe, concern about sodomy was intensifying already before 1348, while the main growth of anxiety came in the fifteenth century, not in the second half of the fourteenth. It may be that the key influence on courts and governments was not plague, but the moral reform agenda of two generations of popular preachers (San Bernardino and his followers).

Like blasphemy, sodomy was proclaimed a sin that endangered the whole of society. Sodomy indeed was a form of blasphemy, a wilful rebellion against God's creation, a sin against nature. This was because it not only avoided procreation, which was the 'natural' function of human sexuality, and misused a God-given organ, but also because it violated gender roles. It perverted God's creation by turning men into women. Behind the theology, it has been argued, lay fear of the undermining of male dominance through effeminacy. Sodomy was so feared by 'normal' male society that it remained literally unspeakable and unspoken. 'Sodom-ite' was never used as an insult, unlike 'thief' or 'traitor' (contrast 'You're gay' in the contemporary British playground). In literature the fear of being sodomised could be used to trigger the dénouement of stories. In the French *fabliau* 'The priest and the knight', a knight lodging with a priest asks for the sexual services first of the priest's niece, then the priest's mistress and finally of the priest himself. The knight's servant is shocked at this last suggestion: 'Make the sign of the cross, cross yourself, my lord! How could you dare to say this? Abominable thing!' It is this very suggestion, however, that resolves the debt relationship between the priest and the knight. In a late fifteenth-century Italian tale, a young priest, dressed up as a woman, is pursued by a friar. When the friar tries to kiss him, the priest throws off his disguise, but the friar says he is so aflame with lust that he does not mind whether the priest is man or woman. The priest cries out and is rescued by his friends. Again the imminence of an act of sodomy – only threatened, never performed – serves as the turning point of the story and resolves the situation.[36]

Goodich has suggested that there were three phases to the ecclesias-tical campaign against sexual deviance: a period in the eleventh and twelfth centuries when theological definitions were worked out and applied, through penitential manuals, to sinners confessing their sins; a second phase in the thirteenth century when secular governments were prompted to legislate against sodomy; and a third phase, from the fourteenth century, in which a willingness grew to execute sodomites.[37] In the first phase of definition, sodomy was linked to the most serious of errors, heresy, and charges of sexual deviance were levelled against heretics. In the second phase in the later thirteenth century, rulers and governments, in response to calls from the Church, enacted secular penalties for sodomy, often death by burning (France, England, Italian cities). Finally, the third phase brought criminal prosecutions and executions. There are some flaws or problems in this general schema. In England there seems, in fact, to have been no specific legislation on sodomy until the sixteenth century, only some jurisprudential statements that the penalty for sex with persons of the same gender, as for sex with Jews or animals, was burial alive.[38] It is not clear either when the earliest secular prosecutions occurred. Boswell and Goodich each found a late thirteenth-century case (Germany 1277, Ghent 1292), and these coincide roughly with an early case in Venice (in 1282), but these could well be isolated instances. Four volumes of decisions by the French royal court between 1254 and 1318 contain only two cases of prosecution for sodomy, and in both of those the suspect was acquitted, once because the accusation was malicious, and once because it was found to be groundless.[39] Boswell claimed to have found no sodomy prosecution in court records for the kingdom of Aragon before 1500. Ultimately, he thought that the strict language of new laws against sodomy was merely rhetorical, not matched by actual punishment.

However, in some parts of Europe, more frequent implementation of capital penalties is evident in the late fourteenth and fifteenth centuries. This process was far from universal. Was there ever any prosecution in late medieval England? When the London authorities discovered a man who had engaged in paid sex with other men while dressed as a woman, and calling himself Eleanor, they appear not to have known what to do with him. In contrast, Venice executed just such a male transvestite prostitute in 1357.[40] A study of the London Church courts found only one man accused of sodomy among over 20,000 defendants across thirty-five years.[41] In the France of King Charles VI, sodomy seems very rare, and judges were more concerned about bestiality.[42] The case of Gilles de Rais, who confessed to sodomising the many children he abducted, must therefore be taken as exceptional. Among the cities of the Low Countries, Bruges was alone in executing considerable numbers of sodomites: twenty-four in the first half of the fifteenth century, forty-nine in the second half. This upward trend has been explained by one historian in terms of the convergent interests of both the local elites and of the Burgundian dukes in strengthening their respective powers in what was the key city of the Burgundian Netherlands. 'Repression of sodomy had become a matter of the highest political importance.'[43]

Most of the sodomy, and most of the historiographical discussion of it, comes from late medieval Italy. As is well known, Florentines were so renowned for sodomy that the very name 'Florenzer' in German meant a sodomite. Again, however, there was no equal distribution. Most cities had laws penalising sodomy, and these might be refreshed from time to time with decrees and proclamations, but prosecutions are in general quite rare. In Milan in the late fourteenth and early fifteenth centuries, there was only one prosecution, which resulted in a fine. In Mantua in the mid-fifteenth century, there was no prosecution of sodomy between males. In the Ferrarese countryside in 1454, a judge dealing with a case of sodomy wondered whether he should expel the culprit or put him in the pillory: the issue of corporal or capital punishment does not seem to have arisen.[44] In nearby Bologna, the pace of prosecutions for sodomy seems to have picked up in the 1450s, and some of these accused were indeed burned to death; but there was a tendency for the death penalty to be commuted into whipping and exile.[45] In other words, sodomy was still treated as a sin, not a crime.

The main centres of sodomy prosecutions were Venice and Florence. In Venice, nearly 300 cases were investigated between 1326 and 1500 (the vast majority after 1400), involving over 500 people. In Florence a new, specific magistracy investigated over 10,000 accusations of sodomy, and convicted nearly 2,500 men, in the period from its inception in 1432 to 1502.[46] In both cities an intensification of anxiety about sodomy is evident in the fifteenth century. In 1464 a law reminded Venetians that 'God had submerged Sodom, sparing no one, covering every inch of earth with sulphurous water so that to the present day the land still stank, and so he might plunge Venice back into the salty Adriatic swamp from which he had raised it, if the crime of sodomy was not obliterated there'.[47] Already competence in such cases had been removed from the 'Lords of the Night' in 1418, as they were seen to have been too weak in investigating a scandalous case involving thirty-five men, seventeen of them nobles and three claiming to be clerics. The role of investigating and prosecuting was given instead to the powerful state security committee, the Council of Ten: an indication of the gravity accorded to this crime. Subsequent decades brought changes to the law and stricter policing. In 1424 a new law allowed for the punishment of boys aged under 14 years who partici-pated in sodomy, presumably as passive partners. In the 1450s patrols were set up to tour the taverns looking for male 'companions of inappro-priate ages', or to keep a look-out throughout the city for men in the company of boys. In 1496 the attention of these patrols was especially directed at 'shops, schools, porticoes, taverns and brothels'. As at Bruges, the political aspects of anti-sodomitical concerns seem uppermost: Labalme has argued that concern was 'calibrated to external pressures', such as lost battles, natural disasters and plague. Similarly, the Adriatic city of Ragusa (modern Dubrovnik) introduced Venetian penalties for sodomy in 1474, despite the absence of any homosexual problem, but against the background of growing political and military threat from the Ottoman Turks.[48]

What is extraordinary about Florence is the precocity and elaboration of its laws on sodomy. In the early fourteenth century, it was far from the case that every Italian city had an enacted legal penalty for this crime. Verona and Arezzo, for example, did not. Some statutes give penalties in terse one-liners. Bergamo, for example, simply decreed that the penalty for sodomy was burning to death. Siena, more unusually, appointed a hefty fine, or, if it was not paid within a month, the culprit was to be hanged by the genitals for a day on the marketplace. In Treviso the penalty for 'unnatural' sex between either men or women was a day spent tied naked to a pole on the piazza (by the penis in the case of a man), followed by burning to death.[49] In contrast, the Florentine law of 1325 is lengthy and ramified. Above all, though, it makes plain what crime is targeted in a way that no other statute does: sodomy with boys. The active partner in such 'contaminations' was to have both testicles cut off; the boy, if aged between 14 and 18, was to be fined, or, if aged under 14, was to be whipped naked through the city. Anyone promoting, persuading or inducing the commission of this crime was likewise to be fined. The house where such an act took place with the house owner's consent was to be destroyed. Anyone found with a boy in an enclosed space who was not from his own family was to be treated with strong suspicion. Even the writing or singing of songs about 'this filthy crime' was to be punished.[50] The desire to pursue those who enticed boys into this sin suggests the anxiety of a city under siege: and that was explicitly expressed in that part of the statute that blamed foreign vagabonds for bringing the 'contagion' of sodomy to Florence. The language of this statute is extreme: these foreigners have sowed the seeds of this abominable crime at the suggestion of the devil, and they have rendered the city 'sickly' with the horrible stench of their wickedness. If convicted, they were to be burned 'such that the heat of the fire extinguishes the heat of their perverse desires'. It also loosened criminal procedure in order to capture and convict such men: minimal proof of suspicion and notoriety would be sufficient to allow the *podestà* to torture them.

A criminal 'anti-society'?

The idea of 'an army of crime, a confraternity or realm of criminals, an anti-society' aiming to destroy the normal social world likewise grew in fifteenth-century France.[51] The chief piece of evidence for this claim is the famous trial of the so-called 'Coquillards' in Dijon in 1455, a case often referred to, but seldom examined in detail.[52]

> For two years there have been in this town of Dijon many *compaignons*, idlers and vagabonds who, when they arrived and since they have been here, do nothing except eat, drink and run up great bills, play at dice, cards, board-games and other games. They spend all their time at the brothel, especially at night, where they lead the filthy, base and dissolute lives of pimps and procurers, losing and spending all their money, such that they end up without a penny. And then, once they have taken all they can from their poor whores whom they keep at the brothel, some of them leave for who-knows-where, and they stay away for two, four or six weeks. Then they come back, some on horseback, others on foot, well-dressed and kitted out, flush with gold and silver coins, and they start again their habitual games and debaucheries with those who stayed behind or others newly arrived. And truly these *compaignons* speak a secret language among themselves and use signs by which they recognise each other. And they are called, these brigands, the Coquillards, that is the *compaignons* of the *coquille*. And they have a 'king' who is called 'king of the *coquille*'. And truly, so it is said, some of them are picklocks, others are pilferers who rob people in changing gold into coin or vice versa, or in buying merchandise; the others carry and sell or pawn fake gems as diamonds, rubies and other precious stones. Others sleep at an inn with a merchant, rob themselves and the merchant, have one of their own men to whom they consign the booty, and then they join the merchant in lodging a complaint. Others play with false dice, and win all the money of the other players. Some of them know such tricks in card- or board-games that one cannot win against them. What is worse, many of them are highway robbers, thieves and murderers: it is to be presumed that this is how they maintain their dissolute lives . . . It is also true that they often get drunk and fight each other, striking good dagger blows, and uttering great insults and profanities, accusing each other of the thefts and tricks they have done . . . And sometimes they make these accusations when they don't want to distribute faithfully to each other what they have earned by some trickery or theft, or when one asks for his share and another refuses to give it. Also, every trick they practise has a name in their jargon, and no one who is not a sworn member of their group can understand them. And it is said that the master of the brothel, Jaquot de la Mer, knows them all or most of them . . . and harbours and helps them sometimes to do their business and to sell stolen horses or other goods, as much for the profit he makes from their spending as from the share in the booty that he is likely to have. Likewise it is notorious that . . . Jaquot used to walk around town with them, arm-in-arm, at all hours.

The authorities were always suspicious of those who appeared to do no work yet had money to squander in tavern and brothel, but what is exceptional about this text is the belief that the Coquillards formed an organised, criminal conspiracy, an association or fraternity, with a leader, a secret language and a sharing of profits. Their trickery is honoured with the term 'science' and their thieving with the term 'earning'. There are hints of them being seen – or seeing themselves – as workers who had learned a craft.

Having received initial information on the gang from an informant whose name is prudently kept silent, the local authorities, in the person of the prosecutor (*procureur*), Jean Rabustel, proceeded to interview a number of potential witnesses. The chief witness was a barber, Perrenet le Fournier, in whose shop the Coquillards were in the habit of gathering, to have their hair combed and their beards shaved, or just to pass the time. Perrenet admits to playing dice with them (and losing), and to wheedling his way into their confidence by pretending to be a trickster himself. So it is that he learned their language and their identities. He gives a list of sixty-four members of the band, though combining those he has seen with others who he had only been told about. They include the exotically named Dimenche 'the wolf', also known as 'Bar-sur-Aube', Guillemin 'Thin Soup', Little John the sword master, Nicholas the stammerer, The One-eyed Burgundian, Simon le Double, whose upper lip is split, Godeaul, who has only one ear, and Jean Colin, known as 'Johannes' and said to be a runaway friar. Their earlier encounters with the law are attested in these split lips and lopped ears; and subsequent encounters are noted in the trial record, with eleven of them being hanged, two banished and one boiled as a counterfeiter. Perrenet also provides three dozen words or expressions from their secret language, perhaps the earliest example of thieves' cant or anti-language.[53] These terms fall into three groups. First we can distinguish ironic names for various types of thief or for thieving: a 'harvester' was a cutpurse, a 'picker' stripped his victim of everything, a 'planter' supplied fake jewels, 'King David' meant opening and closing a locked door or chest, and 'la soye Roland' meant opening by force. Second come terms for their victims and their dupes, for stolen goods, and for the various roles they played in their confidence tricks. Thus, a *beffleur* attracted naive players into card games, a 'pruner' won all their money, a 'balladeer' approached a cleric (or 'crophead') and offered to sell him a 'gold' chain, a 'swindler' carried fakes around pretending to be a poor servant, and a 'white dove' shared a room with a travelling merchant, robbed him and threw the booty out of the window to a waiting accomplice. The third category comprises terms for justice and its officials and procedures: *sergents* are 'hookers' justice itself is *la marine* or 'the wheel', torture is 'day'. There are expressions too for informing to the authorities, giving pursuing officials the slip, fighting off the *sergents*, deceiving the judge, refusing to confess and escaping unscathed. What we seem to have here is a system of words in which the values and referents of 'normal' society have been inverted: an Old Testament king and a chivalric hero are associated with house-breaking; goodness and skill are identified with deceit.

After this build-up, the specific crimes alleged against the Coquillards seem rather small beer. Perrenet says that five of them went to Lorraine on an expedition, hoping to do 'a fine bit of pilfering', but came back empty-handed after most of them were arrested. Some of them, however, managed to talk their way out of gaol, one pretending to be a soldier passing through, another to be a servant of the Duke of Burgundy. Perrenet also gives some information of other thefts – a stolen horse, some stolen coins – and of some fraudulent trading in meat. Other witnesses confirm hearing these stories too, and they add their own experience of encounters with one or more of the Coquillards: a smith who had been asked to make what he suspected were picklocks, and had been offered a stolen horse; a barber whom they had laughed at when he reproached them directly; a prostitute from the brothel, who knew that the father of one of the group wished him dead. None of these other witnesses confirms Perrenet's detailed revelations about the secret language, indeed one says that if they notice people listening to their crime talk, one of them spits like 'a man with a cold who can't get his breath', and they fall silent or speak of something else. Moreover, most of these witnesses say they had not seen the gang doing any wrong, other than playing at dice, having a good time, and keeping themselves in comfort without working. Only one witness claims to know about their practices of 'King David', 'planting', and so forth, but this from hearing them speak of them. In these circumstances, the official prosecutor decided to offer a deal to one of the gang who had been arrested and interrogated, but had confessed nothing: if he confessed what he knew of the others' crimes, he would be released. But the results of this tactic were disappointing. This prisoner acknowledged that some of the group were thieves and 'planters', but refused to link any of them to specific incidents. The reason for his evasiveness is clear. These men, he says, are of the sort who, if they find out that someone has revealed any of their secrets, will kill him. He knows that, when he is released, they will kill him if they can get him on his own.

Were the Coquillards unique? Tales of associations of criminals forming guilds or teaching the tricks of their trade are found in other cultures at other times, for example Roman Egypt, Elizabethan England and modern Sicily.[54] Even at the beginning of the fifteenth century, we find the King of France complaining of the coming and going, across northern France, of 'thieves, murderers, high-way robbers, ravishers, church-violators, hired thugs, tricksters, dice-cheats, counterfeiters and other criminals, with their associates, receivers and accomplices', maliciously moving around from one jurisdiction to another in order to avoid arrest.[55] Another such gang, with a secret language and secret signs, with oaths and a pooling of ill-gotten gains, has turned up in Provence in the 1430s.[56] Some of these features too have been found in a band of thieves in Venice in 1359.[57] However, the best place to look for analogies would be another French document, the equally celebrated register of the Parisian Châtelet for the years 1389–92.

This is an extraordinary register: over a thousand pages in the two-volume printed edition, with over a hundred trials involving almost 130 accused; but what makes it special is that these prisoners give us their life histories and extensive details of their numerous crimes.[58] The register opens in September 1389 with the case of Simon de Verrue, a squire from near Poitiers, who had been plundering the countryside for eight years, and had made off with a horse from a nunnery and a devotional book from the grandest of French abbeys. It closes in April 1392 with the case of Colette Phelipe, a maidservant who was dismissed after she became pregnant, found a wet-nurse for her infant, and rented a room where she made a living from spinning; but when she could no longer afford to pay the wet-nurse, Colette angrily abandoned her 15-month-old daughter in the church of Notre Dame in Paris. However, the immediacy of criminals narrating their own careers is not the only unusual feature of the register: the pattern of criminality that we find there, and the type of punishment meted out to its prisoners, are out of the ordinary too. Theft predominates (67 per cent), and over three-quarters of the penalties were capital (of the 85 thieves, 74 were executed). A number of historians have tried to relate these peculiarities to the social and economic conditions of the late fourteenth century.

Geremek extensively uses this register and its colourful cast of characters in his study of 'marginals' in Paris. These Châtelet criminals may be seen as marginals in many ways. First, they are migrants. Of the 127, only four were definitely Parisian by birth; many of the others came from the towns and regions of northern France. Second, they had no fixed occupations and no stable employment. Although they might have served as apprentices, they are mostly wage earners, not qualified craftsmen, and many of them took a succession of manual jobs in unrelated crafts or in agriculture. Third, their patterns of association were impermanent, fluid, based on the tavern and the road: accomplices did not form a compact criminal gang, but a loose association of collaborators and receivers, who combined and recombined in various small groups, exchanging news and tricks of the trade, travelling together, drinking together. Finally, their lives had been disrupted by war, particularly the Anglo-French conflict, in which they had become familiar with violence and accustomed to live by plunder.

The register also provides grist to the mill of those who see professional, organised crime on the model of the Coquillards. Many of the prisoners have false names. They take oaths and share their profits. They have a special language of secret signs. They call theft a 'craft' and thieving 'earning'. They swap advice on tonsuring in the hope of evading punishment.[59]

Out of the scores of criminals in this register, Geremek focused on the figure of Jean le Brun, 'the principal character of the drama', whose initial confessions opened up a nest of thieves to the authorities in Paris.[60] Jean le Brun was a product of the war in more than one sense. He was the illegitimate child of a soldier and his mistress. Although he had learned the craft of a smith, he promptly abandoned smithing once he left his father's house to go to work in Rouen, and he spent the next six years serving an English garrison in the Limousin, taking part in raids and ransoms. Eventually, not being paid what he considered his share of the plunder, he made off with a horse and came to Paris. There he sold the horse and lived on the proceeds for a while, spending his money on dice games, the tavern and a whore. After about six months, his criminal career began. He and two others took a prostitute to the Bois de Vincennes, where he cut her throat, removed her clothes, sold them, and spent the money eating and drinking. It was at this point that he was advised to get a tonsure, so as to escape punishment. Over the following months more murders followed, with the bodies stripped and the proceeds spent on food and drink in Paris. Jean also stole from craftsmen and traders, disposing of the stolen goods through an innkeeper's wife. Jean le Brun thus presents as a soldier who, having left the theatre of war, could not put his plundering habits behind him. But how many like him were there? Was he typical of demobbed soldiers, or of prisoners in the Châtelet? His accomplices seem to be rather different men. Jehanin la Grene, also known as Raoulet de Laon, also came from Rouen, but he left it as a young man, and learned his trade in Paris. His thieving began two years before his arrest, starting when he was a furrier's servant in Chartres: entrusted with a robe for furring, he ran off with it and sold it in Paris to a second-hand dealer in Les Halles. His subsequent thieving, usually committed with others, consisted of stealing from shops, inns and markets. Another of le Brun's accomplices was Jehan de Soubz le Mur, called Rousseau. He had been born in Orléans, where he learned a leather craft. He left Orléans to go to work at Coulomier-en-Brie, where he married a young woman. He was arrested a first time for theft in Paris, but successfully claimed to be a cleric and was then released as an act of grace by the queen. On his second arrest, he confessed to further thefts, of a silk purse, cheese, partridges, wax, cloth and a rabbit-fur coat, as well as two acts of violence. As we shall see, this variety among Jean le Brun's partners in crime provides a strong critique of Geremek's interpretation.

Although Geremek's aim is to explore the whole connected, marginal world of late medieval Paris, from beggars and prostitutes to peddlers and *jongleurs*, his treatment of criminals does contain explanations in terms of the social and economic context. Warfare, epidemic disease and economic disruption impoverished on the one hand and accelerated social mobility on the other. Warfare plunged some into destitution, while providing others with ladders of social advance.[61] Other historians have cultivated this theme more intensively. In the 1970s, Misraki made a point of contrasting the material of the Châtelet register with evidence from other Parisian criminal courts in the first half of the fourteenth century: these earlier records show a predominance of violence over theft. The reversal of this pattern by 1390 is related by Misraki to social and economic upheavals following the great plague epidemics. In her view, the pool of under-employed, unskilled workers in Paris was constantly refilled by refugees from the countryside, demobbed soldiers and the victims of economic failure, and this led to the formation of criminal gangs. Cohen too has ploughed the same field. She notes that the Châtelet prisoners were poor men, wage earners, servants and farm workers from northern France, migrating to Paris under either the push factor of unemployment or the pull factor of higher wages. They were, she says, the provincial poor, victims of dislocation caused by warfare in northern France or of crisis in the Flemish textile industry. They stole frequently, but opportunistically, as they travelled, thieving from other guests at inns, from houses, or from stalls and customers at markets. Their needs and circumstances defined their main targets: portable items of small value, such as food that could be consumed, money that could be spent, and clothing or household goods that could be pawned or sold.[62]

These interpretations, linking the peculiar features of the Châtelet criminals with the fourteenth-century economic crisis, have been roundly criticised by Claude Gauvard. She has launched a veritable barrage against the sociological use of this register, on the supposition that it discloses Parisian criminality to us. First, she undermines the representative qualities of the register. The *prévôt* of Paris, she points out, had jurisdiction over a wide swathe of northern France, and a good number of his prisoners were in fact arrested outside Paris. This means that the register does not tell us only about Parisian crime. Second, there were other jurisdictions in Paris – the Parlement, and various seigneurial courts – and their criminal trials display the classic features of 'ordinary' crime, that is, of a preponderance of violence, not theft. Gauvard then argues that we need to look more closely at who compiled the Châtelet register and why. Here she maintains that the register is *deliberately* skewed towards certain crimes and procedures of investigation. Most of the prisoners were tortured; many claimed to be clerics. The compiler of the register, the clerk to the criminal court, was appointed by political reformers in 1389. He was in harmony with the actions of the vigorous *prévôt* of the time, Jean de Folleville, and he translated into the register the reform agenda of redress of abuses and intransigent devotion to official recti-tude. The register was thus intended as a model of correct practice, especially in the application of torture and as a record of a conscious campaign against the abuses of clerical status. Finally, Gauvard raises doubts about the links between crime and displacement (by migration or mobility). The population of Paris, she argues, had always been fed by constant immigration, and the Châtelet prisoners therefore had a profile no different from that of the Parisian populace as a whole. Even had it been different, Gauvard questions whether displacement itself can lead to crime: many migrants do not engage in crime.[63] All this derives from the finding of Gauvard's own study of pardons for this period, which show that crime was not committed by young, unmarried, marginal men, but by middle-aged, married, settled men.

Having battered the views of Geremek and Cohen, however, Gauvard then lets the phoenix of Parisian criminality fly once more, but in a different guise. If we look, she says, at pardons granted to criminals in Paris, we do find some peculiar features that place Parisian criminality outside the 'ordinary' patterns of the time. Recidivist thieves are more numerous than elsewhere. They do show signs of poverty linked to displacement. The typical portrait of a Parisian 'bad lad' would be of one who had no craft, supported a girl, frequented taverns and brothels, and assaulted respectable folk. However, Gauvard relates these features not to economic crisis or warfare, but to the profile of the Parisian population, with its many students and servants, and to the greater contrast there between wealth and poverty, between the opulence of royal and noble palaces and the destitution of vagabonds sleeping rough in boats along the Seine.[64] The only problem with this conclusion is that it reinforces, rather than undermines, the views of Geremek and Cohen: they could well counter that this gap between rags and riches had grown *because of* economic and social upheaval. Gauvard, in trying to escape the fourteenth-century crisis, ends up heading straight back towards it.

Did economic crisis generate new levels or types of criminality? It is difficult to give a clear answer. None of the crimes, none of the concerns about crime, that feature prominently in the later fourteenth and early fifteenth centuries was new: vagrancy, gambling, prostitution, blasphemy and sodomy were all penalised already in the thirteenth century. To some extent governments' anxieties about these crimes arose from political, not socio-economic concerns. Yet in the immediate aftermath of the Black Death a rise in criminal prosecutions, and perhaps in criminality, seems beyond question. Historians have found it difficult, however, to stretch this crime wave into the late fourteenth century or beyond. Even the Châtelet register, which promises so much, cannot be related in a straightforward way to economic conditions: more trials of thieves, it seems, did not mean more theft.

Notes

1. B. Schnapper, 'La répression du vagabondage et sa signification historique du XIVe au XVIIIe siècle', *RHDF* 63 (1985), pp. 145–6.
2. *The Chronicle of Jean de Venette*, trans. J. Birdsall (New York, 1953), p. 51; W.M. Bowsky, 'The medieval commune and internal violence: police power and public safety in Siena, 1287–1355', *American Historical Review* 73 (1967), pp. 15–16; *Venezia e la peste, 1348/1797*, 2nd edn (Venice, 1980), p. 78.
3. G. Ruggiero, *The Boundaries of Eros: Sex Crime and Sexuality in Renaissance Venice* (New York and Oxford, 1985), pp. 72–3.
4. C. Caduff, 'I "publici latrones" nella città e nel contado di Firenze a metà Trecento', *Ricerche storiche* 18 (1988), p. 500; S. Piasentini, *'Alla luce della luna': I furti a Venezia, 1270–1403* (Venice, 1992), pp. 85–6; P. Roqué Ferrer, 'L'infrazione della legge a Cagliari dal 1340 al 1380', *Quaderni sardi di storia* 5 (1985–6), pp. 13–15, 18; P. Dubuis, 'Comportamenti sessuali nelle Alpi nel Basso Medioevo: l'esempio della castellania di Susa', *Studi storici* 27 (1986), p. 591.
5. G. Pinto, 'Un vagabondo, ladro e truffatore nella Toscana della seconda metà del '300: Sandro di Vanno detto Pescione', *Ricerche storiche* new ser., 4 (1974).
6. R.C. Palmer, *English Law in the Age of the Black Death, 1348–1381* (Chapel Hill and London, 1993). See, for example, the review by W. Ormrod in *English Historical Review* 109 (1994), pp. 962–4.
7. J.G. Bellamy, *Criminal Law and Society in Late Medieval and Tudor England* (Gloucester and New York, 1984), pp. 14–15.
8. A. Zorzi, 'The judicial system in Florence in the fourteenth and fifteenth centuries', in *Crime, Society and the Law in Renaissance Italy*, pp. 46–7; idem, *L'amministrazione della giustizia penale nella repubblica fiorentina: aspetti e problemi* (Florence, 1988), p. 38; W.A. Morris, *The Frankpledge System* (London, 1910), pp. 151–60.
9. C. Gauvard, *'De grace especial': Crime, état et société en France à la fin du Moyen Age* (Paris, 1991), pp. 532–4, 549–51; B. Geremek, *The Margins of Society in Late Medieval Paris* (Cambridge, 1987), pp. 126–7; J. Misraki, 'Criminalité et pauvreté en France à l'époque de la Guerre de Cent Ans', in *Etudes sur l'histoire*

de la pauvreté, ed. M. Mollat (Paris, 1974); H.R.T. Summerson, 'The structure of law enforcement in thirteenth-century England', *American Journal of Legal History* 23 (1979), p. 327; A. Musson and W. Ormrod, *The Evolution of English Justice: Law, Politics and Society in the Fourteenth Century* (Basingstoke, 1999), pp. 78–9; J.G. Bellamy, *Crime and Public Order in England in the Later Middle Ages* (London, 1973), pp. 5–11.

10. S. Cohn, 'Criminality and the state in Renaissance Florence, 1344–1466', *Journal of Social History* 14 (1980), pp. 214–15; Zorzi, 'Judicial system in Florence', pp. 41–2; E.D. Jones, 'Summary executions at Spalding Priory, 1250–1500', *Journal of Legal History* 16 (1995), pp. 190–1.

11. Gauvard, *Crime, état et société*, pp. 218, 524–52; Musson and Ormrod, *Evolution of English Justice*, pp. 82–4; D. Potter, ' "Rigueur de justice": Crime, murder and the law in Picardy, fifteenth to sixteenth centuries', *French History* 11 (1997), pp. 288–90.

12. *Oeuvres complètes de Eustache Deschamps* (11 vols, Paris, 1878–1903), VI, pp. 230–1, 232, 237, 279–80.

13. Geremek, *Margins of Society*, pp. 37–9; E. Cohen, 'Le vagabondage à Paris au XIVe siècle', *Le Moyen Age* 88 (1982), p. 297; C. Lopez Alonso, 'Conflictividad social y pobreza en la Edad Media segun las actas de las Cortes castellano-leonesas', *Hispania* 38 (1978), pp. 528–9; I. Delabruyère-Neuschwander, 'L'activité réglementaire d'un sénéchal de Toulouse à la fin du XIV s.', *Bibliothèque de l'Ecole des chartes* 143 (1985), p. 89; *Statuty Kazimierza Wielkiego*, ed. O. Balzer (Poznan, 1947); *Statutes of the Realm* (9 vols, London, 1810–22), II, 32.

14. *The Laws and Acts of Parliament made by . . . Kings and Queens of Scotland* (Edinburgh, 1681), pp. 4, 34. The first of these laws is also in *Scottish Historical Documents*, ed. G. Donaldson (Glasgow, 1974), p. 79.

15. Morris, *Frankpledge*, p. 151; Piasentini, *I furti a Venezia*, pp. 101–3; *Bandi lucchesi del secolo decimoquinto*, ed. S. Bongi (Bologna, 1863), p. 169; A. Casali, 'L'amministrazione del contado di Lucca nel '400: il Capitano del contado', *Actum Luce* 7 (1978), pp. 128–30.

16. S. Andreescu, 'La pauvreté à la fin du Moyen Age roumain', *Revue roumaine d'histoire* 22 (1983), p. 344.

17. *Inventari e regesti dell'Archivio di Stato in Milano*, vol. III, *I registri dell'ufficio degli statuti di Milano*, ed. N. Ferorelli (Milan, 1920), pp. 254, 257.

18. *ORF*, I, pp. 73–4, 99–101.

19. Archivio di Stato, Modena, Gridario, Gride manoscritte, busta 1, 1 Apr. 1496.

20. J-M. Mehl, *Les jeux au royaume de France du XIIIe au début du XVIe siècle* (n.p., 1990), pp. 297–306.

21. *Statuty Kazimierza*, pp. 33, 35.

22. I. Taddei, 'Gioco d'azzardo, ribaldi e baratteria nelle città della Toscana tardo-medievale', *Quaderni storici* 92 (1996).

23. A. Zorzi, 'Battagliole e giochi d'azzardo a Firenze nel tardo Medioevo: due pratiche sociali tra disciplinamento e repressione', in *Gioco e giustizia nell'Italia di commune*, ed. G. Ortalli (Treviso and Rome, 1993), pp. 93–105.

24. J. van Humbeeck, 'Exploitation et répression des jeux d'argent en Flandre aux XIVe et XVe siècles', *TRG* 46 (1978).

25. J-M. Cauchies, *La législation princière pour le comté de Hainaut: Ducs de Bourgogne et premiers Habsbourg* (Brussels, 1982), pp. 504–5.
26. M.K. McIntosh, 'Finding language for misconduct: jurors in fifteenth-century local courts', in *Bodies and Disciplines: Intersections of Literature and History in Fifteenth-century England*, ed. B.A. Hanawalt and D. Wallace (Minneapolis and London, 1996), p. 93.
27. *ORF*, V, p. 172; *The Laws and Acts of Parliament made by . . . Kings and Queens of Scotland*, pp. 3, 45.
28. Mehl, *Les jeux au royaume de France*, pp. 345–58.
29. *Statuti di Verona del 1327*, ed. S.A. Bianchi and R. Granuzzo (Rome, 1992), pp. 494–5; C. Santoro, *La politica finanziaria dei Visconti* (3 vols, Varese and Gessate, 1976–83), I, pp. 305–7.
30. *Le livre 'Potentia' des Etats de Provence (1391–1523)*, ed. G. Gouiran and M. Hebert (Paris, 1997) p. 370; *Le très ancienne coutume de Bretagne*, ed. M. Planiol (Rennes, 1896) p. 383; Zorzi, 'Battagliole e giochi d'azzardo a Firenze', pp. 93–4.
31. *ORF*, VIII, pp. 130–1.
32. *ORF*, XX, pp. 46–7.
33. *Cortes de los antiguos reinos de Leon y de Castilla* (5 vols, Madrid, 1883–1903), III, pp. 712–13.
34. W.J. Connell and G. Constable, 'Sacrilege and redemption in Renaissance Florence: the case of Antonio Rinaldeschi', *Journal of the Warburg and Courtauld Institutes* 61 (1999), p. 76.
35. J.A. Brundage, *Law, Sex and Christian Society in Medieval Europe* (Chicago and London, 1987), p. 533.
36. *Nouveau recueil complet des fabliaux*, ed. W. Noomen (10 vols, Assen, 1983–96), IX, pp. 116–17; L. Martines, *An Italian Renaissance Sextet: Six Tales in Historical Context* (New York, 1994), pp. 71–91.
37. M. Goodich, *The Unmentionable Vice: Homosexuality in the Later Medieval Period* (n.p., 1979), pp. 3–15 and *passim*.
38. J. Boswell, *Christianity, Social Tolerance and Homosexuality* (Chicago and London, 1980), p. 290. Edward I's legislation contains no penalty for sodomy. An Act of Parliament in 1534 made 'buggery commyttid with mankynde or beaste' a felony: 25 Hen. VIII, c. 6, *Statutes of the Realm*, vol. 3, p. 441.
39. *Les Olim ou registres des arrêts rendus par la cour du roi*, ed. A.A. Beugnot (4 vols, Paris, 1839–48), III, p. 572; IV, pp. 1202–4.
40. R.M. Karras and D.L. Boyd, '"Ut cum muliere": a male transvestite prostitute in fourteenth-century London', in *Premodern Sexualities*, ed. L. Fradenburg and C. Freccero (New York and London, 1996); P.H. Labalme, 'Sodomy and Venetian justice in the Renaissance', *TRG* 52 (1984), p. 249.
41. R.M. Wunderli, *London Church Courts and Society on the Eve of the Reformation* (Cambridge, Mass., 1981), pp. 83–4.
42. Gauvard, *Crime, état et société*, pp. 597–8.
43. M. Boone, 'State power and illicit sexuality: the persecution of sodomy in late-medieval Bruges', *Journal of Medieval History* 22 (1996).
44. E. Verga, 'Le sentenze criminali dei podestà milanesi, 1385–1429', *Archivio storico lombardo* 3rd ser., 16 (1901), p. 114; D.S. Chambers and T. Dean, *Clean*

Hands and Rough Justice: An Investigating Magistrate in Renaissance Italy (Ann Arbor, 1997), p. 71; Archivio di Stato, Modena, Archivio Segreto Estense, Rettori dello Stato, Ferrara, busta 46, 11 Feb. 1454.

45. Archivio di Stato, Bologna, Curia del podestà, Inquisitiones, 360, reg. 1, fol. 111; 360, reg. 2, fol. 171; 361, reg. 2, fol. 199; 362, reg. 2, fol. 57; Sententiae, reg. 40, fol. 29–v; T. Dean, 'Criminal justice in mid-fifteenth-century Bologna', in *Crime, Society and the Law in Renaissance Italy*, ed. T. Dean and K.J.P. Lowe (Cambridge, 1994), pp. 28, 31.

46. Ruggiero, *Boundaries of Eros*, ch. 6; M. Rocke, *Forbidden Friendships: Homosexuality and Male Culture in Renaissance Florence* (New York and Oxford, 1996), p. 47.

47. Labalme, 'Sodomy', p. 221; cf. Ruggiero, *Boundaries of Eros*, p. 109.

48. B. Krekic, '*Abominandum crimen*: punishment of homosexuals in Renaissance Dubrovnik', *Viator* 18 (1987).

49. *Lo statuto di Bergamo del 1353*, ed. G. Forgiarini (Spoleto, 1996), p. 208; *Il costituto del comune di Siena* (2 vols, Siena, 1903), II, p. 354; *Gli statuti del comune di Treviso (sec. XIII–XIV)*, ed. B. Betto (2 vols, Rome, 1984–6), I, pp. 436–7.

50. *Statuti della repubblica fiorentina*, vol. II, *Statuto del podestà dell'anno 1325*, ed. R. Caggese (Florence, 1921), pp. 218–19.

51. B. Chevalier, *Les bonnes villes de France du XIVe au XVIe siècle* (Paris, 1982), p. 290.

52. The trial record was edited by J. Garnier, *Les compagnons de la Coquille* (Dijon, 1842), which I have not seen, and by L. Sainéan, *Les sources de l'argot ancien*, 2 vols (Paris, 1912), I, pp. 87–109, on which the following discussion is based.

53. Cf. P. Burke, 'Languages and anti-languages', in *The Historical Anthropology of Early-Modern Italy* (Cambridge, 1987), pp. 86–7.

54. B.D. Shaw, 'Banditry in the Roman Empire', *Past and Present* 105 (1984), p. 42; J.A. Sharpe, *Crime in Early Modern England, 1550–1750* (London, 1984), p. 114; D. Dolci, *Poverty in Sicily* (Harmondsworth, 1966), pp. 26–30.

55. *ORF*, VIII, p. 443.

56. N. Coulet, 'Une enquête criminelle au XVe siècle', *Provence historique* 39 (1989).

57. Piasentini, *I furti a Venezia*, p. 52.

58. *Registre criminel du Châtelet de Paris* (Paris, 1861–4).

59. Ibid., pp. 61, 63, 69, 70, 74–8, 89–90, 97, 106.

60. Geremek, *Margins of Society*, pp. 114–15.

61. Ibid., pp. 167, 242.

62. E. Cohen, 'Patterns of crime in fourteenth-century Paris', *French Historical Studies* 11 (1979–80).

63. Gauvard, *Crime, état et société*, pp. 33–45, 271–4.

64. Ibid., pp. 277–80.

chapter 4

WOMEN AND CRIME

Three trials from late medieval France introduce the three themes of this chapter: the crimes that women committed, the crimes against women, and the treatment of female victims and offenders in the courts.

First, the case of a widow and a gentleman: Jehane Hemery, once the wife of a spicer, and Regnault d'Azincourt. In February 1405 Regnault and two others – one man, one woman – were arrested for making an armed, nocturnal invasion of Jehane's house in the Rue St Denis in Paris. It was said that they were accompanied by a priest and several other men, and had the intention of betrothing and/or abducting Jehane, without her consent or that of her father (which was claimed to be a capital crime). In attempting to do this, so it was said, they had caused her to faint and to fall into a near-fatal 'frenzy', which provoked a long period of illness, leading to the loss of her senses as well as her good name. Regnault and his accomplices were interrogated over several days: Regnault confessed some of the charges, but his chief male accomplice denied doing any wrong. The Parlement of Paris condemned Regnault to pay a fine (*amende*) to the king, his female accomplice to the pillory and his male accomplice to be questioned further under torture. All three appealed against these decisions, and it is at the point of appeal that the record of the case opens. During the subsequent pleadings, it transpired that Regnault had been wooing Jehane for some time: she claimed that she had always rebuffed his inquiries, saying that she had no intention of remarrying, and that when she did, she would marry someone who was her social equal, not someone of higher rank, and would take her father's advice. Regnault maintained, to the contrary, that Jehane had spoken to several people of her love for him – how handsome he was, how much she cared for him, how willing she was to have him. He was, she was alleged to have said, 'the sweetest, the most handsome and the best talker she had ever seen'. Regnault also denied that on the night in question any forced entry had been made to her father's house (the servant had let them in, he said), or that any armed offences had been committed (he was a nobleman and was acting without malice) or that Jehane had been in a continuous illness since that night (she was faking, and had got up from her bed as soon as he left). Both Regnault and his male accomplice identify Jehane's father as the obstacle to her remarriage, which they claim was desired by both Jehane and Regnault. The father was reported as declaring that Jehane was not the woman for Regnault, that Regnault was 'too great a master', and that he would rather pay taxes every week than see his daughter taken by force. Both of these versions – Jehane's and Regnault's – have their attractiveness and logic. Jehane was a respectable widow being pestered by a man from a different social class. The potential for such a situation to damage her reputation was high. The ideal, as urged by the Church, was for social equality between marriage partners: this was the best way of ensuring harmonious and happy marriages. Such an ideal was, in any case, supported by the widespread practice of social endogamy, by which inter-class marriages were the exception. So Jehane and her father were at one in rejecting the unwelcome advances of Regnault. Regnault's version is perhaps slightly more compelling. Widows, especially those who returned to the paternal home, did not escape parental control of their future lives, yet Jehane, mature, once married, continuing her husband's spice business, had grounds for believing that she could control her own life. The father's strong-willed objection to this match could be circumvented only through elopement and clandestine marriage, and that is what was arranged. In eventually appearing to prefer Regnault's version to Jehane's, the Parlement was aligning with the nobleman against the bourgeois and with the man against the woman (though also with the suitor against the father).[1]

For the second case we move forward in time and further south in space to Dijon in 1447: the case of Sancerot Bauchet and Katherine, a carpenter's wife. One night, Sancerot, with his brother and two others, broke into Katherine's house while her husband was away. When she protested, she was hit about the head and face and threatened with daggers. She was then raped. While this was going on, two of the group stood guard in the street, throwing stones to intimidate the neighbours, 'so forcefully, that it seemed that all the demons of hell were there'. However, against the clarity of this indictment, one witness said that, although she had never seen any man enter Katherine's house except for her husband, Katherine had an easy laugh, was a 'joyeuse femme', had previously been a servant and a nurse in several parts of town, and knew and spoke to many people in the street, such that bad people, who speak ill rather than good, might say that she was a woman of loose morals.[2] Again the question of the woman's reputation is put in the scales of justice and weighs against her: a woman so loose with her company, it was implied, deserved all that she got.

The third case takes us to Magny-en-Vexin in 1369, when Even Dol was murdered by his wife and her lover, Roland de Santeuil. Even Dol was a high-placed, wealthy nobleman, a councillor of the king, but also a man who pursued quarrels, who lent money but was pitiless in recovering it. Among his debtors was Roland, a less well-off nobleman of the Vexin, who had borrowed money from Even in order to pay his ransom follow-ing capture during a military expedition to Spain. Roland had two motives for Even's murder: he loved Even's wife, Ameline, and he could not repay his loan. By one stroke, he could wipe out his debt and consum-mate his love. So, frequenting Even's house on the pretext of courting his daughter, Roland was able to plot the murder with Ameline. Even was ambushed on the road to Paris and slain with a sword. Both Roland and Ameline were arrested. Both confessed, but their subsequent fate is unclear: the properties of both were confiscated, but Roland at least was still alive in 1387.[3]

Three women in three different situations: one is claimed to be the victim of a near-abduction that left her bedridden and dishonoured; the second is raped in her own home; the third is the accomplice in the murder of her own husband. What links the three cases is marriage. In one case, a widow finds it impossible to contract marriage without her father's consent, and this precipitates an attempted abduction; in the second, a woman had failed to frame her conduct to that of the respect-able wife, and her reputation as a loose woman – to call her a 'joyeuse femme' perhaps came close to calling her a 'fille de joie' or whore – left her open to sexual violence in her husband's absence; in the third, what looks like an arranged marriage, of Dol's status coupled with Ameline's money (her father was the king's wealthy war-treasurer), failed to satisfy the wife, who preferred a young soldier to her quarrelsome husband. In this sense, we could say that all three women were victims; but in fact their ability to act was graduated. Least powerful, most impotent is Katherine, who not only suffers rape but also has her reputation com-promised or diminished. It was the classic male defence in rape cases to argue that the woman was a prostitute, thus mitigating, if not excusing, the offence. Numerous trials in Bologna show this defence being deployed. Another case in Paris in 1393, studied recently by Prevenier, shows the same courtroom contest over a woman's reputation, with the rape victim asserting that she was a 'good, worthy woman', while her attackers claim to know her as a whore.[4] More complicit was Jehane: if the accused are to be believed (as they apparently were), she was on the edge of consenting to a clandestine marriage, perhaps to an elopement as well, and had been shocked into a retreat only by Regnault's appearance in such armed force. Jehane was almost in the situation of those 'girls who let themselves be abducted', against whom various rulers passed punitive legislation (for example, Count Jaime I of Catalonia, 1258).[5] Only a single step separated her from the girls who organised elopements with their lovers, against their father's wishes, in Italian cities such as Bologna.[6] Most complicit of all was obviously Ameline; but even her impotence is evident: as in many husband killings, the wife does not act alone, nor does she deal the fatal blow. Women were not in a position to organise road-side ambushes or to kill with a sword.

Marriage thus forms the essential background to all these women's involvement in crime. The argument of this chapter is that the situation of these women was not unusual, and that marriage, and the social forces acting to contain women that marriage served, significantly controlled women's involvement in crime. This is not to say that it accounts for all female criminality, which would be obviously false. The records of female petty-thieving and brawling often leave little or no indication of motive or context, and it would be wrong to assume that marriage lay at the root of such offences.

Take these examples, selected at random, from Bologna. In 1430, Magdalena, the wife of a smith, was prosecuted for pushing a widow to the ground in the street, then punching her in the face and tearing her tunic and veil. In 1444 a butcher's daughter threw a stone at another woman, hitting her in the eye. In 1450, a Polish woman was charged with stealing money from the clothes and purses of female travellers staying at a hostel. In 1375 a prostitute by the name of Lisia was convicted on ten counts of stealing money and clothes – a cloak here, a shirt there – from houses and shops over the previous two years. Although we might glimpse in these latter cases the poverty and migration that brought one woman from Poland to Bologna, and that reduced another first to prostitution and then to larceny, we have no grounds at all for explaining the face-punching, dress-ripping and stone-throwing of violent women in the other cases. In minor crimes such as these, the court record is fairly uninformative.

Nevertheless, when we look at more serious crimes in which women were either the victims or the offenders, we do find that marriage forms an important part of the explanatory context. This argument is not entirely new. Chevalier, in explaining violence in French medieval towns, placed female crime in the context of oppressive marriages and women's exclusion from commercial or professional activity: female crime was that of the vanquished and the victims in a society that offered them few prospects or opportunities.[7]

Gender and crime

When considering women and crime, the broader issue of gender also needs to be addressed. It is often claimed that crime, especially crimes of violence, are a gendered behaviour, that is, that violence is a part of masculinity itself. It is not a part of the social or cultural construct of femininity, and this explains the low participation of women in crime. This view has recently been challenged, and it has been argued that the violence of medieval women, rather than being an aberration from norms of female behaviour, was part of the culture of honour and shame, in which women participated as much as men.[8] Women at all social levels certainly do respond to attacks on their honour, usually through insult, so to this extent it can be said that violence defended honour without reference to gender. However, the problem with this interpretation lies in the statistics. Across late medieval Europe, women figure little in criminality. Numbers from various courts in various periods tell the same story. In England in the mid-thirteenth century, less than 10 per cent of accused killers were women; in the first half of the fourteenth century women were accused of only 10 per cent of felonies. In France during the reign of Charles VI (1389–1422), women petitioned the king for only 4 per cent of pardons for serious crime. Slightly higher figures come from some southern French cities. In Lyon in the years 1427–33, 20 per cent of convicted criminals were women. Prosecution of women in Manosque reached a similar level.[9] So, although women as well as men might participate in the culture of honour, which dictated a violent response to challenges, they did so at very different rates, and it is gender that explains this difference.

However, the picture is not as simple as this. If women participate in crime but only at lower levels than men, we might expect to find the pattern of women's crimes mirroring that of men. In broad outline it is true that the distribution of female crime followed that of total prosecuted criminality (and therefore of men's): violence bulked largest, followed by theft, sex crimes (adultery, prostitution) and insult. However, women's participation in crime did not simply copy men's at a lower level of frequency. It had its own pattern. Women were more or less absent from some crimes, and their participation in others had its own structure. Some transgressions were even predominantly female. Women were prosecuted very little for homicide. Their involvement in physical violence had different objects and means from men's: women assaulted other women more than they assaulted men; and they fought with hands, feet and teeth, rather than with weapons or tools; as a result the wounds they inflicted were rarely life-threatening. In property crimes, women were prosecuted little for fraud or counterfeiting, and their involvement in theft again had its own objects and means: they committed petty theft more than robbery; they targeted small items for immediate consumption or sale; and they acted as receivers of stolen goods. The classic female thieves were the servants who stole from their mistresses, the innkeepers who stole from their guests, and the nurses who stole from their patients. Women did not take part in highway robbery or cattle-rustling: they abused positions of trust, rather than confront victims with force. When women were involved in greater crimes of violence, it was as accomplices to men or as instigators. Finally, by contrast, some crimes had an incidence that was predominantly or even wholly female: few men were ever prosecuted for infanticide; and no men, except tailors, for infraction of the sumptuary laws, which punished extravagance in dress.[10] Gender dictated not only women's generally lower participation in crime, but also the specific pattern of their criminality.

Gender also affected the treatment of women in the law courts. It has been suggested that they were arrested less often and punished less severely; and there is some reason to think that women's disputes were taken less seriously and denounced less often. A thirteenth-century manual on English court procedure states that 'all bloodshed by force . . . is to be presented in the hundred [court], save mere squabbles among boys and old women': thus reducing some women to the role of children, impotent and with no criminal responsibility.[11] In England, a woman was allowed to make a private accusation (appeal) only in three specific cases (her husband killed in her arms, her own virginity ravished, an infant slain in her womb), and accusations made outside those limits were not allowed to proceed.[12] As we shall see, even victims of rape in England found it difficult to press their cases. However, if women found it more difficult to bring cases, they found it easier to escape severe punishment. In law penalties were to be equal in gravity, with variation only in mode of execution: death by fire for women, rather than by the rope. In practice, women found it easier to obtain pardon or release from prison, and were less frequently subject to corporal punishments such as whipping.[13] In addition, the argument of feebleness (*fragilitas sexus*) was used by jurists and judges to justify lighter punishment of women.[14] The statutes of Arezzo (Tuscany), for example, declared that 'the female sex is to be somewhat indulged', and ordered that for crimes between women the ordinary penalties were to be halved, and for crimes by women against men, the penalties were to be mitigated at the judge's discretion.[15] In England, when husband and wife acted together in committing a crime, jurors would convict the husband but acquit the wife, on the grounds that she 'could not contradict her husband's wishes': in such cases, marriage was seen as removing some of the woman's moral responsibility.[16] In the same way, it was the husbands in England who were prosecuted when their wives were suspected of thieving.

Infanticide

Infanticide has been called 'the female crime *par excellence*', but the number of prosecutions was very low. In the diocese of Canterbury, about one a year; at Stockholm only ten in a period of 150 years. They were more frequent in the sixteenth century, though, for the Parlement of Paris dealt with ten cases in 1535 alone, and the bishop of Fiesole, in Tuscany, between 1500 and 1540, absolved nearly 300 married couples of causing the deaths of their children. In Italy, cases turn up in the secular courts: for example in Bologna in 1344 a woman was tried by the *podestà*, convicted and beheaded for stifling her newborn infant by pressing on its throat with her hands. In England, by contrast, infanticide was dealt with entirely by the ecclesiastical courts, which meant that it was treated as a sin requiring penance, not a crime requiring punishment. The forms of penance imposed were similar to those for sexual offences such as adultery or fornication. For example, the Canterbury court imposed the following penances on Joan Rose, convicted of killing her son in 1470: to 'go before the procession in the parish church of Hythe on three Sundays with a wax candle of half a pound in her right hand and the knife with which she killed the boy . . . in her left', and to repeat this parade around the markets of Canterbury, Faversham and Ashford. Child-killing was also undifferentiated in the Canterbury Church court: cases of negligence or overlaying (when parents accidentally stifled an infant sleeping in the same bed) were dealt with on the same basis as deliberate killings through abortifacient herbs or through drowning, suffocation or exposure. In this way, one writer concludes, infanticide was considered 'something less than homicide'.[17]

Ecclesiastical court records seem not to take us very close to the circumstances of child-killing women. In an extraordinary article, Y-B. Brissaud used petitions for royal pardon in France to explore the 'psychological motives' of infanticide. The petitions deploy elements of a repertoire of excuses for killing: that the woman was of previously good repute, perhaps a mother to other children or from an honourable family; that the death was accidental; that the woman did not know what she was doing because of the *maladie* of childbirth. Most of all, however, the petitions focus on the woman's fear: fear of what husbands, lovers, parents or masters would say or do to them, and fear of the shame and dishonour they would incur for bringing a bastard into the world.

Such fears were fully justified, as Brissaud provides examples of husbands, lovers and masters who assaulted and beat their illicitly pregnant wives, mistresses or servants until they miscarried. It was such fear that led women 'to conceal pregnancy, to give birth secretly, and to dispose of the infant'. The physical pain and suffering of childbirth in such circumstances induced a *folie meutrière*: women might abandon infants where they fell, or push them out of the way under the nearest bench, into the nearest cupboard or down the nearest privy. Often, however, this *folie* resulted in a deliberate act of extermination, in which the infant was strangled, battered against a wall, or thrown into a well or river.[18]

The situations of child-killing women reflect all the positions of unmarried lay women in medieval society: the priest's mistress, the live-in servant, the unmarried twenty-something, the newly-wed, the widow. None of these could afford, financially or morally, the burden of an illegitimate child. Marital status was important here. The mistress and the servant would face dismissal; the unmarried woman in her twenties could say goodbye to any lingering hopes she nursed of marriage; the newly-wed would most likely receive a battering from her husband; the widow would lose her chance of remarriage and would struggle to rear a child on her own. In Flanders in 1453 a noblewoman in her twenties had an affair with a man (a *compaignon*) while staying at a relative's castle. She became pregnant and one Sunday in December she give birth. Though at first she kept the child with her, the following morning, afraid of her uncle's anger, she took a knife and cut its throat. Then she tied a weight round its neck and threw it into a ditch. She returned to her room and pretended to be having menstrual pains, so that no one would suspect anything.[19] The paths towards and from infanticide would thus be littered with lies and deceptions. In Florence in 1407 a newly wed woman was convicted of killing her newborn son by throwing him into a river: she had been pregnant already by another man when she married Cecco, and 'although she had been questioned by Cecco and his brothers about her swollen stomach, [she] had insisted that she had a pain in her stomach and that the swelling resulted from that'.[20] When such women had a child that did not survive, suspicions were bred, as can be illustrated in a case from Manosque, in Provence, in 1298. A widow became pregnant and feared dishonour as a result. She was visited several times by a Jewish physician, and this was noticed by the neighbours. After the birth, both she and the child died. Rumour apparently tied together 'dead child', 'widow' and 'Jewish physician' and came up with 'infanticide'. The Jew, called Isaac, was consequently prosecuted for preparing a poisonous medicine that caused the infant to be born dead.[21]

Plate 1. Scene of thief brought before a judge. Staatsbibliothek Preußischer Kulturbesitz, Berlin, (MS Lat., fol. 332, f. 185v).

Plate 2. Scene of a violent criminal brought before a judge. Universitätsbibliothek, Tübingen, Foto Leutner Fachlabor, (Ms 294, f. 77v).

Plate 3. J. Millaeus Boius, *Praxis criminis persequendi* (Paris, 1541). Roger-Viollet.

Plate 4. Domenico Beccafumi, 'A man subjected to torture' (Paris, Louvre).
D.A.G. © Photo-Michele Bellot.

Plate 5. Master of Alkmar, 'Comforting prisoners' (from 'Seven Acts of
Mercy', dated 1504). Rijksmuseum-Stichting, Amsterdam.

Plate 6. Florentine master, c. 1450, 'A Saint feeding and consoling prisoners'.
Scala.

Plate 7. Master of St Gudule, 'Delivering prisoners' (from 'Seven Acts of Mercy'). Paris, Musée de Moyen-Age. Cluny © Photo RMN.

Plate 8. a & b Scenes of branding and pillory, Coutumes de Toulouse,
Bibliothèque Nationale de France, Paris, (MS Latin 9187, fols. 29v&30).

Plate 9. Scene of amputation of a foot. Österreichische National-bibliothek.
FOTO: Bildarchiv, ONB Vienna.

Plate 10. Bernardo Martorell, 'St George dragged at a horse's tail'. Louvre, Paris. © Photo RMN-Daniel Arnaudet.

Plate 11. Perugino, 'St Jerome saves two hanged men'. Louvre, Paris.
© Photo RG Ojeda.

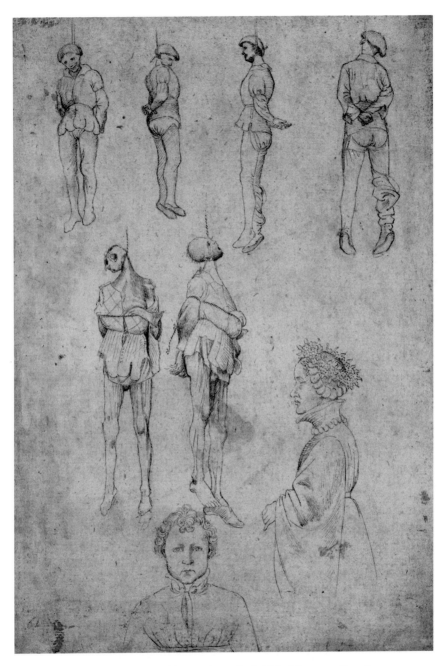

Plate 12. Pisanello, 'Study of hanged men'. British Museum, London.

Plate 13. Leonardo da Vinci, 'The hanged Bandini'. Musée Bonnat, Bayonne.
© Photo RMN RG Ojeda.

Plate 14. 'The prostitute', in 'La danse macabre des femmes'. Bibliothèque Nationale de France, Paris, (MS fr. 995, fol. 37v). Roger-Viollet.

Death
Worthless woman,
Living in carnal sin,
You have led a dissolute life
In every season, winter and summer.
Feel terror in your heart,
For you will be held tight.
One is tormented for doing bad things.
When one keeps doing it, sin is harmful.

Prostitute
I gave in to this sin
For unbridled pleasure.
Hang the ones who led me there
And left me to the trade.
If I had been well brought up
And guided in the first place,
I would never have been found like this.
(Ann Tukey Harrison's translation)

Plate 15. Legend of St Quentin 'Man arrested for stealing a horse', Paris, Louvre. © Photo RMN.

According to the hagiographical record, St Quentin, a Christian martyr during persecutions under Emperor Maximian, was miraculously released from prison in Amiens, by an angel, and converted his own prison guards to Christianity. One of the miracles later attributed to him was this intervention on the gallows to save a horse-thief. (Source: *Acta Sanctorum*, October, vol. XIII (Paris, 1883), pp. 781–2, 804).

The thief who stole a priest's horse: how he was hanged on a gallows, but freed. In this town [of Vermandois], one of the robbers stole a horse belonging to a priest. When the priest tracked him down, he notified the judge, who immediately arrested the thief and held him confined in chains. The thief confessed the deed by his own mouth, and was sentenced to death. At this point the priest grew concerned that his personal loss should be the cause of imperilling a man's soul, so he begged the judge to spare the thief's life and absolve him of the penalty, on the grounds that he had already undergone enough, having confessed after all types of torture. But the severity of the judge could in no way be deflected, and he ordered the thief to be hanged. The priest, in tears, prostrated himself at the tomb of St Quentin, and humbly prayed to him, saying, 'Glorious champion of Christ, I beg you to save this poor man from an unjust death, lest his dying by my accusation dishonour me. Show your holy power, I entreat you, so that where human hard-heartedness has declined to absolve, you may liberate, through the mitigating gentleness of your holiness.' Following this prayer, the chains holding the thief to the gallows broke, and he fell to the ground. When the judge heard this, he was struck with fear and wonder at divine power and dared do no further harm to the thief.

Plate 16. Martin Schongauer, 'Les apprentis orfèvres' (The apprentice gold-smiths, fighting) (Musée d'Unterlinden, Colmar, Engraving, B91). Photograph © 2001 Board of Trustees, National Gallery of Art, Washington, c. 1480.

Pauperis et regis cõmunis lex moꝛiendi Dat caufam flēdi: ſi bene ſcripta legis
Coꝛpoꝛis et aie ſocietas non firmo viculo Ferro. peſte. flama. vinclis. aꝛ
coheret: facile dirimitur. Stultum eſt in doꝛe. caloꝛe. Mille modis leti:
eo confidere: quod leui perditur caſu. miſeros moꝛs vna fatigat.

Le moꝛt
Pꝛomoteur venez a la court
Tantoſt: et ſoyez aduiſe
Reſpondꝛe le long. ou le court.
Du cas qui vous eſt impoſe.
Ceſt: car vous eſte accuſe
Nauoir pas touſiours iuſtement
De voſtre office bien vſe.
En mal fait git amendement.

Le pꝛomoteur
Jeuſſe demain receu ſiꝝ ſolz
Dun homme qui eſt en ſentence
Pour confentir qui fut abſoulz
Se icuſſe eſter a laudience.
Plus ne me fault penſer en ce
Moꝛt ma ſoupꝛiz en ſon embuche
Pꝛandꝛe me fault en pacience
Bien charie dꝛoit qui ne trebuche

Le moꝛt
En ſouffy. peine. et traueil.
Auez garder pꝛiſons geolier
Souuent on vous a fait refueil
Cuidanz doꝛmir. ou ſommellie.
Vous nen ſerez plus traueillie
Venez danſer ſans plus de plait
Cy eſt: ou vous deuez veillier
Il fault moꝛir quant a dieu plait.

Le geolier
Je tenoye de bons pꝛiſonniers
Deſquelꝛ iatendoye recepuoir
Plenne ma bourſe de deniers
Pour deſpence. et pour auoir
Les garder. et fait mon deuoir
De les penſer bien loyalment.
Quant on meurt on doit dire voir.
Dieu ſcet qiu dit vꝛay. ou qui ment.

Plate 17. The gaoler, in *La danse macabre de Guy Marchant*, ed. P. Champion
(Paris, 1925). Roger-Viollet.

Death says to the gaoler: 'Gaoler, you have kept prisoners in worry, pain and torment
. . . You won't be doing any more of that: Come, dance, and no complaining'.

The Gaoler replies: 'I guard good prisoners, and I keep my purse full of the money
I receive from them, for the expenses of guarding them. I do my duty in caring right
faithfully for them'.

There were thus clear psychological and social motives for infanticide, which took some of their force from the economic burden of child-rearing and some from the dishonour of unmarried parenthood. It is also argued that there were demographic factors at play: in fourteenth-century Catalonia, five out of six infant victims were girls. That medieval societies practised female infanticide has often been supposed, from the demographic profiles of children, and occasional evidence such as this seems to confirm the possibility: girls were a cost and a liability, so were extinguished; boys were an asset and a benefit, so were preserved.

Gauvard, also relying on the evidence of pardons, draws a picture very different from that of Brissaud: infanticide as a last resort, not a first move. The young, poor mothers who typically committed this crime wanted to raise their children, but surrendered to murderous instinct when this proved beyond their means. Moreover, where historians usually see the few prosecutions for infanticide as the tip of an iceberg, given the difficulties of proof, and as an indication of emotional indifference to childhood, Gauvard argues contrariwise: that infanticide *was* rare; and that plenty of other evidence suggests respect for pregnant women and love for infants.[22]

This forms a major disagreement with more demographically minded historians. Richard Trexler, for example, in his study of infanticide in fifteenth- and sixteenth-century Florence, produces two types of evidence in support of his contention that child-killing was widespread and common. First, he draws attention to the gender imbalance among young children to be found in the great Florentine fiscal survey of 1427. At age 0 there were 115 males for every 100 females, and this ratio rises, at every year up to age 4, reaching 119:100. The number of girls, he argues, was 'abnormally low', especially given girls' naturally higher rate of survival of infancy. Something 'unnatural' must therefore have been happening to reduce the number of girls in the population. What that was is suggested by two other types of information. Statements by the promoters of foundling hospitals suggest that the alternative for the abandoned children was violent death, and the records of such a hospital in Florence indicate that girls received a lower standard of care from wet-nurses. Girls were more likely to be abandoned; and girls were treated less well by wet-nurses. Trexler also makes an important challenge to the historiographical treatment of infanticide. Late medieval society tended to associate infanticide with unmarried mothers or with witches, ignoring the disturbing possibility that married couples might kill their children. The ideology of the family smothered this idea at birth (so to speak). Most historians have followed the same path, seeing infanticide as 'culturally alien' and rare because incompatible with Christian ideals.[23]

Rape

Of the crimes perpetrated against women, rape stands out for the apparent ineffectiveness of the law. In modern Britain the proportion of reported rapes that result in trial or, even less, conviction, is low and falling; and reported rapes are only a small proportion of total rapes that take place. Nothing should surprise us, then, in the fact that similar figures arise from late medieval courts. In England between 1202 and 1276, one historian has counted 142 prosecutions for rape; in only 23 of these cases did the accused appear in court. Of these accused, 20 were acquitted, and of the remaining three, one was fined and the remaining two, who were clerics, were transferred to a Church court and therefore lost to the record. In Edward Powell's study of the English Midlands in the first three decades of the fifteenth century, there were 280 indictments for rape, but not a single conviction ('a remarkable statistic even by medieval standards'). In the fragmentary register for Cerisy in Normandy in the fourteenth and fifteenth centuries, there are only eight rape cases out of a total of 344 violent crimes. Only eight cases, too, are to be found in the fourteenth-century outlawry books for Nuremberg, out of over 700 cases. Only four rapes appear among over 400 criminal sentences in the north Italian city of Brescia in the years 1414–17, and the main Venetian criminal court heard, on average, only three cases a year.[24] When he correlated age and status of victim with severity of penalty, Ruggiero found that in Venice 'unmarried girls of marriageable age . . . found their rapists penalized with little more than a slap on the wrist'. Two major questions are suggested by such figures: first, why are they so low? And second, would we be justified in seeing them as only a tiny proportion of total instances of rape?

   In England, rape was not, until 1275, a crime for which royal justice could initiate prosecution: justices in eyre did not ask for presentments of rape (see above, pp. 6, 12 for this procedure).[25] Prosecutions happened only in the form of private accusations (appeals) by the victim, and few of those resulted in a jury verdict. For example, of 49 accusations of rape between 1194 and 1216, only one reached a legal conclusion (the accused was acquitted, because of the previous sexual relationship between himself and the victim). What happened to all the other cases? In most the accusing woman simply discontinued the legal action. Such defaults were higher in rape than in other crimes, and were the result of the parties reaching an out-of-court settlement, either in the form of monetary reparation or of marriage (we shall return to these 'rapes' that resulted in marriage). Another reason was the very infrequency of punishment for rape: charges were difficult to prove anyway, and starting a prosecution must often have seemed futile. This was compounded by the perceived disproportion, as far as the male jury was concerned, between the penalty and the crime: the penalty was blinding and castration, but it was applied on only one known occasion (1222). It was in 1275 that English law was changed to allow state prosecution of rape, but even then the state claimed only a residual power: only if no private accusation was made within forty days of the offence did the right to prosecute pass to the Crown. Nevertheless, this new statute did develop the law in several ways. First, it covered the rape of married women as well as virgins, thus moving the law on from the older view that only virgins could be raped (that is, that rape consisted of taking away virginity). Second, it altered the penalty: in place of physical mutilation, two years' imprisonment and a fine.

However, judicial practice seems to have allowed suspects to make objections in order to nullify prosecutions. For example, in Shropshire in 1256, Agnes, a poor woman, accused ('appealed') Adam of rape. He appeared and denied the accusation, and, among other objections, argued that she seemed unsure of the date of the offence (at an earlier hearing she had said it was on a Saturday, now she was saying it was on a Sunday). As a result, Agnes withdrew her accusation, and was imprisoned for making a false appeal.[26] Far from remedying this sort of situation, a further statute in 1285 took English rape law in an entirely new direction. This new statute made the rape of any woman, without her consent before or after, a capital offence. The inclusion of rapes that were consented to has caused some puzzlement: what sort of rapes could these be? It was common for European rape laws to concede that any penalty could be lifted if the rapist married his victim or facilitated her marriage through provision of a dowry. The image that this conjures up in the modern mind – of a woman being more or less coerced into marrying a stranger who had violated her – is distasteful in the extreme. Feminist historians might be right in pointing to such laws as evidence of the denial of women's autonomy: victimised twice over, once by the rape and again by the law. However, it can be argued that we should resist this image, even though the danger of doing so, as Hanawalt has argued, is to discount the brutality of rape and of its impact on the life of its victims. Put simply, too little is known about the circumstances in which this 'get-out' clause might have been applied. Clearly the aim was to repair the damage done by restoring to the woman what had been taken from her, namely her marriageability. It may be that the law had in mind those rapes that are better described as elopements: where parents expected to arrange their daughter's marriage and viewed her virginity as their property, any exercise of choice by the girl would appear as abduction and rape to her parents. These were the 'rapes' to which the 'victim' consented before or afterwards.

English law took an increasingly severe attitude to such autonomous choice. As Post has argued, 'by discounting the woman's consent, the wishes of others (the crown, the family) were allowed to override her own', and these statutes 'turned the law of rape into a law of elopement and abduction'. The law pushed injury to the woman into the background and injury to the father or husband into the foreground. This development was then perfected by the Statute of Rapes of 1382: this completed the transfer of injury from the woman to her family by disinheriting both the ravisher and his 'victim', and laid the ravisher open to prosecution by the woman's family. By extension, a further law of 1487 made abduction of women itself a felony, even without sexual assault (abduction of propertied women, heiresses, was clearly intended).

Two important points need to be made about these changes. The first is that most of them were examples of what was later dubbed 'bad law made in a hurry'. These statutes were passed in the heat of response to particular episodes. The 1275 statute seems to have been a response to a recent 'abduction feud' in Sussex. The 1382 statute grew out of Sir Thomas West's petition following the 'horrible assault' by Nicholas Clifton on his daughter Eleanor – 'horrible' in that Nicholas was a landless younger son deemed unsuitable for his daughter by the ambitious Sir Thomas. The 1487 statute 'agaynst taking awaye of women' was prompted by the abduction of a Coventry widow and heiress by a gentleman from Warwickshire (they subsequently married). Scandalised and well-connected fathers thus pulled and pushed the law into a series of rough and ready reforms aimed at protecting their property against the actions of their daughters and their lovers.

The second point follows on from this. The direction of reform was not towards greater protection of women from sexual assault. Rape prosecutions were not facilitated, but made more difficult. Indictments for rape fell by one-fifth in the dozen years following the 1487 law. In the one attempt by a woman to bring a prosecution under this law, the courts were easily smothered by the social influence and legal know-how of the abductor's noble family. As Ives despairingly commented: 'the legal machine had brought forth perjured juries, legal ingenuity and a blanket of frustration'.[27]

The clear evolution of the English law on rape seems unusual, but continental laws did share many of the same features. In France and the Low Countries too there was a confusion of rape (sexual assault) and abduction, with the latter more often prosecuted. Here too the interests of the parents could be substituted for those of the victim. Here too accusatory procedure persisted as the sole means of prosecution for much longer than for other serious crimes: in France it was only during the fourteenth century that state prosecutions of rape became possible, in Ghent only in 1438. Even with inquisitorial procedure and torture, convictions for rape remained rare and punishment rarer, largely because of the difficulty of proof: in the absence of witnesses, it was her word against his, and her word was more easily impugned.

The heart of the problem lay in the tension between canon and secular law in the area of consent to marriage. Canon law did not require parental consent for the creation of a legitimate marriage; secular law did. As one historian has put it: propertied families 'could not tolerate that a twelve-year-old heiress endanger the property of her lineage'.[28] As a result, governments legislated not only to penalise marriages contracted without parental consent, but also to allow the prosecution of elopement as rape. That abduction was perceived as an attack on property rather than personal violence is indicated by the penalties: at Ghent the abductor of a poor girl was hardly punished at all, whereas the abductor of a girl from a propertied family was banished for three years. The case law seems to show clearly that families used rape charges to punish and disinherit daughters who took their own decisions in choosing a partner. In 1457 Hanse de Lisvelt and Katherine Colins, 'who loved each other', arranged an abduction/elopement, because her parents had gone back on a previous agreement that Hanse could wed her when she came of age. Despite the fact that she consented to the abduction, the prosecution defined the act as violent and against her will, with the result that Hanse was banished (although he subsequently made peace with her parents and married her). Thus, 'the definition of violence depends not on the woman's consent, but on the family seeing it as an attack on their rights'.[29]

The low level of rape convictions can thus be related to difficulties of proof, prejudices against the word of women, and a disproportion, in the eyes of an all-male courtroom, between the crime and the designated penalty of death: to adapt Hanawalt's verdict, in the scales of justice the woman's broken hymen counted for little against the rapist's life. It remains to ask whether the low level of rape prosecutions represent the tip of an iceberg of sexual violence. There are two contrasting views here. On the one hand, it is often reckoned that in contemporary society reported rapes represent only one-tenth of actual rapes committed. Is this true of the Middle Ages too? Many historians think so. Porteau-Bitker points out that many medieval rapes involved an abuse of trust or authority by men, for example, kinsmen, employers and officials, and supposes that few women would be in a position to impugn that authority in the courts. Ruggiero, in examining sex crimes in Venice, depicts late medieval sexuality as naturally rough and violent – he writes of the 'easy fluctuation between violence and courtship' – in which context, rape was a minor offence, 'of little importance to government or society'. On the other hand, Gauvard has challenged this view directly by pointing to the protectiveness of late medieval society towards women and to the fact that most rapes were of prostitutes: this indicates, she argues, that sexual violence was channelled fairly strictly and in such a way as to preserve the integrity of the mass of respectable women.[30] Now it is certainly true that men accused of rape liked to allege that their victims were prostitutes, but there is plenty of evidence that women 'of good repute' were also raped: the argument that sexual violence was common is not so easily swept aside. On the other hand, the prosecutions are few, and the successful ones usually have some extreme elements – the rape of under-age girls, for example, or the betrayal of trust – and this could indicate that courts effectively policed the limits of violence against women.

Prostitution

However, it was not just that the victims of rape were prostitutes, but rape victims could also become prostitutes. Because of the dishonour that rape brought, some women could not escape the sex trade once reduced to the level of a prostitute. In his study of prostitution in Dijon, Rossiaud found that one-fifth of prostitutes had entered the brothel following a rape. Records from Cracow give us the case of a woman, tricked by a prostitute into sharing a bed, who was then raped by her pimp, who told her 'This way you'll learn how to do it next time.'[31] Gauvard too recognises this phenomenon. She differentiates rape victims into three groups, the permitted (prostitutes), the vulnerable (servants, concubines, widows) and the respectable (virgins, wives), and argues that the rape of the vulnerable and the respectable aimed to assimilate them to pro-stitutes, and thus 'to maximise and renew the numbers of permitted women'.[32]

Rape was only one route into prostitution. In her study of Florentine prostitution, Mazzi conjectures that women entered prostitution from all the misfortunes that denied them re-entry into normal society: servants dismissed for having sex with their masters, fugitive slaves, abandoned wives, unmarried mothers, girls tricked by brothel recruiters. Rinaldo Comba presents a similar picture for late medieval Piedmont.[33] However, a concentration on such cases risks graphically misrepresenting medieval women's power over their own lives. This at least is the argument of Ruth Karras in her study of prostitution in late medieval England. She does of course acknowledge that some women were drawn into prostitution through force or trickery, and she presents numerous prosecutions of bawds and pimps for preying on vulnerable young women with promises of employment, but she also argues that such evidence is biased towards perceiving prostitutes as victims, and that the vocabulary of condemnation conceals the fact of cooperation. Most prostitutes, she argues, entered the profession willingly, constrained by nothing more than the state of the labour market.[34] Moreover, a focus on girls in the brothel obviously ignores the broader picture of occasional prostitutes, married or working women who engaged sporadically in the sex trade in order to make ends meet. However, the labour market was not gender-neutral: it has been argued that, as women were progressively excluded from certain occupations in the later fifteenth century, they were pushed into prostitution, and that this in turn prompted restrictive legislation from alarmed civic authorities.[35]

Prostitution itself was not a crime (though it was a sin); what was punished was prostitution outside designated areas, and pimping and procuring. Various schema have been suggested for the evolution of public intervention in the sex trade in the later Middle Ages. Rossiaud constructed a sequence for the history of prostitution in France in which thirteenth-century rejection softened into toleration and integration in the fourteenth and fifteenth centuries. Thus he starts with King Louis's famous ordinances of 1254 and 1256 ordering the expulsion of prostitutes at least beyond the city walls or out of respectable streets. He also points to thirteenth-century laws that associated prostitutes with other agents of impurity such as lepers and Jews, and imposed on them various restraints of trade: certain sacred areas of the city, certain special days of the Christian calendar were not to be sullied with whoring, and prostitutes were at all times to be clearly distinguishable in their dress from decent women. Rossiaud then presents the period from 1350 to 1450, however, as one in which all the restrictions on prostitutes fell away: their trade itself was municipalised, with the creation of legalised brothels; prohibitions of residence in respectable streets were ignored; requirements for distinctive clothing lapsed; and prostitutes took part in religious processions and feast-day games.

A similar schema has been adopted to tell the history of prostitution in late medieval Italy. Already in the nineteenth century, the great Italian legal historian Antonio Pertile saw the history of prostitution as a sequence from expulsion to toleration to legalisation, and a similar three-phase development has been more recently taken up by Maria Serena Mazzi for the city of Florence. She sees, first, a period of restriction and segregation in the late thirteenth and early fourteenth centuries, with laws requiring prostitutes to wear distinctive clothing and to keep away from churches. These repeatedly issued laws condemned prostitution as 'offensive to God, noxious to the city's reputation and a source of impurity'. This phase was succeeded during the fourteenth century by a gradual 'reconquest' of the city by prostitutes, as shown in the records of fines imposed on them for walking the central streets without their distinctive clothing. The last phase sees a governmental volte-face, with the authorities putting aside repression and creating a public brothel, regulated by an official magistracy, the *Ufficio dell'onestà*.[36]

Both Mazzi and Rossiaud explain this development by reference to the opinions of theologians and clerical writers in the fourteenth and fifteenth centuries: in the fight against the more serious sexual sins of sodomy and adultery, fornication came to be seen as an ally, not an enemy, especially when it involved unmarried men and unattached, professional prostitutes. Prostitution came to serve the greater good of protecting marriage from sodomites and adulterers. Rossiaud quotes St Augustine as saying that the prostitute 'is in society what bilge is in a ship at sea and the sewer pit is in a palace. Remove this sewer and the entire palace will be contaminated.'

Rinaldo Comba has also used a two-part sequence to describe the evolution of government attitude to prostitution in Piedmont, between an earlier period of urban legislation and a later period of intervention by the Duke of Savoy. In the thirteenth century civic statutes prohibited the residence of prostitutes in the city or their presence on major streets, and attempted to exclude them from taverns. In the early fifteenth century, specifically in the 1430s, towns were prompted to establish municipal brothels, partly by fervent preaching by proponents of moral reform, and partly by ducal decrees. Prostitutes were now to be segregated for two specific reasons: to prevent disorder and to stop 'decent' women being drawn into prostitution: as the statutes of Ivrea put it, 'to avoid the disturbances that usually happen because of prostitutes, and to prevent the prostitutes having cause to associate with decent women'. For Comba, the municipalised brothel had nothing to do with providing more acceptable outlets – more acceptable, that is, than adultery or sodomy – for the sexual energies of young, unmarried men. It was, rather, part of a much broader ducal strategy to impose Christian moral discipline, and was accompanied by a strengthening of regulation of vagabonds and Jews.[37]

However, it is not clear that this chronology is convincing. In the case of Rossiaud and Comba, this is mainly because their sequences are built on a contrast between legal restrictions and later evidence for their non-observance. This ignores the possibility that the restrictions were not enforced in the first place. Of course, it can be countered that what we have is evidence of a change in *attitude* on the part of governments, and this is what Comba would argue. However, as he admits, the ducal order for segregation of prostitutes was slow to be realised, as women could not easily be removed from their houses and did not want to be interned in brothels. Moreover, as expulsions and restrictions continued to happen in many places, it would be difficult to argue for a complete change in attitude.

Second, the sequence of two or three phases does not conform to the currents of thinking among Church lawyers and theologians. Prostitution was tolerated by them already in the twelfth and thirteenth centuries, when it was believed that 'the prostitute had a certain public usefulness', and that 'what was required was to set limits to her practice, rather than to eliminate her from society'. For canon lawyers in the twelfth century, prostitution was 'a minor stain on the social fabric'.[38]

More convincing therefore is the idea of constant tension throughout the period between exclusion and integration. As Gauvard has pointed out, even in the fourteenth century the state used prostitutes as scapegoats and repeatedly decreed purifying campaigns against them.[39] Ill-repute continued to haunt those who frequented brothels, and prostitutes continued to be imprisoned on the denunciation of neighbours for practising outside designated areas. Any clerical ideas of the protective value of prostitution in greater battles against sin seem not to have been transmitted to the lay population.

This oscillation, as Gauvard calls it, between love and hate, repulsion and attraction, provides a better schema for explaining the continuing efforts in the fourteenth and fifteenth centuries to confine prostitution. At Verona, for example, a law of 1327 endeavoured to confine prostitutes to the old Roman Arena. A new law in Cremona, 1349, attempted to keep prostitutes out of the cathedral, baptistery and main square, and to stop them moving more than a few yards from the brothel, and it authorised citizens to upbraid whores found in the cathedral and to expel them, with force if necessary. The Duke of Milan can be found asserting all the old restrictions: in 1390–1 there was an order to restrict access to the brothel area by building a wall and installing a guard; in 1412 prostitutes were ordered to wear white, fustian cloaks, and not to loiter in the Broletto, while no brothel was to be opened except in the designated area and no one was to enter the brothel at night.[40] In London, an ordinance of 1393 prohibited prostitutes from any area of the city except the designated places, 'that is to say the stews on the other side of the Thames and Cock's Lane', because of the 'many and divers affrays, broils and dissensions . . . by reason of the frequent resort of and consorting with common harlots at taverns, brewhouses . . . and other places of ill-fame'. The later fifteenth century also saw other English towns attempting to control prostitution, in contrast to an earlier tendency to exploit them through rents and fines. The Scottish Parliament of 1426 enacted 'that common women be put at the utmost endes of the towne' (although, bizarrely, this was intended as a fire precaution!).[41] In Montpellier in 1469, the licensees of the brothel outside the city walls complained of an inhabitant welcoming the girls to his house within the city: the licensees, specifically recalling King Louis's ordinance of 1254, pointed out that under the terms of their licence no one else was allowed to create within the walls any 'brothel, *cabaret*, hostelry or other stew' for girls. In this case, the local government and clergy amplified the complaint, seeing this unlicensed abuse as causing 'great vituperation and dishonour' and setting 'a very bad example to married women, their daughters and servants'. The result was that the king ordered the new brothel to be closed down.[42] As this last example clearly shows, continuity of attitude over two centuries could be more evident than change.

Sumptuary laws

Problems arising from marriage also stand behind another form of behaviour for which women were subject to legal reproof and correction: their dress. Laws on dress or apparel were common across Europe in the later Middle Ages. Most countries issued such 'sumptuary laws' sooner or later – sooner in France, Italy and Spain, later in England and Scotland. The purpose of such laws was to restrain extravagance in all its guises, from surfeits of food at wedding banquets, to exaggerated mourning at funerals, and luxury and ornament in clothing. In the fifteenth century, however, it has been argued that the increasing focus of this legislation is dress rather than funerals or weddings, and women's dress rather than men's.[43] Restrictions were imposed on styles of dress, materials and ornamentation. The length of trains and sleeves was limited. The use of expensive fabrics – cloth of gold, certain silks or velvets – was prohibited. The numbers of pearls, jewels or rings worn were controlled. The types and amounts of embroidery, trimming and lining were restrained. This narrowing of focus on women's dress was furnished with an ostensible rationale by misogynistic preachers who censured the pride, ruinous extravagance and provocative lustfulness of female attire. Women's sinful pride, which led them to extravagance, also caused the ruination of their fathers and husbands, and provoked other men to lust. According to Diane Owen Hughes, however, we need to look elsewhere for the real motive for such laws, and specifically to the marriage market. A monstrous inflation in dowry levels was often denounced at the time and seems to have been verified by modern historians. This inflation was probably caused by a shift in the ages of marriage in the early fifteenth century – men took to marrying later, women earlier – with a resulting imbalance in the marriage market that forced fathers to offer greater inducements to attract husbands for their daughters. According to Hughes, this bred a sense of impotence among the 'city fathers' who reacted by lashing out at styles of female dress that seemed to signify their loss of control.

There are some problems with this hypothesis. Hughes's emphasis on the misogynistic preambles to sumptuary legislation, and her willingness to explain such laws in terms of hidden psychological impulses, are open to challenge. Catherine Kovesi-Killerby's long-awaited and comprehensive study of Italian sumptuary law will present a wider study, bringing out the complexity of legislators' motives. While not wishing to preempt her forthcoming work, some criticisms of Hughes's argument can be entered here. Although Hughes does acknowledge a range of motivations for sumptuary law, she minimises the role of economic objectives in order to stress the moral ones: 'at heart', she maintains, the concern was female sexuality. It is not clear that in a European context other motives can be played down so easily. Hughes herself quotes the Venetian law that lamented that 'our state has become less strong because money that should navigate and multiply . . . lies dead and is converted into vanities'. This was not a lone voice. Preachers such as San Bernardino of Siena spread the idea that money should circulate in commerce and not 'lie dead' in unproductive, rarely worn apparel.[44] Indeed, in the sixteenth century, protectionist economics seems to be responsible for new sumptuary laws in England and Scotland, where their declared aims were (in the Scottish example) 'to abridge the use of such forrayn commodities as be not necessary for us', and to provide work for the poor by promoting the use of home-spun wool rather than imported silk.[45] Other sumptuary laws seem to have been purely fiscal in intent, to raise money for local treasuries. Moreover, dress laws in Castile, England and Scotland were more concerned with social rank than with the sinfulness of women – those 'subjectes of meane estaite presuming to counteraict his hieness and his nobilitie in the use and wearing of coastlie cleithing', according to the Scottish law of 1581. Indeed the English Acts on apparel specifically *excluded* women from liability. Conversely, concerns about indecency also applied to men. The sensitivity that was shocked by a *décolletage* that showed the cleavage was equally appalled at men's tight breeches and short jackets that revealed the shape of the buttocks and genitals. The Nuremberg law in the fifteenth century declared as 'unchaste and shameful' the fashion for flies in contrasting colours and 'stuffed and artificially enlarged', and condemned the practice of having the fly at dances 'shamelessly bare and uncovered in the presence of honourable women and maidens'.[46] This is not to deny that nuptiality or marriage-rate was not a concern. One Florentine law did, after all, announce that women had forgotten

> that it is not in conformity with nature for them to decorate themselves with such expensive ornaments when their men, because of this, avoid the bond of matrimony on account of the unaffordable expenses, and the nature of these men is left unfulfilled. For women were made to replenish this free city and to observe chastity in marriage; they were not made to spend money on silver, gold, clothing and gems.[47]

What we have to ask, however, is how common such concerns were and how typical of sumptuary law as a whole. This remains an open question.

The gravity attached to female infringements of the dress laws contrasts, of course, to the levity attached to male violations of female bodies, and would justify feminist descriptions of late medieval criminal law as patriarchal. However, to this male historian things do not look so straightforward. We have no means of knowing the numerical relation between prosecuted and unprosecuted sexual assaults. Although courts in different times and places varied in their ability or willingness to prosecute rape, brutal rapes were punished, and severely. Dress laws were not, on the whole, inspired by misogyny, but by a wide range of other governmental concerns. The sex trade in itself was not criminalised, but seen as having public utility. Women were prosecuted for crimes against other women, in which the role of patriarchy is difficult to discern.

Notes

1. Le Roux de Lincy, 'Tentative de rapt commise par Regnaut d'Azincourt sur une épicière de la rue Saint Denis en 1405', *Bibliothèque de l'Ecole des chartes* 2nd ser., 3 (1846).
2. A. Voisin, 'Notes sur la vie urbaine au XVe siècle: Dijon la nuit', *Annales de Bourgogne* 9 (1957), pp. 275–6.
3. A. Porteau-Bitker, 'Un crime passionel au milieu du XIVe s.', *RHDF* 59 (1981).
4. W. Prevenier, 'Violence against women in a medieval metropolis: Paris around 1400', in *Law, Custom and the Social Fabric in Medieval Europe*, ed. B.S. Bachrach and D. Nicholas (Kalamazoo, 1990).
5. F. Sabaté, 'Femmes et violence dans la Catalogne du XIV siècle', *Annales du Midi* 106 (1994), p. 300.
6. T. Dean, 'Fathers and daughters: marriage laws and marriage disputes in Bologna and Italy, 1200–1500', in *Marriage in Italy, 1300–1650*, ed. T. Dean and K.J.P. Lowe (Cambridge, 1998), pp. 100–1.
7. B. Chevalier, *Les bonnes villes de France du XIVe au XVIe siècle* (Paris, 1982), pp. 295–7.
8. N. Gradowicz-Pancer, 'De-gendering female violence: Merovingian female honour as "an exchange of violence"', *Early Medieval Europe* (forthcoming).

9. J.B. Given, *Society and Homicide in Thirteenth-century England* (Stanford, 1977), pp. 134–49; B. Hanawalt, 'The female felon in fourteenth-century England', *Viator* 5 (1974); C. Gauvard, *'De grace especial': Crime, état et société en France à la fin du Moyen Age* (Paris, 1991), pp. 300–1; N. Gonthier, 'Délinquantes ou victimes, les femmes dans la société lyonnaise du XVe siècle', *Revue historique* 271 (1984), pp. 25–6; R. Lavoie, 'Les statistiques criminelles et le visage du justicier: justice royale et justice seigneuriale en Provence au Moyen Age', *Provence historique* 28 (1979), p. 18.

10. Gauvard, *Crime, état et société*, pp. 300–28; Given, *Society and Homicide*, pp. 134–49.

11. H.R.T. Summerson, 'The structure of law enforcement in thirteenth-century England', *American Journal of Legal History* 23 (1979), p. 318.

12. *The Assizes held at Cambridge, AD 1260*, ed. W.M. Palmer (Linton, 1930), p. 16.

13. Gauvard, *Crime, état et société*, pp. 303–6.

14. A. Porteau-Bitker, 'Criminalité et délinquance féminines dans le droit pénal des XIIIe et XIVe siècles', *RHDF* 58 (1980), p. 50.

15. *Statuto di Arezzo (1327)*, ed. G. Marri Camerani (Florence, 1946), p. 210; and in general see A. Pertile, *Storia del diritto italiano*, 2nd edn (6 vols, Turin, 1896–1903), V, p. 150.

16. H. Summerson, 'Maitland and the criminal law in the age of *Bracton*', *Proceedings of the British Academy* 89 (1996), p. 117.

17. R.H. Helmholz, 'Infanticide in the Province of Canterbury during the fifteenth century', *History of Childhood Quarterly* 2 (1975); E. Österberg and D. Lindström, *Crime and Social Control in Medieval and Early Modern Swedish Towns* (Uppsala, 1988), p. 99; B. Schnapper, 'La justice criminelle rendue par le Parlement de Paris sous le règne de François Ier', *RHDF* 52 (1974), p. 272; R.C. Trexler, 'Infanticide in Florence: new sources and first results', *History of Childhood Quarterly* 1 (1973), pp. 103ff; Archivio di Stato, Bologna, Curia del podestà, Inquisitiones, busta 161, reg. 1, fol. 18; ibid., Accusationes, busta 50/b, no. 15.

18. Y-B. Brissaud, 'L'infanticide à la fin du Moyen Age, ses motivations psychologiques et sa répression', *RHDF* 50 (1972).

19. C. Petit-Dutaillis, *Nouveaux documents sur les moeurs populaires et le droit de vengeance dans les Pays-Bas au quinzième siècle* (Paris, 1908), pp. 19–22.

20. G. Brucker, *The Society of Renaissance Florence* (New York, 1971), p. 147; I. Walter, 'Infanticidio a Ponte Bocci: 2 marzo 1406. Elementi di un processo', *Studi storici* 27 (1986).

21. J. Shatzmiller, *Médecine et justice en Provence médiévale: documents de Manosque, 1261–1348* (Aix-en-Provence, 1989), pp. 80–5.

22. Gauvard, *Crime, état et société*, pp. 657–9, 823–6.

23. Trexler, 'Infanticide in Florence'.

24. M.K. Schüssler, 'German crime in the later Middle Ages: A statistical analysis of the Nuremberg Outlawry Books, 1285–1400', *Criminal Justice History* 13 (1992), p. 22; A. Finch, 'Women and violence in the later Middle Ages: the evidence of the officiality of Cerisy', *Continuity and Change* 7 (1992), pp. 33–5; E. Powell, 'Jury trial at gaol delivery in the late Middle Ages: the Midland circuit, 1400–1429', in *Twelve Good Men and True: The Criminal Trial Jury in England, 1200–1800*, ed. J.S. Cockburn and T.A. Green (Princeton, 1988), p. 101;

B.A. Hanawalt, 'Whose story was this? Rape narratives in medieval English courts', in *'Of Good and Ill Repute': Gender and Social Control in Medieval England* (New York and Oxford, 1998), pp. 131–2; G. Bonfiglio Dosio, 'Criminalità ed emarginazione a Brescia nel primo Quattrocento', *Archivio storico italiano* 136 (1978), p. 115; G. Ruggiero, *The Boundaries of Eros: Sex Crime and Sexuality in Renaissance Venice* (New York and Oxford, 1985), pp. 94–6.

25. For what follows, see R.D. Groot, 'The crime of rape *temp.* Richard I and John', *Journal of Legal History* 9 (1988); J.B. Post, 'Ravishment of women and the statutes of Westminster', in *Legal Records and the Historian*, ed. J.H. Baker (London, 1978); idem, 'Sir Thomas West and the Statute of Rapes, 1382', *Historical Research* 53 (1980); E.W. Ives, '"Agaynst taking awaye of women": the inception and operation of the Abduction Act of 1487', in *Wealth and Power in Tudor England*, ed. E.W. Ives, R.J. Knecht and J.J. Scarrisbrick (London, 1978).

26. *The Roll of the Shropshire Eyre of 1256*, ed. A. Harding (London, 1981), p. 258.

27. Ives, '"Agaynst taking awaye of women"', p. 43.

28. M. Greilsammer, 'Rapts de séduction et rapts violents en Flandre et en Brabant à la fin du Moyen Age', *TRG* 56 (1988), p. 56.

29. Ibid., p. 66.

30. A. Porteau-Bitker, 'La justice laïque et le viol au Moyen Age', *RHDF* 66 (1988), pp. 496–7, 503–5; Ruggiero, *Boundaries of Eros*, pp. 31–2, 93, 96; Gauvard, *Crime, état et société*, pp. 332–3.

31. *Najstarsze Ksiegii i rachunki miasta Krakowa od r. 1300 do 1400*, ed. F. Piekosinski and J. Szujski (Cracow, 1878), p. 58 (1384).

32. Gauvard, *Crime, état et société*, pp. 333–9.

33. M.S. Mazzi, 'Il mondo della prostituzione nella Firenze tardo medievale', *Ricerche storiche* 14 (1984); R. Comba, '"Apetitus libidinis coherceatur": strutture demografiche, reati sessuali e disciplina dei comportamenti nel Piemonte tardomedievale', *Studi storici* 27 (1986), pp. 563–4.

34. R.M. Karras, *Common Women: Prostitution and Sexuality in Medieval England* (New York and Oxford, 1996), pp. 48–64.

35. P. Goldberg, 'Women in fifteenth-century town life', in *Towns and Townspeople in the Fifteenth Century*, ed. J.A.F. Thomson (Gloucester, 1988), p. 121.

36. Pertile, *Storia del diritto italiano*, V, pp. 539–42; Mazzi, 'Il mondo della prostituzione'.

37. Comba, '"Apetitus libidinis coherceatur"', pp. 566–73.

38. J.A. Brundage, *Law, Sex and Christian Society in Medieval Europe* (Chicago and London, 1987), pp. 226, 308, 463–4.

39. Review of J. Rossiaud, *Histoire de la prostitution*, in *Annales*, 45 (1990), p. 1240.

40. *Statuti di Verona del 1327*, ed. S.A. Bianchi and R. Granuzzo (Rome, 1992), p. 495; *Statuta et ordinamenta comunis Cremonae*, ed. U. Gualazzini (Milan, 1952), pp. 261–2; *I registri dell'Ufficio di provvisione e dell'Ufficio dei sindaci sotto la dominazione viscontea*, ed. C. Santoro (Milan, 1932), p. 13; *I registri dell'ufficio degli statuti di Milano*, ed. N. Ferorelli (Milan, 1920), p. 240.

41. Goldberg, 'Women in fifteenth-century town life', pp. 118–21; *The Laws and Acts of Parliament made by . . . Kings and Queens of Scotland* (Edinburgh, 1681), p. 11.

42. *ORF*, XX, pp. 181–2.

43. D.O. Hughes, 'Sumptuary law and social relations in Renaissance Italy', in *Disputes and Settlements: Law and Human Relations in the West*, ed. J. Bossy (Cambridge, 1983).

44. M.G. Muzzarelli, ' "Contra mundanas vanitates et pompas": aspetti della lotta contro i lussi nell'Italia del XV secolo', *Rivista di storia della chiesa in Italia* 40 (1986), p. 377.

45. W. Hooper, 'The Tudor sumptuary laws', *English Historical Review* 30 (1915), p. 437; J. Chisholm, 'The sumptuary laws of Scotland', *The Journal of Jurisprudence* 35 (1891), p. 294.

46. K.R. Greenfield, *Sumptuary Law in Nürnberg: A Study in Paternal Government* (Baltimore, 1918), pp. 114–16.

47. R. Rainey, 'Dressing down the dressed-up: reproving feminine attire in Renaissance Florence', in *Renaissance Society and Culture: Essays in Honor of E.F. Rice*, ed. J. Monfasani and R.G. Musto (New York, 1991), p. 232.

chapter 5

OUTSIDE THE LAW?
AVENGERS, CLERICS,
STUDENTS

The Italian short-story writer Giovanni Sercambi tells the following tale of two bandits, Gualfreduccio and Sessanta. Gualfreduccio had been banned from the city of Lucca for many homicides, including that of Sessanta's brother. He made peace with Sessanta, and the two of them became partners in brigandage in the Lucchese countryside. Years passed and Gualfreduccio came to trust Sessanta more than a brother. One summer's day, these bandits were lying in ambush when a young, female pilgrim fell into their hands. She was brought before Gualfreduccio, who at once decided to 'take pleasure of her'. He took her aside, took off his helmet and cuirass, dropped his underpants and forced himself on top of her. At this point, a lad in the bandit gang jokingly said, 'Anyone want to do Gualfreduccio an injury? Now's your chance!' This reminded Sessanta of his dead brother, and he struck Gualfreduccio on the head with a pike. Gualfreduccio could not get up to defend himself because his legs were caught in his underpants, and Sessanta was thus able to rain further blows on his helpless victim and kill him. And so, Sercambi says, for trusting his enemy, Gualfreduccio met his death.[1]

Let us take two further examples of revenge stories from fifteenth-century Flanders. In 1458, Parceval de le Woestine, an inhabitant of Ypres, petitioned the Duke of Flanders for pardon for an old offence of homicide. He did this because some new ducal commissioners had re-vived proceedings against him for this killing. This is how he recounts the events of forty years previously. In 1418 there was a dispute between Parceval's two bastard brothers and two other men, Hellin and Mahieu Annesen. Parceval was then aged about 16. One day he and his mother were passing the house belonging to the uncle of Hellin and Mahieu. His mother was pregnant and rode in a wagon, while Parceval rode on a horse. Seeing them pass by, Hellin and Mahieu, with a group of a dozen or more men, rushed out and chased after Parceval as if to kill him, even though he was a youth who had done them no wrong. Parceval escaped them, but his mother was so shocked by fear that within a few days both she and her unborn child died. This left her husband with seven small children to bring up on very little money. Shortly afterwards, Parceval was drawn into taking revenge. At this point in his narrative Parceval uses all the excuses he can. He was grieving at his mother's death. He was tempted by the devil. He was young and naïve, 'an innocent, not knowing what he was doing'. He was led on by the entreaties of his half-brothers. So, with them, he went to a village near Messines. There they found the uncle of Hellin and Mahieu. While Parceval watched, his brothers killed him. Afterwards, fearing 'the rigour of justice', Parceval fled to a church in Ypres. Meanwhile some of his family and friends negotiated peace and compensation with the family of the dead man: they declared themselves satisfied, and proceedings against Parceval were dropped.[2]

For our third case we stay in Flanders, but move to the town of Audenarde. In 1459 the brothers Jean and Adrien van Coye, and their servant, also petitioned the duke for pardon. This is the story they told. That January, Jean had been in a tavern, sitting at the same table as Laurens Bertin and Rasse du Bois, who were talking about a cloth deal. To assist the deal, Jean said something, thinking he was helping. Laurens got cross at his intervention and began insulting him, repeatedly calling him a liar, among other things. Jean suffered this in silence at first, but eventually his patience snapped and he made a move to punch Laurens, 'to avenge himself'. Actual violence was prevented, however, by other people in the tavern. Later, when everyone had gone home, Jean's brother Adrien came to his house to find out what had happened. He then returned to his own house, which was situated opposite Laurens's. Laurens and his nephew spotted Adrien, came out and assaulted him with knives, wounding him so badly that he had been confined to bed ever since. Hearing of this, Jean felt he could no longer endure the 'enormous and excessive' actions of Laurens, so he went out with his servant and killed him with axes and sticks. The authorities in Audenarde imposed a truce between the parties, but despite this Laurens's son found another of Jean's brothers, Lievin, and attempted to kill him with his dagger, and would have done so had Lievin not wrested the weapon from him. Jean says in his petition that he and his kin have repeatedly sought to make peace with Laurens's family, offering compensation, but this has always been refused. This refusal has forced Jean and his family to keep away from Audenarde, out of fear, such that they cannot earn their livings and are in danger of falling into poverty.[3]

The revenge stories of Sessanta, Parceval and Jean van Coye come of course from two very different genres of text: an entertaining novella and petitions for pardon. However, what might be thought to be an unbridgeable gap between these types of source has been filled in recent years, as the idea has spread that all 'historical' sources are forms of 'fiction', and as modern techniques of literary criticism have been applied to them. In the case of petitions for pardon, Natalie Davis has famously studied these as forms of narrative, under the title 'fiction in the archives'.[4] In the three tales just told, the link between historical and fictive narration can be seen in two elements. First, both narrative forms have moral lessons to tell, whether of distrust or compassion. They are both exercises in persuasion, ordering their material to achieve specific responses. The difference between them relates to their attitude to pacification: Sercambi discourages it, the petitioners hope to benefit from it. Second, we might surmise that they both depart from verisimilitude at certain points. In the tale of Sessanta, this point comes when Gualfreduccio drops his pants. In petitions, it is the point at which they claim personal innocence. Again, though, the purposes are different. The novella aims to evince a smile through a combination of realistic, serious and unusual elements. The petition aims to arouse the ruler's clemency through adherence to a common stock of excuses. When viewed as tales, the petitions are clearly constructed around a small, fixed group of exculpatory themes. For example, the avengers are innocent and well-meaning people, provoked beyond endurance, in these cases by the death of a mother and child or by aggressive insults. They have offered peace and compensation to their victims' families. They have suffered poverty as a result of their own and others' actions. Their victims were in the wrong.

Both fiction and pardon tales can therefore tell us about the culture of vengeance. The stories of Sessanta, Parceval and Jean together encapsulate many of the features of revenge that will occupy us in this chapter. The primary element is escalation. In Parceval's case the violence flows from his bastard brothers to himself and then to his attackers' uncle, claiming his mother as a victim on the way. In the van Coye example, Laurens extends the conflict by attacking Jean's brother, who was not involved in the original quarrel. After Laurens's death, his son extends it further by assaulting another brother. The second element is incitement, evident in the tale of Gualfreduccio: the memory of old injuries could be revived uncontrollably by the words of bystanders or by the sight of an old enemy in a vulnerable position. Another petition from Flanders illustrates this same phenomenon.[5] Last, all three tales show that revenge attacks could be pacified, and that the forces of pacification were strong. None of the cases shows us an endless cycle of revenge and counter-revenge.

Examples from Italy and Flanders thus seem to point in the same direction. However, it has been said that

It is not easy to generalise about bloodfeud. The form it takes in any one place will depend variously on the structures of kinship, the rules regarding residence, the economic system and ecology, among other things. So too the actions that will incur the feud will vary from culture to culture, depending on the underlying normative order.[6]

Historians have, consequently, differed in their presentations of feud and vengeance. Miller himself gave two rules of feuding: the idea of equivalence, that is the biblical idea of 'an eye for an eye'; and the limitation of the targets of revenge, as women, children and old men were seen as 'inappropriate expiators'. Stephen White, in his study of feuding in France, produced a different list of common features: the participants were all upper-class, adult males; they waged feuds in groups, not as individuals; their declared aim was to take revenge for alleged injury; but their conflicts could be pacified because they belonged to the same local community.[7] Studies of Italian vendetta would present a different picture again: here the stress would be on family solidarity and on revenge as obligation or sacred duty. Family solidarity was the key to the exaction of revenge: a claim to vengeance bound the generations and branches of a kindred together and was transmitted as part of the heritage. 'Grudges were carried across the generations.'[8] The target for a revenge attack could be any of the offender's kinsmen. Conflicts were escalated either by secondary revenge of this sort, or by returning a greater injury than that received. Either way, revenge threatened to create an endless cycle of actions and reactions. 'It was the tendency of vendetta to escalate and expand', says Kuehn.

However, the reader will have noticed that many of these elements are present in our three tales from Flanders and Lucca. This raises the possibility that one *can* generalise about bloodfeud. Historians seem to have selected different features of the same general phenomenon, as they appeared to them in their documents, and stressed cultural variation, overlooking the connections between them. Those connections would include: ideas of limitation, through equivalence or the exclusion of certain groups; the nature of the avenging group; the differentiation between revenge, of a specific injury, and feud; and the possibility or impossibility of pacification. These elements in turn lead us to consider the relationship between feud/vengeance and four cultural variables: peace, time, law and family.

Peace

There was a time when historians saw feud and vengeance as forms of lawlessness that were inimical to peace and justice. For such historians, the essence of modernisation lay in curtailing and suppressing feuding and in drawing all violent conflicts into the ambit of the law and the law courts. However, in the second half of the twentieth century anthropological influences began to propagate the idea that feud was not lawless or anarchic, but had its own rules and aimed at restoring peace. This argument has been developed by branches of analysis known as 'legal anthropology' and 'processual analysis', in which disputes are not seen as breaches of law that are rectified by the courts, but as social processes that are resolved outside the law. The argument was also classically advanced by Max Gluckman in a famous article in the interdisciplinary history journal *Past and Present* in the 1950s. In 'The peace in the feud', Gluckman used the example of the Nuer people of East Africa to argue that, once a disturbance had taken place, the threat of feud itself was sufficient to bring about the restoration of peace. This was because the community was not divided cleanly into two warring groups: there would always be many individuals with connections to both sides in a conflict, and these cross-cutting ties would work to prevent feud and to arrange for pacification and compensation. As one anthropological historian has suggested: 'the fundamental function of feud was to regulate conflicts and to enable and keep open a process of pacification based on the principle of reciprocity'.[9] Another has written that 'feud implies the presence of arbitrators, it generates them and imposes on them the difficult task of resolution desired by the participants in the conflict'.[10] Thus, to conceive of law and government bearing down on vengeance is to misunderstand the nature of feuding, which generated its own self-limiting and self-resolving mechanisms. This is the picture of vengeance presented by Gauvard in her great study of crime in France in the reign of Charles VI (1389–1422). Vengeance was self-regulating, she says, and had its own rules for self-limitation. The avenger would flee from the locality of the crime, thus giving his family time and space to intervene and negotiate peace.[11]

Was there peace in the feud? Numerous historians doubt it. White points out that the 'cross-cutting ties' could be too weak or too few to prevail, that the bonds of family or lordship could be too strong. Miller too is doubtful of the effectiveness of the pacifying efforts of such intercessors, and suggests that feuding could also get out of hand: 'when it exceeded the limits of its own rules, there was surely no peace'. We also have to consider the quality of the peace: pacification could in fact be an instrument of oppression or an opportunity for vexation. This takes us to consider the extent, purposes and effectiveness of the arbitration of disputes.

Many disputes, which might include acts of violence, were resolved through private arbitration rather than judgment in a court of law.

Arbitration was attractive because it was quicker and cheaper than litigation, especially when judicial corruption was rife, and because it offered the prospects of higher compensation as well as reconciliation between the parties. 'Arbitration settled problems which could not be settled in the courts ... without the rancour and humiliation of legal defeat for one party.'[12] However, it would be wrong to think of arbitration and judgment as opposite methods of conflict resolution, private and public remedies. The arbiters were likely to include judges or lawyers, disputes could flow from litigation to arbitration or vice versa, and arbitral awards were enforceable at law. The range of disputes settled by such means varied across Europe. In England, arbitration in cases of violence, even of homicide, was not unknown, in one historian's words 'commuting "blody strokes" into hard cash'; but it was used chiefly in land disputes.[13] In Saragossa it seems to have been used more widely in crimes: in a society where, it is claimed, justice was ineffective and clans were strong, noblemen could promote the limitation of violence through arbitration, with victims and relatives formally releasing offenders from responsibility for injuries and deaths.[14]

To arbitration were added other methods, formal and informal, of restoring social peace following the disturbance of violence. Clayton has studied over 4,000 'peace bonds' from the county of Cheshire in the middle and late fifteenth century. These bonds provided guarantors for indicted suspects to keep the peace or to appear in court. Members of the local gentry acted as guarantors either for the lower orders or for other gentlemen. Such peace bonds acted as 'preventive and precautionary' measures to control disorder or to maintain peace. They also bound the local community together.[15] More developed was the system of 'pacifiers' in many northern French or Flemish towns, for example in Ghent. Here there was a formal tribunal of 'pacifiers' (*paysierders*) who, between arrest and trial, could settle any crimes when the parties wanted to make a private composition. It was because of this institution that only one criminal case in ten went to formal trial in Ghent: settlement by pacification was the norm. Composition was preferable to both plaintiff and defendant: to the plaintiff because it offered larger sums in compensation than were awarded under the fixed tariff applied by the trial courts; and to the defendant because he thus avoided punishment in the form of exile, execution or mutilation. Even this tribunal, though, was but the formal aspect of a wider informal practice: among the lower classes, and among women, insults and minor acts of violence would be pacified by neighbours or guilds.[16] However, historians have disagreed on the relation between such pacifying mechanisms and feud. Nicholas sees pacification as being triggered only when feuds went too far, in other words as a last resort amid normal practice of retaliation; others see pacification as controlling and restricting feuding. Thus Cattier presents the practice of 'forswearing' and 'assurance' (*forjur* and *asseurement*) in Hainaut as a means of limiting vengeance. The kinsmen of a killer who fled the scene were obliged to 'forswear' him. This amounted to a legal repudiation of their kinsman, the killer. In return, the victim's family would assure them that they would suffer no harm (the *asseurement*).[17]

Between England, where arbitration was formally separate from institutions and used mainly for land disputes, and Ghent, where it was institutionalised and used mainly for crimes, sits France. Here too the royal attitude tended to be an exclusive one. At times the king pronounced against compositions. In 1356 he prohibited all judges, royal and seigneurial, from receiving compositions for crimes, which resulted in crimes going unpunished. Later, in a capacious ordinance on justice in 1493, the king objected to compositions made between injured parties and prisoners released on bail, which had the effect of stifling prosecutions. The king saw this as detrimental to the public interest, as it allowed many great crimes to go unpunished, and he ordered closer supervision of bail, to ensure, if a composition was made, that justice was done too.[18] The king here is not setting his face against all private accords, but against officials trading in public justice and the disregarding of the public interest. Private accords were accepted, but only when accompanied by royal justice. Nevertheless, royal justice did succeed in excluding some crimes from private composition: during the fourteenth century, royal lawyers (*procureurs*) challenged such accords in major crimes, confining them mostly to minor crimes. The path to private settlement was not, however, closed off completely: it now had to pass through the royal chancery via the mechanism of pardon. For a royal pardon to be valid, the recipient had to make satisfaction to the injured party. Royal courts now supervised that process.[19]

Time

How were injuries remembered? Were grudges carried across the generations? Were there, in every town or village, families divided for decades by 'mortal hatreds'? Italian treatises stressed the value of waiting for the opportune moment, and of learning to lull one's target into a sense of security. 'Don't spoil it through haste', one recommends. 'He who conceals the injury can better take revenge', says another.[20] Examples of just such revenge, apparently long meditated and long nursed, are certainly made. One such is a Florentine murder of 1267 which was not avenged until 1295. Another is a Flemish case in 1458, in which the murder of a man was avenged by his sons forty-two years later.[21] There are also some graphic accounts of the ways that feuds were remembered from one generation to the next. The Frisians had a custom of keeping the body of a murdered man unburied at home, until vengeance had been accomplished, although they were later persuaded to abandon this practice by a holy man, Dodo the Frisian.[22] In the Icelandic sagas the severed head of the victim might be used to remind his kinsmen of their duty to take revenge.[23] The French writer Joinville recalls the case of a knight, Geoffroy de Rançon, who had been greatly wronged by the Comte de la Marche and 'vowed on the Holy Gospels never to have his hair cut short, as is the custom with knights, but to wear it long like a woman's until such time as he should be avenged on the count'.[24] Not achieving vengeance was thus seen as un-manning, emasculating, acting like a woman. Perhaps this explains the prominence sometimes given to women in recalling injuries and calling on men to take revenge: the presence of a woman implied that the victim's kin were not acting like men. But it was not only women who called on reluctant men to take revenge. It was difficult for men, having once suffered an injury, to forget, to resist opportunities for revenge, to ignore incitements from bystanders. For this reason, Italian laws penalised verbal incitement to revenge, of the type 'Go on, avenge your brother who was killed by so-and-so.' Social memory of unavenged injury could thus outlive and conflict with family or individual memory. Individuals might wish to forget, but society expected them to remember. This was not, however, everywhere the case. In France, vengeance did not have the Italian characteristic of 'a dish best eaten cold': instead, revenge was taken swiftly, within a day or two of the original offence. French noble families lacked the means for recording and transmitting memory of injuries that Florentine families had in their family diaries. But most Italian families outside Florence lacked these too, and this is what makes Florentine practice of vendetta untypical.

However, there is strong argument that long feuds are constructs after the event. Keith Brown has attempted to distinguish between the beliefs of participants or observers and the objective continuity of feuds. Some-one like the Bishop of Ross might observe that 'gret families they feid, and that perpetuallie', but Brown is doubtful that quarrels separated by years were 'directly linked by an unbroken chain' of enmity. 'The partici-pants in such feuds may have liked to connect such events in their minds', but this was only an appearance. Halsall too has argued the same for the early Middle Ages: feuds were 'periodically reinvented to justify discrete acts of violence'.[25] In an age in which states were increasingly punishing homicide, to present a killing as revenge was to open the way to pacifica-tion rather than penalty.

Law

The coexistence of formal justice and composition varied in its forms. So too did the transition from private vengeance to public punishment. In that transition a unique place has been claimed by England. One theme of Pollock and Maitland's great history of English law is the alien nature of blood-feud: already in the Anglo-Saxon period, they argue, royal laws bore down on feuding, making vengeance a substitute only for unpaid compensation, and replacing composition with punishment. The twelfth century then sees the sudden effacement of feud and composition: homicide becomes a capital crime, and the victim's family loses its right to compensation. 'So fierce is [English law] against self-help that it can hardly be induced to find a place even for self-defence.' 'The ordinary criminal law is strong enough to suppress anything we could fairly call private war.'[26] Although recent work on arbitration seems to run counter to such views, they have received support from John Gillingham's argument that blood-feud was indeed taken out of English political history for 200 years by the king's habit of treating aristocratic rebels chivalrously.[27]

Nevertheless, the robustness of English law could not stifle revenge as a motive. In Wiltshire in the 1240s, when one man was hanged on the accusation of another, his kinsmen went to the accuser's house and killed both him and his son.[28] Nor, it seems, could it stifle feuding. Although English historians often make the mistake of seeing simple quarrels as feuds, some mild variant of continental feuding clearly persisted, as Kaeuper argues: English gentry combined litigation with violent self-help just like French noblemen.[29]

Although in England it seems that a sudden transition was made from vengeance and composition to trial and punishment, from private war to public law, this applies barely anywhere else, not even among England's immediate neighbours. In the Welsh Marches composition for murder survived the English conquest by over a century, though in diminishing incidence. It merged with the English import of jury trial, occasionally surfacing after conviction in the form of private accords between a killer and his victim's kin. In return for money payments the killer redeemed his life.[30] If awareness of the 'otherness' of vengeance crystallised in consonance with the development of the state, we can see this clearly in English contact with alien cultures. When English lawyers encountered feud and compensation (*galanas*) in Wales, 'they greeted it with quizzical surprise . . . followed by unconcealed abhorrence'. As the archbishop said to the last Prince of Wales, 'in every way your customs seem to be a travesty of justice, as you fail to condemn homicides, and many other crimes, formally and specifically'.[31] Similarly, on the Anglo-Irish frontier, there was the same concern to uphold the principle of punishment against the Irish practice of compensation for homicide. In 1351 an order was issued that English common law, not frontier (March) law was to be used in disputes between English settlers. March law, it was firmly declared, 'is not law and ought not be called law'; another archbishop condemned it as 'the law of the devil'.[32]

Such condemnation was rare, but the coexistence of vengeance and law achieved different balances. In only one part of France does an evolution similar to England's seem to have occurred. Revenge had already been limited in Normandy by the duke in 1075 – a 'milestone' according to John Gillingham – and the later book of Norman legal customs forbad private war altogether. 'Let no man dare to wage war against another', it ruled, 'but for an injury done to him, he is to complain to the duke or his judge.' The effectiveness of this prohibition seems to be shown by the Norman demands against the French Crown in 1314–15: when the nobility of other regions of France were demanding recognition of their right to private war, the Normans were silent on the issue.[33] Confirmation perhaps also comes from the findings of Andrew Finch in his study of violence at Cerisy: in the hundreds of assaults and fights recorded there between 1314 and 1458, very few were explicitly motivated by revenge, and even in those that were, the participants were punished.[34] Elsewhere in France, however, revenge and private war were recognised.

So there was no straightforward replacement of vengeance and composition by state justice and punishment, but a transitional phase in which the two coexisted. In France in the 1320s and 1330s, revenge and private war emerge strongly as motives in cases that came before the Parlement of Paris. For example, Jourdain de l'Isle, Lord of Casaubon, who was tried and convicted for many acts of brigandage committed over several years, excused his actions by saying 'that it was in war' and 'that it was to maintain himself and his men in their war, and that this is what was done in his region'. In another case, Guillaume de Léans confessed to ordering his sons to assault the daughter of a man called Adam, so as to be revenged, 'as Adam is threatening and mocking us and has done us much harm'. Guiart de Noirterre, before he died of his wounds from a fatal attack in the Rue de la Harpe in Paris, attributed the assault to his support for a cousin's lawsuit against a knight, Jean de la Forêt; a witness confessed that Jean had said to him that he wanted Guiart assaulted 'for he has done me too much damage'. Last, an accomplice to the murder in 1333 of Perrant Buiron, a burgess of Rheims, testified that one of the killers had said after the event, 'Perrant once wounded me in the leg, now I've wounded him in the legs.'[35]

What is noticeable in these cases, however, is that the suggestion of private war or revenge does nothing to save these suspects from the gallows. Vengeance might be recognised as a response, but only if the avenger petitioned the king for pardon. But the numbers even of such cases are small. Only one-eighth of pardons in the reign of Charles VI explicitly mention vengeance (though Gauvard believes vengeance can be surmised in another quarter of cases), and in the fifteenth century new currents were diminishing and transmuting revenge culture. Royal ordinances continued to condemn private war. Crown prosecutors tried to claim that royal judges (*baillis*) could take action in cases of vengeance. Kin solidarity was now more likely to work in the direction of pacifying rather than supporting vengeance. Ideals of Christian and royal peace overcame the ideal of honour.[36]

A similar fifteenth-century transformation is evident in the Low Countries. In Abbeville, the practice of pacification disappeared after 1421. In Flanders, as soon as the Valois dukes took over in the 1380s, a statute was issued allowing criminal trials even after private settlements had been made. In Ghent, the numbers of sentences passed by the 'pacifiers' (*paisierders*) fell precipitately and irreversibly from the 1470s. In Hainaut the system of forswearing by the killer's kin was passing out of use before the end of the fourteenth century: people had begun to lose sight of what sort of cases it applied to, and had to consult the authorities to find out if it was necessary to 'forswear' in the case of a physician who accidentally cut a man's hand.[37]

The same evolution at a similar time has also been urged for Florence. Gene Brucker contrasted a thirteenth-century vendetta to a fifteenth-century pacification to suggest that the general cultural changes of the Renaissance also affected inter-personal behaviour. Others have criticised this hypothesis. Not only is the evidence insufficient to support such a conclusion, but earlier pacifications and later revenges can be signalled to throw its chronology into doubt. Anyway, according to processual analysis, pacification is a natural part of feud, not something that emerges only in the fifteenth century.

Throughout Europe rulers responded to the escalation of feud with horror and restrictions. The intention was everywhere the same: to confine vengeance to the two parties originally involved, aggressor and victim, and to prevent conflict spilling over and touching other kinsmen of either party. The King of Norway declared in 1270:

> May it be known to all men that a barbaric custom has prevailed in our countries for a long time: when a man has been killed, his kinsmen want to remove the best man in the [killer's] family, even though he is ignorant and innocent of the slaying. And they do not want to avenge themselves on the real killer, even when they have an opportunity to do so.[38]

A similar complaint was made by King Pere III of Catalonia in 1360. This time it was a 'damnable and pernicious custom'

> that if anyone is killed or injured by another, the kinsmen or friends of the victim dare to claim vengeance, in contempt of our justice, and not only plot the death or wounding of the killer or wounder, but also kill or injure his kinsmen and friends though they are innocent and distantly related.

The king's remedy was to institute a series of obstacles to the pursuit of vengeance: no revenge was to be taken until the would-be avengers had registered their claim in writing, nor in the ten days following delivery of this letter to the house of their target; even after the ten-day period, all revenge attacks on the family and friends of the aggressor would be punished. As Ferdinand II said in confirming this law in 1503, 'by this law we do not intend to enable private war [*guerrejar*]'.[39] Protection of innocent kinsmen in this way was also a feature of the law in Ghent and other Flemish towns, where they were covered by an immediate truce varying in length between fourteen and forty days.[40] In eastern Europe, 'rulers insisted that the victim or his family could take revenge only as specified by court judgment', forbidding injured parties to decide on punishment themselves. The law in Mazovia allowed revenge only against the murderer, not against his relatives. In Poland would-be avengers had to notify the authorities of their intentions. These were then broadcast as a means of encouraging the offender into court to make monetary compensation.[41]

The most complex of these laws restricting revenge come from Florence. Four elements are distinguished: the avenging group, the revenge target, the mode of revenge and the role of public justice. Laws on the avenging group were the most permissive of any, and became increasingly so. Vendetta was allowed to the victim and any of his relatives up to four degrees of kinship (1295), to the victim and 'anyone of his house' (1331–4), to the victim and all 'of his house and clan-group, and his descendants in the male line' (1355), or finally to the victim 'with any support whatsoever' (1415). Restrictions, however, applied in all the other elements. Revenge had to be proportionate. Assistance to a revenge target from his family was discouraged. Additional penalties applied for revenge taken against the relatives of the original aggressor. The victim's right to vengeance was displaced by public justice when the original aggressor was executed, or if he was a convict, bandit or rebel.[42]

Family

A mid-fourteenth-century family partnership agreement from Florence contains the following clause: 'Item, in the event of any one of us being injured by any person, each and every one of us will be obliged to aid, defend and avenge, in person and with his resources, and to take on the quarrel as if it was done against his own person.'[43] This expresses clearly the key principle of vengeance, that injuries received were considered family property. Consequently, the family as a whole should decide how to respond to such injuries. Violation of this rule could split a family apart, as Kuehn has shown with the example of the Lanfredini of Florence. When the father made peace with his enemy without consulting his sons, he was considered to have dishonoured them all. 'You're a traitor to yourself', his wife angrily told him, 'since you've brought such shame to your sons by making peace without them or me knowing anything about it. You've robbed them of stuff, of honour, of everything.' One of these sons was so ashamed that he abandoned both father and Florence and went to find work in Venice, changing his name to avoid its dishonourable associations.[44] 'All members of a family take up offensive weapons, for an injury to one stains the whole house', noted one fourteenth-century lawyer.

However, this ideal of family solidarity was often difficult to achieve or to maintain. Kinsmen refused to be held responsible for the actions of their hot-headed brethren. They might band together to wash their hands of troublemakers, literally or effectually surrendering them to their enemies. Where they were expected to contribute to compensation payments to the victim, they might decline to do so. Perhaps it was this lack of solidarity that explains the features of vengeance in France: it was mostly kept within one or two generations of a family, and avenging groups rarely encompassed wider kin than brothers or uncles.[45] In Avignon, revenge might motivate individual acts of violence, but cycles of vengeance and the mobilisation of family solidarity were rare, confined to Florentine immigrants.[46]

Using these four cultural variables – peace, law, sense of time, family solidarity – we have found that it is possible to make some generalisations regarding vengeance. Pacification was conscripted by local authorities in order to support public order. Injuries could be forgotten, as well as forgiven: remembering was a social, not a personal event. Laws uniformly aimed to curtail escalation. Family solidarity was not a given, but a construct, and one that often failed.

Clergy

The fate of clergymen who committed crimes is but one part of a much wider history of relations between secular institutions and the Church which embraced tithe, wills, marriage disputes, debt and defamation. The two issues that concern us in this section are criminous clerks and sanctuary. Some of the issues arising from crimes committed by clergymen may be seen in a case from Chartres in the early fifteenth century. Jean le Vacher, a rural priest, was suspected of murdering a parishioner. The dead man's widow pressed charges and Jean was summoned to the bishop's court. He fled, travelling instead to Rome to obtain a pardon from the pope. However, the judicial clock kept ticking against him in Chartres and he was eventually convicted in his absence and deprived of his benefice. When he returned, with his pardon, he was arrested and held prisoner by the bishop's court. Jean naturally confessed the homicide, and after some months was acquitted, in consideration of his 'poverty and bodily infirmity', of the travails of his journey to Rome, and of his sufferance of long detention, in which he had daily said his prayers and devotions, as well as performing many fasts and vigils. The only matter to be settled was the size of damages due to the widow. The widow, however, was not easily satisfied. She wanted corporal punishment and refused damages. After months of wrangling, the court ignored her plea and condemned Jean to pay her 10 *livres*, and to endow an annual mass for the soul of his victim.[47] In this case, it is difficult to see what more the court could do. Church courts lacked the power to impose 'penalties of blood': their only punitive option was imprisonment. Moreover, their greater aim, dictated by Christian charity, was to heal the hurt of crime through penance and reconciliation. Lay people might find this unsatisfactory. In England in 1351, for example, the chief judges complained that criminous clerics were not sufficiently punished by imprisonment (and the Church responded by tightening the rules for release).[48]

In the case from Chartres the culprit was a priest, but a far worse problem arose with clergymen who had chosen not to progress up the clerical ladder. These were the minor clergy who, though they might be married, could enjoy clerical privileges as long as they had a tonsure and wore clerical dress. Not only was this privilege easily abused by clerics, but criminals too had their hair tonsured in order fraudulently to claim clerical status (as we have seen in Chapter 3). Disputes over jurisdiction of minor clergy were legion in late medieval Europe. In Castile the Cortes in 1401 complained that 'most ruffians and malefactors' in the kingdom were tonsured, and that when royal judges laid hands on them they were excommunicated by local bishops. The Cortes returned to the theme in 1406, lamenting the great harm done by those who live in lay dress, but escape royal justice on account of their tonsures. In the same year, the *prévôt* of Paris declared that 'the clergy release prisoners too easily and it is these who do the misdeeds'. In 1448 the Count of Hainaut tried to limit the criminal jurisdiction of the Church courts so as to exclude minor, married clerics, but such was the clerical protest at this measure that it had to be withdrawn, and no other solution to the problem was agreed. Other rulers in the fifteenth century made similar efforts: for example the Duke of Milan in 1419 decreed that clerics not wearing clerical dress were to be treated as lay men.[49]

One of many conflicts between the bishop and the *bailli* of Amiens reveal many of the day-to-day problems. In 1408 the bishop claimed numerous infringements of clerical privilege by the *bailli*. When any cleric was held in the royal gaol and the bishop requested his transfer to his own custody, the *bailli* found one pretext after another to delay this. He tortured clergymen. He claimed the right to decide what constituted clerical dress. He constrained imprisoned clerics to reach settlements with the injured parties or to enter promises not to breach the peace. If and when he did transfer suspects to the bishop's court, he led them bare-headed, with ropes at their necks, and threatened to take them to the gallows. Even after prisoners had been surrendered, the *bailli* tried to prevent the bishop releasing them, by declaring their crimes triable only in the king's court. The *bailli* defended himself against all these charges. The Church court, he said, is lenient because it does not want the death of sinners, but the city is swarming with cut-throats, hired killers, ravishers and other criminals, who are often clerics, but who deserve to be arrested. And he gave examples. There was Jean Bonne, a *jongleur*, impostor and trickster, who abducted a girl at night and raped her. The *bailli* arrested him, and he confessed, but he was forced to surrender him to the bishop, who merely put him in the pillory and then released him. Then there was Jacquemart de Fayel, who was charged with raping an 11-year-old girl. He was imprisoned, but later demanded by the bishop's court; the Crown prosecutor objected to his surrender, because one sleeve of his tunic was made of various different fabrics, and insisted that it be sent to Paris for inspection. There were other cases of so-called clerics: one who ambushed a labourer while he was working and cut his face in a revenge attack; another who, in order to free himself of having to pay rent to a poor, old woman, had her ambushed as she bathed and thrown into a lake.[50]

Two issues thus became hotly disputed ones: clerical dress and tonsure. Church courts were prepared to allow some latitude to clergymen in their dress, while secular courts insisted on the ecclesiastical dress code being strictly followed. The bishop's court in Toulouse allowed that a cleric who had added to his habit some parti-coloured hose should nevertheless enjoy clerical privilege, whereas the Parlement of the Dauphiné decided that a murderer should not, even though he had a tonsure, because he was wearing a short robe, six inches above the knee, which was deemed not proper clerical dress. The Parlement's decision was supported by the argument that, though proof of clerical status is a Church matter, proof of dress is a lay matter. English judges too insisted that deciding on suspects' claims to clerical status was their duty, not the bishop's.[51] Church courts would also allow immunity to a cleric who usually wore his hair tonsured, but happened not to have it so when arrested for a crime, on the grounds that 'a married cleric, by letting his hair grow, does not irreparably lose his privilege, but recovers it as soon as his head is shaved again'.[52]

A further accusation made by the Bishop of Amiens against the local *bailli* was the infringement of sanctuary by dragging people out of churches. He cited the case of Guillemot Bachofeu who fled into a church after hitting a man over the head with a stick. The *bailli* sent thirty *sergents* into the church, disrupting divine service, and swore he would keep them there until he had his man. The main problem was that sanctuary was used by all manner of fugitives, debtors fleeing their creditors as well as criminals fleeing their pursuers. In theory sanctuary was limited to those who killed or injured by accident. Deliberate killers, habitual criminals, thieves and convicts should all have been excluded. The key principle was that the crime should be unpremeditated and should inflict serious injury or death. The Parlement of Grenoble in 1457 declared that it was no violation of sanctuary to remove from a church a deliberate killer, who did not deserve to enjoy the Church's protection. However, to judge from some English sanctuary registers, these restrictions were far from observed in practice. It is true that at Durham between 1464 and 1524 most of the sanctuary-seekers were killers, and that the debtors and thieves were in a minority. But at Beverley between 1478 and 1539 most were debtors or minor criminals, and the killers were in a minority.

The civic authorities were understandably vexed by what they saw as indiscriminate abuse of rights of sanctuary. In 1368 the authorities in Ghent complained to the bishop that convicted criminals were using churches as bases from which to make 'armed forays' against their enemies in the town. A similar complaint was made by the London authorities against St Mary le Grand in 1402. The response of the civic authorities was to mount guards outside churches in order to starve fugitives out, or to seize them if they set foot outside holy ground. Such a case arose in London in 1402. John Giffard had fled to a church following an accusation against him of robbery. That night he briefly left the church in order to visit a public latrine to defecate. On his way back the sheriff's men seized him. Cases such as this led to protests from the ecclesiastical authorities of violation of their rights.[53]

University towns

All these problems were doubled in university towns. These have often been portrayed as the most lawless and turbulent places of the later Middle Ages. The universities themselves had numerous privileges, both fiscal and judicial, which put them beyond the reach of urban taxation and justice. Student lifestyles – the proverbial licentiousness of groups of young men in foreign cities – clashed with the demands of bourgeois decorum. Students, because they were clerics, were not subject to secular courts for their wrongdoing, but were remitted to the court of the local bishop or to a university tribunal. Le Goff's general picture is often quoted:

> Academics constituted a group of males, largely young bachelors, in the midst of the urban population. The clerical nature of this group was sufficiently loose that a good many did not feel constrained by certain ecclesiastical rules of conduct, such as continence, sobriety and non-violence. Instead, encouraged by legal privileges which granted them, if not immunity at least milder punishment, a great many academics (including masters as well as students . . .) took part in the sort of violent acts to which they were driven by their age, their uprootedness, and the fact that a majority of them belonged to the two social classes most given to violence, the nobility and the peasantry.[54]

In his magisterial history of the medieval universities, Rashdall too reflects this image: in depicting the 'wilder side of university life', he narrates half a dozen bloody episodes, four from Paris, one each from Orléans and Toulouse, in which crowds of students were confronted and usually worsted by other groups in the city. Thus an abbot, disputing with the university the ownership of a meadow, arranges a punitive expedition against the students, to shouts of 'Death to the clerks!' In a second case, the servants of the royal chamberlain ride their horses through a university procession and some students are trampled on or shot at in the ensuing mêlée. A third example has a citizen hiring some thugs to attack an academic who had seduced his wife: when he is tried and convicted for this, a riot erupts against the student population. In another incident, the civic authorities attempt to disperse a noisy and unruly student street party, but one of their number receives a sword-blow to the head that cuts off his nose, slices off parts of his lip and chin, and knocks out eleven teeth. The list of such *flambées paroxystiques*, as they have been called, could be extended: the student wars, for example, in Salamanca, 1410–11, and Heidelberg, 1422. At Toulouse it has been noted how the decrees issued to prohibit arms-bearing were frequent and followed the academic year, their numbers rising during term-time and falling in vacation. In Louvain, to judge by the university statutes, student gambling and violence were serious problems. Of actual violence, Oxford seems to provide the worst (or best) example: the homicide rate peaks at an extraordinary 110 per 100,000 of population per annum, which is several times worse than the most violent of US cities in the later twentieth century. In Gurr's famous graph of the historical trend of violence in England, this figure from Oxford is truly off the scale.[55]

However, there is reason to be cautious. Let us take the homicide rate in Oxford first of all. Hammer calculates this exceptional figure in the following manner. The best continuous set of coroners' records for Oxford runs from 1342 to 1348. From this run, he takes five years' figures out of seven. These yield an average of eight homicides a year. For the population of Oxford before the Black Death of 1348, he takes Russell's estimate derived from the Poll Tax returns of 1377 (3,500), inflates it by 57 per cent to account for plague losses (5,500), then adds in 1,500 for the students (total 7,000). The resulting ratio of 8:7,000 equals 110:100,000. Several things seem doubtful about this calculation. First, why discard two of the seven years' figures from 1342 to 1348? This seems to be purely on numerical grounds: because they are lower figures than for the other years, they are discarded as 'untypical' and 'incomplete'. But if we count them in and recalculate the average, we get six homicides per year. Second, Russell's estimates of the population are now recognised to be too low, and need to be inflated by at least one-third.[56] Recalculating the homicide rate on this basis, we arrive at a figure of 66:100,000 – still high, but no longer stratospheric.

Other considerations take more of the certainty away from the picture of extreme violence in university towns. Even Hammer admits that only a minority of killers in Oxford were actually students, and even fewer of the victims. At Louvain, though the university statutes are full of violence, it is less clear in practice that this amounted to more than nocturnal rowdiness. It is argued in relation to the universities in Castile (Salamanca, Valladolid) that conflicts were not generated within the academic community, but were extensions of more general social conflicts in those towns: the universities were permeated by urban disputes, not towns by academic ones.[57] The same might be said of Toulouse in the sixteenth century, where riotousness, as measured by the frequency of bans on arms-bearing, was highest during periods of national conflict. At Orléans the rioting against the university in the 1380s was in part at least a local variation on the general tax revolts in many cities of northern France. Moreover, students everywhere were the victims of crimes: their books, which were costly and in short supply, were prime targets for thieves. A thirteenth-century friar, Etienne de Bourbon, tells an exemplary tale of the thief who enters a student's lodgings at Vespers on Christmas Eve and steals his law books, which he later pawns to a Jew. This seems to hit verisimilitude in many respects, from the vulnerability of student accommodation, and the cloaking hour of dusk, to the disposal of stolen goods through Jewish pawnbrokers.[58] Bologna in particular, the major centre for law studies in Europe, has yielded numerous cases of such book thefts.[59] It has to be acknowledged that the figure of the student victim seems not to be as prominent as in the university towns of modern Britain – where, it is said, 'thieves see students and pounce', and where nearly one-third of street robberies are committed against students.[60] Nevertheless, theft was only one way in which medieval students were victimised: they were exploited and swindled in other ways too, and urban authorities were obliged sooner or later to put in place a range of protections and guarantees regarding fair rents and the provision of loans, food and other services. Last, we need to recognise the picture of student excess – pleasure, amorous adventures, dice, dancing and drink – for what it is: 'the distorted product of cautionary tales'. This stereotype makes the historian's task 'a wretched one', because of the lack of other material beyond 'the anecdotal and the haphazard'.[61] Yet what can be said is that more effective regulation of student life did emerge over the course of the period. The most spectacular riots in French university towns occurred in the thirteenth and fourteenth centuries; in the fifteenth a twin-track reform, of abolishing riotous games and celebrations, and 'interning' students in small, disciplined hostels, reduced the turbulence of university life.[62]

Notes

1. Giovanni Sercambi, *Novelle*, ed. G. Sinicropi (Bari, 1972), II, pp. 522–3.
2. C. Petit Dutaillis, *Documents nouveaux sur les moeurs populaires et le droit de vengeance dans les Pays-Bas au quinzième siècle* (Paris, 1908), pp. 173–4.
3. Ibid., pp. 179–81.
4. N.Z. Davis, *Fiction in the Archives: Pardon Tales and their Tellers in Sixteenth-century France* (Cambridge, 1987).
5. Petit Dutaillis, *Documents nouveaux*, pp. 161–2.
6. W.I. Miller, 'Choosing the avenger: some aspects of the bloodfeud in medieval Iceland and England', *Law and History Review* 1 (1983), p. 160.
7. S.D. White, 'Feuding and peace-making in the Touraine around the year 1100', *Traditio* 42 (1986), pp. 196–8.
8. T. Kuehn, 'Conflicting conceptions of property in Quattrocento Florence: A dispute over ownership in 1425–26', in *Law, Family and Women: Toward a Legal Anthropology of Renaissance Italy* (Chicago and London, 1991), p. 150.

9. O. Raggio, 'Etnografia e storia politica: la faida e il caso della Corsica', *Quaderni storici* 75 (1990), p. 946.

10. Torre quoted in Kuehn, *Law, Family and Women*, p. 151.

11. C. Gauvard, *'De grace especial': Crime, état et société en France à la fin du Moyen Age* (Paris, 1991), pp. 772–83.

12. I. Rowney, 'Arbitration in gentry disputes of the later Middle Ages', *History* 67 (1982), p. 376.

13. C. Rawcliffe, 'The great lord as peacekeeper: arbitration by English noblemen and their councils in the later Middle Ages', in *Law and Social Change in British History*, ed. J.A. Guy and H.G. Beale (London, 1984), pp. 44–5; Rowney, 'Arbitration', p. 367; E. Powell, *Kingship, Law and Society: Criminal Justice in the Reign of Henry V* (Oxford, 1989), pp. 101–3.

14. J-P. Barraqué, 'Le contrôle des conflits à Saragosse (XIVe–début du XVe siècle), *Revue historique* 279 (1988), pp. 44–8.

15. D.J. Clayton, 'Peace bonds and the maintenance of law and order in late medieval England: the example of Cheshire', *Historical Research* 58 (1985).

16. D.M. Nicholas, 'Crime and punishment in fourteenth-century Ghent', *Revue belge de philologie et d'histoire* 48 (1970), pp. 294–8, 311–16, 1141–9, 1166–8.

17. F. Cattier, 'Evolution du droit pénal germanique en Hainaut jusqu'au XVe siècle', *Mémoires et publications de la Société des sciences, des arts et des lettres du Hainaut* 5th ser., 7 (1894), pp. 136–7.

18. *ORF*, III, p. 130; XX, p. 405.

19. Gauvard, *Crime, état et société*, pp. 20–3.

20. I. Del Lungo, 'Una vendetta in Firenze: il giorno di San Giovanni del 1295', *Archivio storico italiano* 4th ser., 18 (1886), pp. 385–6.

21. Petit Dutaillis, *Documents nouveaux sur . . . le droit de vengeance dans les Pays-Bas*, p. 53

22. H. Platelle, 'Vengeance privée et réconciliation dans l'oeuvre de Thomas de Cantimpré', *TRG* 42 (1974), p. 278.

23. Miller, 'Choosing the avenger', pp. 175–80.

24. Joinville, 'Life of Saint Louis', in Joinville and Villehardouin, *Chronicles of the Crusades*, trans. M.R.B. Shaw (Harmondsworth, 1963), p. 189.

25. K.M. Brown, *Bloodfeud in Scotland 1573–1625* (Edinburgh, 1986), p. 6; G. Halsall, 'Violence and society in the early medieval West: an introductory survey', in *Violence and Society in the Early Medieval West*, ed. G. Halsall (Woodbridge, 1998), p. 20.

26. F. Pollock and F.W. Maitland, *The History of English Law before the Time of Edward I*, 2nd edn (Cambridge, 1968), I, p. 303; II, pp. 449–59, 489, 574.

27. J. Gillingham, '1066 and the introduction of chivalry into England', in *Law and Government in Medieval England and Normandy: Essays in Honour of Sir James Holt*, ed. G. Garnett and J. Hudson (Cambridge, 1994).

28. J.B. Given, *Society and Homicide in Thirteenth-century England* (Stanford, 1977), p. 45.

29. R.W. Kaeuper, *War, Justice and Public Order: England and France in the Later Middle Ages* (Oxford, 1988), pp. 263–6.

30. R.R. Davies, 'The survival of the bloodfeud in medieval Wales', *History* 54 (1969), pp. 344–7.

31. Ibid., p. 339.
32. B. Smith, 'Keeping the peace', in *Law and Disorder in Thirteenth-century Ireland: The Dublin Parliament of 1297*, ed. J. Lydon (Dublin, 1997), pp. 62–3.
33. J. Yver, 'Le "Tres Ancien Coutumier" de Normandie, miroir de la législation ducale?', *TRG* 39 (1971), p. 364.
34. A.J. Finch, 'The nature of violence in the Middle Ages: an alternative perspective', *Historical Research* 70 (1997), pp. 262–7.
35. *Confessions et jugements de criminals au Parlement de Paris (1319–1350)*, ed. M. Langlois and Y. Lanhers (Paris, 1971), pp. 39, 40, 53, 67, 105–6. See also pp. 112, 172–3.
36. Gauvard, *Crime, état et société*, pp. 753–88.
37. Ibid., p. 784; Nicholas, 'Crime and punishment in fourteenth-century Ghent', p. 1174; R.C. Van Caenegem, *Geschiedenis van het strafrecht in Vlaanderen van de XIe tot de XIVe eeuw* (Brussels, 1954), p. 321; Cattier, 'Evolution du droit pénal', pp. 143–5.
38. Miller, 'Choosing the avenger', p. 165.
39. *Constitutions y altres drets de Cathalunya*, vol. 1 (Barcelona, 1704), pp. 180–1, 426–7.
40. Petit Dutaillis, *Documents nouveaux*, pp. 59–60.
41. J.W. Sedlar, *East Central Europe in the Middle Ages, 1000–1500* (Seattle and London, 1994), p. 322.
42. U. Dorini, 'La vendetta privata al tempo di Dante', *Giornale dantesco* 29 (1926), pp. 59–61.
43. Del Lungo, 'Una vendetta in Firenze', p. 390.
44. T. Kuehn, 'Honor and conflict in a fifteenth-century Florentine family', *Ricerche storiche* 10 (1980), p. 294.
45. T. Dean, 'Marriage and mutilation: vendetta in late-medieval Italy', *Past & Present* 157 (1997), p. 21; Davies, 'Survival of the bloodfeud in Wales', pp. 344–5; Gauvard, *Crime, état et société*, p. 774.
46. J. Chiffoleau, *Les justices du Pape: délinquance et criminalité dans la région d'Avignon an quatorzième siècle* (Paris, 1984), pp. 149–52.
47. L. Merlet, 'Registres des officialités de Chartres', *Bibliothèque de l'Ecole des chartes* 4th ser., 2 (1856), pp. 583–7.
48. J.G. Bellamy, *Criminal Law and Society in Late Medieval and Tudor England* (Gloucester and New York, 1984), pp. 123–4.
49. C. Lopez Alonso, 'Conflictividad social y pobreza en la Edad Media segun las actas de las Cortes castellano-leonesas', *Hispania* 38 (1978), pp. 531, 539; Gauvard, *Crime, état et société*, p. 274; J-M. Cauchies, *La législation princière pour le comté de Hainaut: Ducs de Bourgogne et premiers Habsburgs (1427–1506)* (Brussels, 1982), pp. 536–41.
50. *Documents inédits concernant la ville et le siège du bailliage d'Amiens*, ed. E. Maugis (2 vols, Amiens and Paris, 1914), II, pp. 54–65.
51. *Decisiones capelle sedis archiepiscopalis Tholose una cum additionibus additis per egregium virum dominum Stephanum Auffrerii* (Lyon, 1508), fol. 9v; *Decisiones per excellentissimum legum doctorem dominum Guidonem Pape* (Lyon, 1512), fol. 42; Bellamy, *Criminal Law and Society*, pp. 128–9.
52. *Decisiones . . . Tholose*, fol. 19v.

53. Nicholas, 'Crime and punishment in fourteenth-century Ghent', pp. 331–2; *Documents inédits concernant la ville . . . d'Amiens*, p. 67; *Decisiones per . . . Guidonem Pape*, fol. 36; N.M. Trenholme, 'The right of sanctuary in England', *University of Missouri Studies* 1 (1903), pp. 322–36, 351–67.

54. J. Le Goff, *Time, Work and Culture in the Middle Ages* (Chicago and London, 1980), p. 143 (from an article originally published in 1965).

55. H. Rashdall, *The Universities of Europe in the Middle Ages* (3 vols, Oxford, 1936), III, pp. 427–41; J. Verger and C. Vulliez, 'Crise et mutations des Universités françaises à la fin du Moyen Age', in *Histoire des Universités en France*, ed. J. Verger (Toulouse, 1986); S. Cassagnes-Brouquet, 'La violence des étudiants à Toulouse à la fin du XVe et au XVIe siècle (1460–1610)', *Annales du Midi* 94 (1982); C.I. Hammer, 'Patterns of homicide in a medieval university town: fourteenth-century Oxford', *Past & Present* 78 (1978); E. De Maesschalck, 'The relationship between the university and the city of Louvain in the fifteenth century', *History of Universities* 9 (1990), pp. 53–5; R.C. Schwinges, 'Student education, student life', in *A History of the University in Europe* (2 vols, Cambridge, 1992), I, pp. 223–6.

56. J.L. Bolton, *The Medieval English Economy, 1150–1500* (London, 1980), pp. 50–6.

57. I. Del Val Valdivieso, 'Universidad y luchas urbanas en la Castilla bajomedieval', *Mayurqa* 22 (1989), pp. 217–19.

58. C.H. Haskins, *Studies in Mediaeval Culture* (Oxford, 1929), p. 68.

59. A. Palmieri, 'Furti di libri e di vivande a scolari dell'antico studio bolognese', *Studi e memorie per la storia dell'università di Bologna* 9 (1926); M. Bellomo, 'Studenti e "populus" nelle città universitarie italiane dal secolo XII al XIV', in *Università e società nei secoli XII–XVI* (Pistoia, 1982), p. 67; Archivio di Stato, Bologna, Curia del podestà, Inquisitiones, busta 259, reg. 6, fol. 68; busta 260, reg. 1, fol. 60; busta 263, reg. 1, fol. 47, etc.

60. *The Guardian*, 25 September 2000.

61. Schwinges, 'Student education, student life', pp. 223–4.

62. J. Verger, *Les universités françaises au Moyen Age* (Leiden, 1995), pp. 249–51.

chapter 6

PUNISHMENT

In 1330 a Hungarian baron called Felician made a murderous attack on King Charles of Hungary and his wife Elizabeth, as they dined unguarded in their castle at Wischegrad. Charles was lightly wounded in the hand, but Elizabeth was more seriously injured, as four fingers of her right hand were cut off, later earning her the nickname of 'Kiktawa' in Polish, or 'cripple-hand'. Felician was immediately killed by royal servants. His son and other accomplices were seized, tied to horses' tails and dragged around the streets and squares until they died, their flesh ripped off, exposing the bones. Their bodies, strewn around the streets, were cut up and eaten by dogs. Felician's head was sent to Buda, his hands, feet and other limbs to the chief cities, to be affixed to the city gates as a mark of abhorrence of such a heinous crime.[1]

Public punishment for the political crime of treason often involved the tearing or hacking apart of the body of the traitor. Just such a description of an eighteenth-century execution, for an attempt to kill the king of France, opens the pages of Michel Foucault's highly influential book *Discipline and Punish: The Birth of the Prison*, first published in 1975 and quickly translated into English. Foucault's influence on the study of modern modes of punishment means that his presence cannot be ignored for the Middle Ages either. Foucault starts with the shocking description of a traitor's death in torment, but then suddenly moves forward by eighty years to quote the rules issued for a juvenile delinquents' prison in Paris, which divides its inmates' time into monotonous blocks of prayer, work, instruction and exercise. 'We have, then', he writes, 'a public execution and a timetable.' Foucault puts these two documents side by side in order to convey, with chilling immediacy, the theme of his book: the disappearance of public execution, the disappearance of 'torture as a public spectacle', and the transformation of systems of punishment between the *ancien régime* and the modern world. No longer is the body of the criminal made to suffer through varieties of corporal and capital punishment, but the object of punishment has become the criminal's mind or character or soul. He is deprived of liberty in institutions whose aim is to reform or correct his character and behaviour. The purpose of these institutions is announced in their titles: reformatories and penitentiaries. Thus punishment has become 'the most hidden part of the penal process', where before it was the most public. Foucault's intention is not to explain this shift, but to describe it and place it in the context of the institutions of modern disciplinary society: factories, schools, barracks, hospitals, prisons. It is no coincidence, he says, that these regulatory institutions of control all appeared in the late eighteenth and early nineteenth centuries. These modern developments are outside the scope of this book, but what does fall within it is Foucault's assumption that the penal system of eighteenth-century France stretched back into the Middle Ages.

Foucault quotes and makes use of a Marxist analysis of changes in penal systems, in which the mode or production – servile, feudal, capitalistic – determines the nature of punishment. Thus, in a slave economy, punishment takes the form of enslavement; in a feudal economy (broadly speaking, the Middle Ages), 'at a time when money and production were still at an early stage of development, we find a sudden increase in corporal punishments, the body being the only property accessible'; and finally, under capitalism, 'the industrial system requires a free market in labour', but labour of a regular and ordered kind, hence the emergence of houses of correction with the purpose of producing that labour from those who had not yet learned how to behave 'properly' in a capitalist society. Foucault uses this analysis, but he also distances himself from it when he argues that we must regard punishment as a 'complex social function', and must look not only at how it might be determined by the economic structure, but also at its positive role in the assertion and exercise of political power.[2] This connection between punishment and power then becomes a major theme of the book.

Foucault, it must be said, is not a historian in the conventional sense of the word, and has been taken to task by some practitioners in the discipline. 'By traditional standards of scholarship', wrote one reviewer of *Discipline and Punish*, 'the book is a scandal, lacking in original research and making only the merest gesture toward modern scholarship.' The book 'belongs to no recognizable genre', said another, echoing Clifford Geertz's description of Foucault as 'a kind of impossible object: a non-historical historian'.[3] Nevertheless, these faults are commonly taken to be outweighed by Foucault's brilliant, provocative insights and generalisations. As one reviewer has put it, 'even his most historical enquiries . . . are unreliable guides', but 'whatever exactly may have been true about the history of imprisonment . . . , no one has written more deeply about what it is to punish'.[4]

From this discussion of Foucault, I wish to take three themes for this chapter: the notion that the major form of punishment in the centuries before the eighteenth was physical, the infliction of pain on the body; the corresponding idea that imprisonment was not used punitively in those centuries; and the key arguments that punishment patterns can be related both to economic structure and to political processes. Foucault knew what he was doing: he was not writing a history of punishment, but locating and describing the moment of transition between two 'penal styles', one changing the convict's body and the other changing his mind. However, *Discipline and Punish* has had the unfortunate consequence of encouraging the views that medieval punishments were inflicted mainly on the body of the criminal, and that those punishments were unchanging, static. This Foucault effect has merely reinforced older opinions, represented for example by Huizinga's *Waning of the Middle Ages*, which allowed their idea of late medieval justice to be filled by images of extreme cruelty. This view is deceptive for several reasons: first, because imprisonment as a penalty was in fact imposed increasingly during the later Middle Ages; second, because punishment evolved, and was not a static phenomenon; third, because a manifest contrast between the exceptional punishment meted out to a traitor and the punishments administered to the vast mass of offenders could be made for any period of pre-modern history; last, because in the Middle Ages, as in the eighteenth century and today, most offenders paid money fines, and were subject to neither physical punishment nor incarceration.

Imprisonment

It is often claimed that prison was not used as a punishment in the Middle Ages, but only for pre-trial custody or as a means of compelling fulfilment of the actual penalty, say, the payment of a fine. This was the background thinking to Foucault's location of the 'birth of the prison' in the early nineteenth century. However, the birth of the prison, in the sense of punitive incarceration, at least, and perhaps too in the sense of confinement for the purpose of reform, is more correctly located in the later Middle Ages.

It should be acknowledged that the evolution of punitive imprisonment was uneven across Europe. It was also hampered by what was thought to be a Roman-law rule that sentencing criminals to be kept in prison was forbidden, as 'prisons should be used for confining men, not punishing them'. However, this barrier was breached first in the Church, then in the lay world. Because churchmen were prevented by canon law from shedding blood, some other means of punishing wayward clerics was required. Monasteries had had prisons for the correction of monks from an early date, and in the twelfth century bishops did too. These were, in Peters' words, 'the first instances of confinement for specific periods for the purpose of moral correction'. Pope Boniface VIII in 1298 then overturned the 'rule' that prison should be for custody, not punishment, in allowing bishops to incarcerate clerics who committed crimes: although prison is known to be appointed for the custody, not the punishment, of offenders, he announced, we shall not disapprove if you subject clerics convicted of crimes to indefinite or fixed terms of imprisonment in order to undergo penitence. Meanwhile, secular law in some areas (England, Germany) continued to allow imprisonment only for custody pending trial or as replacement for a fine. In France, Italy and Spain, however, imprisonment was increasingly introduced into the modes of penalty. This means, as Peters argues, that it was medieval Europe that invented punitive imprisonment.[5]

Imprisonment as a penalty can thus be found in both secular law and secular practice. It was mainly prescribed either as one element in a mixed penalty, combining with exposure in the pillory or banishment, or as substitute penalty for those who could not afford to pay a money fine.[6] For example, already in the 1260s, King Louis IX of France ordered that those unable to pay their fines for the offence of blasphemy should spend a period in prison, from one to eight days depending on the gravity of the offence.[7] It was also the case that time spent in gaol could be discounted against an eventual sentence, or used as a supporting argument in a petition for pardon. 'This man has already suffered enough' would be the implication. An example of this comes in the pardon of the priest, Jean le Vacher, in 1413 (see above, p. 109): his long detention, patiently endured, with daily saying of prayers and observation of fasts and vigils, was one factor that earned him acquittal for a murder he acknowledged.

Although the intention of governments, as expressed in legislation, may have tended to an increasing use of punitive imprisonment, did this actually happen? What evidence do we have of prison sentences served? Recent studies of fifteenth-century prisons offer some support for the argument developed here. Records of those admitted to the Parisian Châtelet over six days in 1412 show that periods in prison were very short: out of a total of just over one hundred prisoners, most (70 per cent) were released the same day or the following day, and all but six were set free within two weeks.[8] In the much more extended records from Arras, covering over 3,000 cases in the years 1407–50, over half of prisoners were released within two days; but this still left 30 per cent held for up to a week, and 10 per cent for one week, two weeks or more.[9] In

Bologna, more significantly, a prison register for 1439 shows that over half of those unmistakeably detained for crimes were held for longer than a week, and some of them for over a month.[10] The weakness of building any argument on such registers is that they do not distinguish between terms spent in prison on remand and terms spent as punishment. Also, to modern eyes, prison sentences of a few days are very slight punishment. However, we need to remember that to late medieval people even a fortnight behind bars was intolerable, and that laws often prescribed brief periods of penal incarceration. The medieval version of the 'short, sharp shock' was short indeed, but it seems to have been a growing element in the penal repertoire.

At the same time, prison conditions bore none of Foucault's disciplinary controls. Treatment was largely determined by rank. Prisoners had to pay for their use of the service. If they were moneyed, they could choose greater light, warmth and comfort, taking rooms higher in the building, having a bed to sleep on, and buying in food from outside. If they were poor, then they could enjoy none of these amenities, but were dependent for food on the charity of the local community or of friends in the outside world. The idea that the external hierarchy of social rank should be reproduced within the prison walls was a common one. At Cambrai the local law urged judges not to put 'decent people or people of worth with common folk, criminals, pimps and procuresses'. Prisons were often run as profit-making enterprises by gaolers who sub-contracted ('farmed') the prison from the local authorities. Even where, as in England, prisons were not farmed out, but run by paid agents of the sheriff, the same regime of fees and charges obtained. As one historian has put it, gaolers were 'part warders, part inn-keepers'.[11] They naturally did not like to see prisoners walk out without paying, and would try to claim release fees even from those who had been acquitted. Even worse, they might try to prolong a prisoner's stay in order to maximise revenue. Such practices are attested, for example, in Catalonia in the fourteenth century and Provence in the fifteenth.[12] The distribution of alms, collected for the poor prisoners, was a further area of possible abuse: the money could be intercepted before the poor prisoners saw any of it, as in fifteenth-century Bordeaux, or it might be paid out to the rich instead, as apparently happened in Siena in the 1290s.[13] Last, gaolers permitted gambling and visits from prostitutes, perhaps as a way of maintaining order and filling the prisoners' time.

The overriding concern of medieval prison regulations was to prevent excessive profiteering, even extortion, and the infliction of pain. Gaolers who forced prisoners to buy their food and drink from themselves, who appropriated the alms intended for relief of poor prisoners, who used damp dungeons and heavy chains to extort bribes, or who raised fees to extortionate levels: these were the abuses addressed by such regulations. Other records confirm that prisons were dangerous and unhealthy places. The Bishop of Lyon's chief judge in 1305 objected to the gaolers' practice of stripping prisoners of their clothes even before they were convicted and of torturing them, such that, when they were eventually released, they died or barely subsisted because of the cold and disease they had suffered.[14] In 1398 the king's council was informed that many paupers were dying in gaol from poverty or disease because they could not pay their fines. In Venice, the stench from the prisons in the doge's palace was at one time so high that it was thought best to move the prisoners elsewhere. Earlier, the Venetian prison was described as a 'nauseating pit'.

In many prisons the toll of disease and despair was high. In the Florentine Stinche, seventy prisoners died between October 1347 and March 1348. In Siena twenty-two poor prisoners died in January and February 1340, and a further nineteen in the following two months. In the years 1315–17 scores of prisoners died in gaols in England: over sixty in Newgate, London, in 1315–16, twenty-eight in Wallingford in 1316, and seventy-one in Maidstone in 1316–17. In Amiens in 1408 it was claimed that far more prisoners died in prison than on the gallows.[15] Porteau-Bitker has described any prison sentence of more than a few months as amounting to slow death. Some prisoners, fearful of their fate, or in despair, committed suicide in their cells.[16] Overcrowding was another problem. At its height in 1346, the Stinche prison held over 600 inmates, which far exceeded the resources of local charities to support. This forced the Florentine government into a series of measures to reduce numbers by controlling new arrivals and allowing a mass discharge of nearly 200 prisoners at Christmas. Overcrowding of existing buildings was often the explicit rationale for new constructions. In both Venice and Siena in 1326 additional prisons were built to relieve the pressure on space. The press on numbers in the Châtelet in Paris led the *prévôt* to urge the adaptation of some rooms in another building as an overspill. These rooms, he said, would be 'secure and well-ventilated, where men can live without disease or death'.[17]

One prisoner who survived to write about his experience was Jean Regnier, captured and held to ransom for seventeen months in 1432–3. Regnier was in a sense a prisoner of war – as an official of the English occupation of northern France, he was captured by French brigands – but as he was held in the bishop's prison in Beauvais, he did experience ordinary gaol conditions. In a series of poems of personal complaint, he paints a picture, sometimes distressed, sometimes ironic, of cold, hunger, fear and despair. With a bed of straw and a diet of bread and water, assailed by fleas and lice, he dreams of eating poultry and fish, and creates a fantasy of a warm, light room and a purse full of money.[18]

Clearly the late medieval prison served more than one function in the systems of criminal justice: not only holding defendants pending trial, but also the punishment of convicted criminals in austere conditions reminiscent of penitence.

Public execution

If imprisonment was evolving, so too were punishments inflicted on the body. There were certainly some enduring features of public execution and punishment across late medieval Europe. For the most serious crimes, the most serious penalties were reserved: the mutilation of ears, lips and tongue, the amputation of hands, feet and ears, the gouging out of eyes, or death by hanging, beheading or other means (dismemberment, burning, drowning, burial alive, the wheel). There was a code to the assignment of mode of capital execution. Dismemberment was reserved for traitors and conspirators, and would be preceded by dragging the culprit to the scaffold at a horse's tail or on a hurdle. Burning was for crimes requiring 'extreme purification by the total elimination of the offender's body': sodomy, incest, sorcery, infanticide.[19] Throughout this catalogue of ghastliness there was differentiation, or inequality, by class, gender and status. Nobles and bourgeois were given the quicker, less painful death by decapitation. Women were rarely hanged: when one was hanged in Paris in 1445, it was reported that 'a great multitude of people, especially women and girls, flooded in, because of the great novelty of seeing a woman hanged, for this had never before been seen in the kingdom of France'.[20] Townsmen were less likely to be hanged than outsiders: when a bourgeois of Malines was hanged for theft in 1423, it was noted that none had been executed in this manner in the past century.

Despite the apparent stability of the symbolism of executions, there was change in their implementation. Places of execution varied. Some punishments became rare or reserved for specific crimes. Numbers of executions rose or fell. Andrea Zorzi has stressed the variability of the incidence, method and ceremonial of public executions in his study of punishment in Florence.[21] Average numbers fell: one a month in the fourteenth century, one every other month in the fifteenth. The repertoire of methods contracted as forms of execution that preserved elements of ritual purification, such as burning or burial alive, gave way to more straightforwardly secular forms, decapitation and hanging. Then in the later fifteenth century, hanging became the more frequent manner of criminal death. In the thirteenth and early fourteenth centuries, there had been numerous sites for executions, and it was only from the second half of the fourteenth century that one principal site emerged: outside the city walls, near the river bank, in an area populated with numerous hospitals, including one for plague victims, and crossed by streams carrying the effluent of urban manufacturing. The combination was significant: it was 'a zone of pain and reclusion', of discharge and expulsion, but also of cleansing and cure.

Capital punishment also became reserved for the 'incorrigibles', for example recidivist thieves, and for the 'scandalous', that is those who committed intolerable crimes against public or sexual morality. Let us take as an example the executions in the city of Ferrara in the 1490s, ruled by the ageing Duke Ercole d'Este. Here we find a peasant burned to death for impregnating his sister and for bestiality with asses, a 17-year-old youth from the suburbs burned for sodomy, another peasant hanged for theft and incest with his sisters, an 18-year-old hanged for thieving during public celebrations of a ducal marriage, two more peasants hanged for homicide, and soldiers hanged for robbery and counterfeiting. In addition, an 80-year-old draper convicted of sodomy and sentenced to death by burning was spared his life, and a teenage wife convicted of strangling to death her husband's nephew, escaped from prison while awaiting the death penalty.[22] The list is indicative of the real public order concerns of a late medieval government: apart from the predictable executions for theft and homicide, what stands out is the concern for sexual propriety, especially in the countryside, and protection of ducal interests such as the coinage and dynastic celebrations. As Andrea Zorzi has put it, public executions became 'the most sophisticated forms of transmission of key values', foremost among them obedience and discipline.[23]

Lavoie makes the point that there in fact seems to be in the later Middle Ages a horror of spilling blood in punishment.[24] When blood was spilt, it had to be justified by the exceptional nature of the crime: especially inhuman acts, re-offending, a grave threat to public morality. In practice, local inhabitants tended to be spared, while outsiders were made an example of. Spierenberg's study of punishment in Amsterdam in the early modern period comes to a similar conclusion: the main type of person executed was the young, lower-class male, especially from the unmarried, unsettled, marginal groups. Those in their twenties represented nearly half of all those executed; and men vastly outnumber women.[25] The recent study of an 18-year-old burglar, executed in Normandy in 1493, fits exactly this pattern: he was a failed apprentice who wandered from job to job, thieving opportunistically as he went.[26] At Arras in the mid-fifteenth century, crimes of blood in themselves were rarely punished with death; it was only exceptionally horrid acts that attracted this penalty, such as the killing of infants and children, the brutal murder of a young wife, and so on. Two categories especially prominent among such crimes were sexual crimes (rape, incest, sodomy) and theft (in particular highway robbery and repeat offences).[27]

Although these convicts were marginals – young people in cities ruled by greybeards, immigrants in cities where economic and political power was reserved to native citizens – their deaths were far from marginal events. Rather, executions were seen as having great power as warning examples to others. These exemplary and didactic functions of public executions seem to become more evident with time. The Florentine writer of an advice book in the fourteenth century recommended: 'Go to church often, to sermons, because you will learn many good examples and habits . . . and likewise go to see men executed, not out of pleasure at seeing them punished, but so that it can be an example to you.' Similarly, in 1491 a government official describing some beheadings in Mantua noted that 'there was a dead silence such as I never witnessed at any sermon'.[28] Capital punishment was thus both likened to and differentiated from preaching: its message was one of moral edification; and it was a message that people really attended to. The need to drum home that message was also understood by those French parents who whipped their children when criminals were hanged, so that they would remember, thus in a sense writing the message indelibly in weals on their backs. It is no wonder then that spectators at public mutilations remembered for decades the sight of blood flowing from the wound and flooding on to the ground.[29] Town governments too tried to ensure that punishments were not forgotten, and for this reason retained the bodies of executed criminals, either for hanging on the gibbet or for cutting up and displaying on spikes at the city gates. Around the year 1300, the government of Siena declared by law that nothing was more just than that criminals receive their due punishment and that the example of this punishment inspire fear in others: consequently it ordered that new gallows were to be built, high and with iron chains, such that the hanged remain there and might not be removed except by falling down by themselves.[30] The authorities in Strasbourg in 1461 ended the practice of removing corpses soon after execution, because this meant that 'the gallows has stood entirely empty, as if no thief were punished here'.[31] Elsewhere only the fear of infection spreading from corpses on the gibbet could persuade a town council to remove and bury them.[32] The punishment of the criminal was to serve as an example to others. Cruel punishment taught a lesson, not so much to the wrong-doer, as to the populace at large. The sight of punishment deterred crime.

Did the moralising message of public execution have any effect? Following Foucault, historians have focused on the public reception of executions, on the behaviour of the crowd. Foucault found in eighteenth-century gallows crowds a strong element of resistance to the political message of authority, of rejection of punitive power: crowd disturbances, shouts of encouragement to the condemned man, the mocking of authority, and the transformation of criminals into heroes.[33] In contrast to Foucault, however, Gauvard finds the late medieval crowd approving of capital executions, relieved rather than terrorised at the spectacle, and Gonthier agrees: the crowd shouted insults at the convicts and supported the executioners in their work.[34] There is evidence, though, that the responses of the crowd could vary. The following examples show how that response depended heavily on the class of convicts. Compare the following two cases from Ferrara in the 1490s.

> Saturday 1 August 1495. At the windows of the lawcourts of Ferrara a thief was hanged, a peasant from Argenta, who refused to confess [his sins] before dying, or to receive communion or to climb up to the window where he was to be thrown down. Nor would he look on the image of the crucifix, or be escorted by the Company of Death [the confraternity offering spiritual comfort to the condemned], as other convicts do, nor would he say one good word to commend himself to God. And as soon as he was thrown down, the rope was cut without delay, and he fell to the ground in the piazza, and was carried off on a cart by four porters to be thrown into the river Po.

> 1496 Wednesday 13 April. In the morning . . . , at the windows of the lawcourts one of the duke's men-at-arms was hanged, Guglielmo the son of Antonio da Ronco of Modena, aged about 38. This was by command and order of the duke, for his having clipped silver coins and forged 3,000 gold ducats and French crowns, as appears in the records of . . . the notary to the criminal court, who read out the sentence from the balcony of the lawcourts. This man died better than any living person ever did, dying such a death. He was so staunch and steadfast that, when the executioner wanted to throw him down, still he encouraged himself, saying clearly that he was sure that his soul would be saved. And he was from one of Modena's good families, well-educated, industrious, virtuous in all things. He made everyone cry who saw him die so well. And that evening, the Franciscan friars and the Company of Death carried him, honourably accompanied, to be buried in [the church of] San Francesco, where one of his sons was a friar.[35]

The bourgeois from a good family knows how to die well and how to control his actions in even the most convulsing circumstances. The peasant does not. The crowd responds accordingly. It cries for the calm counterfeiter and allows him Christian burial; it inflicts more punishment on the ill-disciplined peasant, letting his corpse be carried off to the watery grave of an outcast. A good death, humbly playing the role of a faithful penitent, evoked the sympathy of spectators; recalcitrance incurred their hostility.

The role of class in executions is even more clearly revealed in executions in Florence and Siena. Here class was mixed with faction. Chroniclers record hostile reactions to a number of executions that seemed partisan, excessive, even illegal. In divided, factional cities, the execution of members of the political class or their supporters drew forth strong reactions and suspicions of partisan illegality. In Siena in 1315 there was a riot when the *podestà* tried to amputate a foot from each of six men who had entered the city contrary to a new security order aimed at weakening one noble faction. Judges sometimes refused to have anything to do with such executions, regarding them as homicide. In 1355 when the Sienese government suspected two men of subversion and condemned them to death, it had to perform the execution itself as the judges viewed it as unlawful killing. Pressing ahead with executions in such tense political conditions could generate crowd disturbances. When the *podestà* of Florence insisted on beheading two aristocrats in 1379, the event brought a huge crowd onto the piazza, and it took just one woman's cry to cause a stampede. In their rush to clear the square, people left their shoes and lost their hats as they fled, and half a dozen people were suffocated to death. Conversely, judicial reluctance to execute noblemen could stir up popular anger. When a band of brigands was captured at a castle held by the Salimbeni family in 1374, the *podestà* of Siena was quick to hang or behead a good number of them, but held back from touching members of the Salimbeni themselves, until a section of the populace threatened to riot.[36]

Contrast the execution of slaves. In Florence in 1379, a slave called Lucia was convicted of murdering her master, a Bolognese wine-seller. Knowing that he had ordered his servants to make him a preparation, she went to a spicer in the Mercato Vecchio and bought some refined silver. She added this to the pan containing the preparation. As a result of applying or ingesting this concoction, he died. The sentence was that she be led around the city in a cart, that her flesh should be torn off with pincers, and that she should then be burned to death, 'so that no female slave dare to poison her master'.[37] No one disturbed this execution.

Among forms of punishment then, imprisonment and public execution were minor forms. This can be judged from numbers. Prisons were mostly small and half-filled anyway with debtors, not criminals. In medium-sized towns of northern Europe, capital executions could run at rates from one to five per year: less than one a year, it seems, at Nuremberg and Lyon, two at Malines, four at Frankfurt, five at Lübeck.[38] In one of the most important cities of southern Europe, Florence, executions were becoming fewer: between eleven and thirteen a year in the second half of the fourteenth century, seven or eight in the fifteenth. At the count of Savoy's town of Ivrea, some fifty executions were inflicted over thirty-five years in the early fourteenth century.[39] At Arras, corporal punishment, mutilation and capital executions were rare in the fifteenth century, with death penalties averaging only one per year. Moreover, capital executions there fell unevenly in time, with irregular concentrations, such that there were many years in which none apparently took place.[40] Such numbers are important. They show how far the spectacle of public capital punishment was reserved for the exceptional.

Banishment

One of the preferred alternatives was exile or banishment, but even this varied greatly in its incidence. It has been said, of late medieval Nuremberg, that 'criminals were not punished, but simply excluded from the city, frequently for only short periods of time'.[41] In Cracow in the second half of the fourteenth century, exile was widely imposed for all manner of offences, though in two different forms: as outlawry, imposed on fugitive killers and wounders who had refused to reach a settlement with the victim's family; and as banishment, imposed by the authorities as a penalty on a much broader range of offenders. Thus, in the 1360s a dozen killers and two or three times as many assaulters were exiled (outlawed) every year. In the 1370s exile (banishment) was also imposed for theft, house-breaking, minor acts of rebellion, gambling and sex crimes such as adultery, fornication, bigamy and rape. The tariff seems to have been one year's exile for violence, one hundred years' for theft and perpetuity for murder. Some of these longer banishments were, however, reduced through intercession and pardon. For example, one Stroenwirsing had been exiled for theft and rape, but was re-admitted at the request of some nobles; he then committed further offences – rape, sexual harassment, threats of violence against the town consuls – and was required to take a vow 'to behave himself and never to re-offend', on pain of beheading. By contrast in Aberdeen in the years 1398–1407, exile was imposed only twice, once for two years on a woman for receiving stolen goods, and once in perpetuity on another woman for unspecified crimes. All other offences were dealt with by fines, pledges for good behaviour and promises to indemnify the victim. These included thieving, assault, wounding, 'perturbing the town' and insolence towards the urban authorities (the *baillies*) or disobedience towards its officers.[42] This great divergence in the use of banishment is not just an effect of distance: at Lyon banishment was rare before 1348, but frequent after, mostly for thieves; whereas at nearby Dijon it was applied to all sorts of crimes, from insults to the authorities and forgery, to sodomy, rape and prostitution.[43] When strictly enforced, exile was a fearful punishment, pushing exiles into destitution and banditry, cutting their contacts with family and friends, and exposing them to the unpunishable violence of bandit-catchers.[44]

Public shaming

Public shaming was also used as punishment. In towns of southern France, couples discovered committing adultery were required to undergo a shaming 'race': if a man is found with a married woman, with his trousers down, or both are found undressed, behind closed doors, then they are to run naked through the town from one gate to another – presumably through a crowd and accompanied by a whipping. However, in the fourteenth and fifteenth centuries, the option often existed to pay a fine instead.[45] The pillory, ladder or stocks was often used for minor offences: the offender was attached to it for a set number of hours on a market day, to the general ridicule of bystanders. In Aberdeen in 1405 a cuckstool was instituted for insults to urban or royal officers: for a first offence, the miscreant was to kiss the stool; for a second, he or she was to be placed on it and defiled with eggs, dung and muck.[46] In France in 1397 the king ordered that for a first offence of blasphemy, the culprit was to stand in the pillory from early morning to mid-afternoon, so that people could throw mud and other filth at them, and then spend a month in prison on bread and water.[47]

Monetary penalties

The dominant forms of punishment in the Middle Ages were in fact the money fine and banishment or exile, penalties that depleted the convict's assets or expelled him from the community. This has been amply demonstrated by the French historian Robert Muchembled in his book *Le temps des supplices*. In contrast to Foucault's focus on horrific pain, Muchembled shows that 'judicial fines were at the heart of the system' in the later Middle Ages. It was not until the sixteenth century that 'the real period of tortured bodies arrives', with more and greater 'punitive festivals, offering to the crowds of spectators a liturgy based on a new sacrality of public power'. Muchembled's study is limited to the town of Arras and its region in northern France, but as we shall see, his conclusion regarding the role of fines applies more generally to western Europe. From 1400 to 1436 the judicial authorities in Arras, a town of some 14,000 inhabitants, imposed over 1,600 fines, equivalent to one for every seven to ten inhabitants. 'The effectiveness of the Arras penal system was largely founded on pecuniary penalties.' The only other major penalty in frequency of incidence was banishment. Together these forms of punishment 'constituted the essential arsenal of repression'.[48]

For the most common of prosecuted crimes, physical violence, the usual penalty was a fine. In many towns and cities of France and Italy these were fixed fines. Two examples from Dauphiné illustrate the variety of local practice here. At St Symphorien d'Ozon, fines were levied at the following levels: 100 *sous* for the rape of a loose woman or for breaking bones; 60s. for wounding with a weapon and shedding blood, for throwing a stone maliciously or for causing a bloody injury without a sword (except for bleeding from the mouth or nose); 30s. for drawing a sword with the intent to wound; 20s. for maliciously pulling someone's hair or kicking without bloodshed; 10s. for slapping; and 7s. for punching without bloodshed. By contrast at St Marcellin, the fine for raising or throwing a knife or sword with intent to injure was 30s. if this were committed against an inhabitant, 15s. if against an outsider; for wounding short of causing death or cutting off a limb, the fine varied from 30s. to 60s.; for the more serious injury of cutting off a limb, the fine would vary from 10 to 20 *livres*; and for slapping or punching, without causing bloodshed or breaking teeth or 'deforming' the face, the fine would be 5s. (for a punch) or 10s. (for a slap).[49] Two places only 55 km apart could thus differ not only in the level of fines, but also in the categorisation of offences. Both places differentiate between injuries caused with or without intent or malice, with or without a weapon, and with or without bloodshed, but St Marcellin also differentiates between permanent and impermanent injury and by status of the victim, that is between inhabitants and outsiders.

Even greater differentiation is found in Italian cities. Let us take the fourteenth-century statutes of the city of Rome.[50] These statutes seem to preserve two separate legislative moments, one envisaging two levels of fine, according to social status, and one envisaging three levels. The distinctions are a combination of the chivalric, the military and the social. At first, knights and magnates are distinguished from the rest of society, those liable to infantry service (*pedes*/foot); later, enhanced penalties were enacted for magnates. For ease of presentation, the latter provisions are given here in tabular form.

- For chasing someone with a weapon, 4 lire, or without a weapon 40s.
- For putting a hand to knife or sword with ill intent, 40s.
- For going with weapons to a 'battle', 7 lire, or to a brawl, 4 lire (a 'battle' being defined as having over twelve armed men on each side, a brawl fewer than twelve).
- For throwing stones at a battle or brawl, 3 lire.
- For deliberately causing someone to fall down, 100s.

- For all the above, penalties are doubled for knights, the sons of knights or anyone with over 2,000 lire of property.
- For disparagingly cutting a woman's clothes above the knee, 100 lire.
- For pushing someone into a fire, 10 lire, and if their clothes are burned, 15 lire.
- For pushing someone into a well or into the river or the sea, 100 lire.
- For breaking or knocking out a tooth, 10 lire per tooth.
- For pulling someone from a horse, 10 lire.
- For putting dung, excrement, mud or other filth in anyone's mouth, 25 lire.

Offence	Foot	Knight	Magnate
Drawing a knife or sword	L 3	L 6	L 25
Wounding with a bladed weapon, without bloodshed	10s.	20s.	L 50
Wounding with a bladed weapon, with bloodshed	L 30	L 60	L 150
Cutting off or mutilating a limb	L 2	L 4	L 1,000
Breaking bones or bruising	L 50	L 100	L 300
Cutting off fingers, hand or foot	L 100	L 200	L 600
Cutting off nose, gouging out an eye, blinding in one eye	L 200	L 400	L 1,000
Blinding in both eyes	L 500	L 500	L 3,000
Wounding in the face with scarring	L 50	L 100	L 500
Wounding in the face, leaving a shameful mark	L 100	L 200	L 1,000
Slapping/punching in the face, without bloodshed	L 15	L 30	L 100
Slapping/punching in the face, with bloodshed	L 30	L 60	L 200
Punching elsewhere on the body	L 5	L 10	L 50
Punching in the throat	L 4	L 4	L 4
Pulling by the hair or beard	L 10	L 20	L 50
Pulling by the hair or beard and dragging along ground	L 20	L 40	L 100
Maliciously cutting or tearing clothes	L 5	L 10	L 50
Participating in a battle in armour	L 100	L 200	L 1,000
Starting a battle	L 25	L 50	L 200
Participating in a brawl with weapons	L 30	L 60	L 600
Starting a brawl	L 15	L 25	L 100

It is of course unwise to attempt to write social history from legislative acts, but what such extensive provisions suggest is high levels of social conflict, and a more nuanced legislative response. Battles are distinguished from brawls. The range of injuries envisaged runs from slaps to tearing of clothes, and from pulling by the hair to wounds on all parts of the body. Aggressive acts are distinguished from actual blows. Various forms of outcome are differentiated: bloodshed, debility, scarring, broken bones. The three most significant variables are using weapons, shedding blood and social rank.

This has been called 'tariff justice', in which the level of penalty is set according to degrees of violence, responsibility and premeditation, and according to the location, the status of the victim and the solvency of the culprit. Such tariffs have been interpreted as a sign of the dominance of the fiscal function of justice. According to this view, judicial powers were valuable assets, yielding valuable sums to their holders. It is argued that financial considerations drove the criminal justice system: dictating its specification of 'a multiplicity of extremely slight crimes', its close policing, and its offering of monetary inducements to denouncers. In an era of rising public expenditure fines were important to the fisc.[51] Financial concerns certainly seem to be behind the evolution of fines in late medieval Cagliari (Sardinia): with a smaller population after the Black Death, the total monetary value of fines was nevertheless maintained, by multiplying the numbers of fines imposed.[52] Nevertheless, the fiscal argument rarely survives an inspection of urban or seigneurial revenue accounts. Fines rarely contributed a significant amount to the income of towns or lords. The city of Constance, for example, was very efficient at collecting fines, but these never amounted to more than 4 per cent of annual revenue.[53]

We should not assume either that the monetary penalties set by statute were always strictly imposed or fully paid. As Peter Schuster has recently suggested, the statutes give the impression that the sentence was the last word on the matter and allow for no discussion or appeal, but in practice the sentence was the opening statement in a fresh dialogue between the authorities and the culprit. In Constance convicts negotiated with the authorities both how to pay their fines and how quickly: they were allowed to pay partly in cash and partly in kind, they could pay in instalments (sometimes spaced over years rather than months), and they could pay off their fines by offering their labour on public works. A similar sort of dialogue is evident in Italy. At Bologna, convicts were allowed to enter a plea of poverty in the hope of obtaining a reduction of any fine: the offender had to provide the names of two people to attest to his poverty, who were then questioned by the magistrate. Reduction of fine could also be obtained by paying a sum to certain public charities before sentence.[54]

This predominance of monetary penalties of course means that the crude Marxist scheme, half-endorsed, half-abandoned by Foucault, is untenable. In a still feudal era, there was sufficient coin and sufficient movable goods to make extensive confiscation a viable penal option.

Repentance, reparation, reintegration

However, punishment in whatever guise continued to exist alongside other obligations laid on offenders which had the aim of securing their repentance, the reparation of their wrong and their eventual reintegration into society. Numerous 'secular' punishments in fact carried associations with penances imposed for sin: imprisonment on bread and water or public whippings were commonly imposed by the Church courts. More-over, as we shall see, as state repression intensified, so too the religious character of its scaffold theatre became more elaborate.

Historians frequently distinguish among punishments between those for 'curable' delinquents and those for the 'incurable'. Another way of describing this distinction is to talk of 'medicinal' and 'repressive' penalties, the one seeking to reintegrate the wrong-doer, the other to expel him from the community. 'Medicinal' penalties can be seen in those punish-ments that sought to bring the criminal to repentance, to compensate victims materially, and to pacify ruptured social relations. 'Repressive' penalties may be seen in those penalties that inflicted on the convict some permanent physical disability, or excluded him permanently from the community through exile or death.

One area where corrective penalties seem uppermost is among the Flemish towns such as Bruges, Ypres, Ghent and Lille, which all used expiatory pilgrimages as part punishment of offences ranging from insult to homicide. They sent offenders to any one of scores of shrines in France and abroad, with Roccamadour and Santiago de Compostella being the most frequent destinations. Pilgrimage might not seem like punishment, but it involved three elements that mixed the remedial with the punitive: cost, absence and penitence. The criminal would have to pay his own travel costs, he would be removed from the community for a period of weeks or months, and he would have to behave as a penitent sinner. In Germany and Central Europe in the thirteenth century, pilgrimage by the offender was one part of a broader settlement between a killer and his victim's family: moral compensation accompanied financial. In the four-teenth century, pilgrimage was incorporated into public systems of justice and began to take the place of banishment, not compensation.[55] In France too the second half of the fourteenth century saw a growing number of royal pardons that included penitential elements: prison on bread and water, or pilgrimage. These letters of pardon also used the vocabulary of penitence, apparently inspired by canon law and ecclesiastical models, and being issued on important Christian festivals such as Easter. Similarly, in Castile a condition of many royal pardons, especially for killing, was a period of service in a frontier fort on the Moorish border, preserving a link between penitence and crusading. The same link can be seen in the condition that Louis IX imposed on a cleric pardoned for homicide (above, p. 37). The connection to religious penitence was further developed in Castile in the fifteenth century when King Juan II ordered that all petitions for pardon submitted during the year were to be kept until Good Friday, called appropriately 'the day of pardons', when the king would select no more than twenty to grant, on the advice of his confessor.[56] Moreover, the prison was to an extent conceived in religious and penitential terms. When work started on building a new prison in Siena, all the clergy were present, saying psalms and prayers, accompanied by musicians. Many Italian cities released a small number of prisoners on important festivals, for example the feast day of the city's patron saint, as an act of state charity.

Executions as rituals

The same stress on penitence has, more debatably, been argued for physical punishments. Public execution has been seen as a ritual process, a drama or spectacle, but the casting of roles in this piece of theatre diverges widely among historians. Spierenburg has seen execution as a drama in which Church and state combined, but with religious elements to the fore. As the prisoner was led to the scaffold, a bell would be tolled. The procession would be accompanied by priests and prayers. On the scaffold the convict would act out the part of the penitent, kneeling, confessing to further crimes, saying a prayer, singing a psalm or giving a speech, telling a moralistic story of his sin that deserved punishment.[57] Cohen too has stressed the religious and penitential elements, especially from the late fourteenth century when the state allowed prisoners to make confession of sins to a priest on the gallows. This confession served as the culmination of a process of acknowledgement of guilt and request for prayers that assisted the reconciliation of the convict to God.[58] Confession on the scaffold has been seen as assisting the criminal on his path to repentance.[59] As for the crowd, Spierenburg has it as passive and receptive, actively intervening in the process only in exceptional circumstances, for example where death seemed an undeserving punishment for a member of the local community rather than the merited end of an undesirable stranger.

However, Gauvard has argued forcefully against the casting of the convict as penitent and the crowd as passive onlooker. The convict did not dress in penitential garb, she argues, but in his normal, secular attire. He was conducted to the scaffold on a dung-cart, a mode of transport not associated with repentance. At the moment of death, the focus shifts to the relation between the executioner and the crowd, not that between the convict and God. The crowd had an active role. It could halt proceedings in favour of clerics in the tumbril crying out 'Clergie!' Individuals in the crowd, specifically women, could stop an execution by offering to marry the convict. Women's pleas for mercy could also reduce the scaffold tortures planned for the prisoner. Any failure of the equipment, any error by the executioner – a rope that broke, for example – might be interpreted by the crowd as a sign from God, a miracle signalling that the convict did not deserve to die.

Confirmation of these active interruptions of the drama is readily found in France. In Amiens in 1443 an execution of four supposed clerics had to be aborted because of attempts to stop the cart and to arouse the crowd with shouts of 'Good people, are you going to let these clerics go to the scaffold?' The body of Gilles de Rais, hanged for the abduction, rape and murder of children in 1440, was saved from burning by the appeals of various noblewomen. A number of cases from the fourteenth and fifteenth centuries show women saving men from hanging. For example in 1374 the *prévôt* of Beaugency, near Orléans, was leading three thieves to the gallows when a young girl approached him and asked for one of them in marriage. She said that 'by the local custom her request had to be granted, but the *prévôt* replied that he knew nothing about this'. The large crowd cried out confirming the custom, so the *prévôt* spared the third thief (echoes of Christ's Passion here), who eventually obtained a pardon from the king. In most of these cases, the woman is described either as a young girl, a poor young girl, a maiden or a repentant prostitute. For the good therefore of providing a husband for an unwed virgin, or of rescuing a whore from sin, the punishment of a thief could be put aside. As for miracles, there is the case in 1395 of an infant-killer who was thrown into the River Charente at Châteauneuf, to drown for her crime, but who survived and surfaced on a sandbank, her hands miraculously untied.[60]

Yet another interpretation of the 'drama' of execution has stressed its ludic or play elements, and has attempted to see execution as a game or as a form of play. Here the historian Balestracci has taken yet another cue from Foucault.[61] Spectators ran up to watch an execution as if to a game. Children and youths played with the corpses of public enemies, dragging them around town, hanging them up and beating them, cutting off the hands and kicking them around. Even dice might be made from their bones. The execution was a contest between the executioner and the flesh and bone of the condemned: the executioner who failed to deliver a clean blow with sword or axe might be turned on by the crowd. On the way to the gallows, convict and crowd would engage in word games, of verbal challenges and burlesque replies. Finally, the treatment of some corpses, with the disembowelled innards thrown to the dogs, reproduces a ritual of another sport, that of hunting. Persuasive though this accumulation of ludic elements might seem, there is a problem, of which Balestracci is quite aware. 'Does this happen with all types of execution?' he asks, thus pointing to the rather small range of evidence he had available. From the many hundreds of executions that took place, evidence of play is recorded in only a small minority of cases. Many of these come from only two cities, Florence and Siena, and from a small group of exceptional cases: the executions of the heretical friar Michele da Calci in 1389, of the conspirator Jacopo Pazzi in 1478, of another friar, Girolamo Savonarola, in 1498. Moreover, only public enemies, traitors and conspirators were treated to a second 'execution' at the hands of boys, and banter is found only in the execution of heretics. This does not, of course, invalidate Balestracci's argument, but it does point to the exceptional conditions required for play elements to be present in public executions.

Private punishment

A further restriction of the role of punishment by the state arises in those special crimes where the injured party or other private persons could inflict punishment on criminals. When anyone captures a thief or robber, declared the laws of Siena, he is not to be punished for any blows he inflicts on the culprit, provided he does not kill or mutilate him.[62] In some places, killing a bandit was no crime: anyone could attack or kill a bandit with impunity. Some governments did, however, restrict this right as they were forced to deal with the bloody consequences.[63] In England, however, the Crown seems to have put an end to such practice and regarded it as an illegality requiring royal pardon: in Lincolnshire in 1391 six men seized an outlawed felon and took him to the 'Playing Place' in Spalding where, 'believing it was permissible to behead and slay anyone outlawed of felony', they struck off his head.[64] What is interesting in this case is that this unofficial posse chose a public recreation ground, on a Sunday, for their action, thus guaranteeing maximum publicity and, in their eyes, legitimacy. Italian governments sometimes, in exceptional circumstances, allowed private vengeance as replacement or realisation of judicial penalty. When Pagnozzino Strozzi killed a member of the Lenzi family in 1387, the Florentine government authorised the Lenzi 'with impunity to pursue a vendetta and to offend by any means and to any degree' Pagnozzino, his brother Nofri, their sons and descendants 'and any other member of the Strozzi clan . . . no matter how remote the relationship'.[65] In some parts of Germany the idea survived that the victim should deal the fatal blow on the scaffold: as late as 1470 in Weimar the oldest relative of a murder victim beheaded the killer, and in rape cases a remnant of this practice can be found where the rape victim held the hair of her rapist's head as he went under the axe.[66]

It was also generally accepted in law that fathers and husbands had the right to chastise their wives and children, and masters their servants and slaves. The fourteenth-century statutes of Perugia, to take only one example, declare that violence by parents against children is not to be prosecuted or punished, but that the killing of a parent by a child is to be punished with beheading.[67] Violence was thus permitted to descend the domestic hierarchy, but not to ascend it. By extension, husbands also had the right to kill wives and their lovers discovered *in flagrante delicto*. Matthew Paris narrates the ghastly tale of Godfrey de Millers, a knight from Norfolk, who secretly entered the house of John Brito at night, intent on sleeping with his daughter, but he was seized in a trap by hidden men, and hung upside down by his feet from beams, his legs splayed. His genitals were then cut off, and he was thrown out of the house half-dead. However, in this case, it was decided that this 'punishment squad' had exceeded the bounds of acceptable reaction, and all of those involved were prosecuted and convicted. The king, 'saddened to sighs and tears' by Godfrey's fate, ordered it to be proclaimed law that 'no one dare to mutilate the genitals of adulterers'.[68] Nevertheless, the theme of the cuckolded husband who castrates the priest who has slept with his wife occurs in a number of thirteenth-century *fabliaux* and the book of legal 'customs' of Toulouse has an illustration of a public castration for sexual crime.[69] In Catalonia, the husband's right was restricted to holding the woman in private prison. A fourteenth-century sentence even set out the conditions of detention: the size of her room was specified; she was to have a straw sack to sleep on, and a blanket to cover herself; there was to be a hole through which she might 'expel the natural discharge of her belly'; and there was to be a window through which specified amounts of food were to be given to her, 18 oz of bread per day and as much water as she wanted.[70]

Examples of kings pardoning husbands for killing their wives' lovers can be found in thirteenth-century France and fifteenth-century Naples,[71] but the later fifteenth-century trend seems to have been towards reluctance to allow such concessions to marital authority. A case in Normandy in 1476 is instructive. Jacques de Brezé, the seneschal of Normandy, went hunting with his wife, the illegitimate daughter of the former king, Charles VII. Also in the hunting party was Pierre de la Vergne, a gentleman from Poitou. At the end of the day, they dined, and Jacques retired to a room by himself to sleep. His wife took Pierre to her room. When this was reported to Jacques by his *maître d'hôtel*, he grabbed a sword, broke down the door to his wife's bedroom and killed Pierre on the spot with sword-blows to his head and body. His wife fled into the children's bedroom, but Jacques dragged her out, and, as she knelt pleading for her life, plunged the sword into her chest. Jacques was arrested, convicted and ordered to pay a huge fine of 100,000 *écus*.[72]

By 1500, with private war restricted and with revenge a less attractive option, state-inflicted violence was about to undergo another period of significant growth. In the sixteenth century, the number of executions rose strongly and their ceremonial aspects became more elaborate. As Muchembled argues for northern France, the centralising force of monarchy generated obedience by intensifying repression. Such too seems the pattern among the principalities of Renaissance Italy.[73] Despite the alleged displacement of religious authority by the secular state in this period, punishment continued to show strong associations with penance, especially on the scaffold, where religion intensified as executions were seen as sermons, as convicts gave edifying speeches, as the crowd accepted accidents as miracles, and as convicts were allowed to confess their sins before being sent to divine judgment. Foucault's dictum, that execution was a way of exercising power, as well as 'mere' repression, needs to be amended: it was also a way for both convict and crowd to regularise their relation to God.

Notes

1. *Joannis Dlugossii . . . Historiae Polonicae libri XII*, in *Joannis Dlugosz senioris canonici cracoviensis opera omnia*, ed. A. Przezdziecki (14 vols, Cracow, 1867–87), XII, pp. 132–3.
2. M. Foucault, *Discipline and Punish: The Birth of the Prison* (Harmondsworth, 1979), pp. 23–5.
3. Reviews by H. White, *American Historical Review*, 82 (1977), pp. 605–6; J. Goldstein, *Journal of Modern History*, 51 (1977), pp. 116–18; C. Geertz, *New York Review of Books*, 26 January 1978, pp. 3–6.
4. J. Dunn, in *Times Higher Education Supplement*, 25 May 2001.
5. E. Peters, 'Prison before the prison: the ancient and medieval worlds', in *The Oxford History of the Prison*, ed. N. Morris and D.J. Rothman (New York and

Oxford, 1998), pp. 25–41; 'Liber sextus decretalium Bonifacii Papae VIII', V.9.3, in *Corpus iuris canonici*, ed. A. Friedberg (Leipzig, 1881), II, col. 1091.

6. A. Porteau-Bitker, 'L'emprisonnement dans le droit laïque du Moyen Age', *RHDF* 46 (1968), pp. 389–405.

7. *ORF*, I, p. 100.

8. C. Gauvard, M. Rouse, R. Rouse and A. Soman, 'Le Châtelet de Paris au début du XVe siècle d'après les fragments d'un registre d'écrous de 1412', *Bibliothèque de l'Ecole des chartes*, 157 (1999), pp. 573–8.

9. R. Muchembled, *Le temps des supplices: de l'obéissance sous les rois absolus, XVe–XVIIIe siècle* (Paris, 1992), p. 44.

10. Archivio di Stato, Bologna, Comune, Soprastanti alle prigioni.

11. Porteau-Bitker, 'L'emprisonnement', p. 411.

12. *Constitutions y altres drets de Cathalunya*, vol. 1 (Barcelona, 1704), p. 187; *Le livre 'Potentia' des Etats de Provence (1391–1523)*, ed. G. Gouiran and M. Hebert (Paris, 1997), pp. 316–17.

13. *Costituto di Siena*, I, pp. 275–6; *Archives municipales de Bordeaux*, vol. 5, *Livres des coutumes*, ed. H. Barckhausen (Bordeaux, 1890), pp. 676–8.

14. *Cartulaire municipal de la ville de Lyon*, ed. M-C. Guigue (Lyon, 1876), pp. 110–1.

15. B. Geremek, *The Margins of Society in Late Medieval Paris* (Cambridge, 1987), p. 18; H. Manikowska, 'The Florentine communal prison – le Stinche – in the fourteenth century', *Acta Poloniae Historica* 71 (1995); *The Towns of Italy in the later Middle Ages*, ed. T. Dean (Manchester, 2000), pp. 27, 32; R.B. Pugh, *Imprisonment in Medieval England* (Cambridge, 1970), p. 331; *Documents inédits concernant la ville et le siège du bailliage d'Amiens*, ed. E. Maugis (2 vols, Amiens, 1914), p. 74.

16. A. Murray, *Suicide in the Middle Ages*, vol. I, *The Violent against Themselves* (Oxford, 1998), pp. 80, 81, 83–4, 100, 101, 156–7, 181–2, 192, 239; H. Summerson, 'Suicide and the fear of the gallows', *Journal of Legal History* 21 (2000).

17. *ORF*, VIII, p. 309; Manikowska, 'The Florentine communal prison'.

18. *Les fortunes et adversitez de Jean Regnier*, ed. E. Droz (Paris, 1923), pp. 28–47, 84–5, 98–9.

19. N. Gonthier, *Le châtiment du crime au Moyen Age* (Rennes, 1998), p. 163.

20. E. Gessler, 'Mulier suspensa', *Revue belge de philologie et d'histoire* (1939), p. 982.

21. A. Zorzi, 'Le esecuzioni delle condanne a morte a Firenze nel tardo medioevo tra repressione penale e cerimoniale pubblico', in *Simbolo e realtà della vita urbana nel tardo medioevo*, ed. M. Miglio and G. Lombardi (Rome, 1993).

22. *Diario ferrarese dall'anno 1409 sino al 1502 di autori incerti*, ed. G. Pardi, *Rerum italicarum scriptores*, 2nd edn, vol. 24, pt 7 (Bologna, 1928–38), pp. 157, 161, 162, 170, 173, 199, 200, 245, 259, 265 283.

23. A. Zorzi, 'La politique criminelle en Italie (XIIIe–XVIIe siècles)', *Crime, histoire et sociétés* 2:2 (1998), pp. 95–6.

24. R. Lavoie, 'Les statistiques criminelles et le visage du justicier: justice royale et justice seigneuriale en Provence au Moyen Age', *Provence historique* 28 (1979), pp. 15, 18.

25. P. Spierenburg, *The Spectacle of Suffering: Executions and the Evolution of Repression* (Cambridge, 1984), pp. 153–65.

26. J. Sweeney, 'High justice in fifteenth-century Normandy: the prosecution of Sandrin Bourel', *Journal of Medieval History* 10 (1984).

27. Muchembled, *Le temps des supplices*, pp. 49, 57.

28. *Mercanti scrittori: ricordi nella Firenze tra Medioevo e Rinascimento*, ed. V. Branca (Milan, 1986), pp. 23–4; D.S. Chambers and T. Dean, *Clean Hands and Rough Justice: An Investigating Magistrate in Renaissance Italy* (Ann Arbor, 1997), p. 244.

29. J. Heers, *Gilles de Rais* (Paris, 1997), p. 204; N. Gonthier, *Cris de haine et rites d'unité: La violence dans les villes, XIIIe–XVIe siècle* (n.p., 1992), p. 189.

30. *Costituto di Siena*, II, p. 402.

31. Spierenburg, *Spectacle of Suffering*, p. 58.

32. *Correspondance de la mairie de Dijon*, ed. J. Garnier (3 vols, Dijon, 1868–70), I, p. 90.

33. Foucault, *Discipline and Punish*, pp. 59–62.

34. C. Gauvard, 'Pendre et dépendre à la fin du Moyen Age: les exigences d'un rituel judiciaire', in *Riti e rituali nelle società medievali*, ed. J. Chiffoleau, L. Martines and A. Paravicini Baglioni (Spoleto, 1994), pp. 204–5; Gonthier, *Châtiment du crime*, pp. 188–9.

35. *Diario ferrarese*, pp. 162, 175.

36. *Cronache senesi*, ed. A. Lisini and F. Iacometti, *Rerum italicarum scriptores*, 2nd edn, vol. 15, pt 6 (Bologna, 1931–9), pp. 350, 583, 649, 653–4; 'Diario d'anonimo fiorentino dall'anno 1358 al 1389', ed. A. Gherardi, in *Cronache dei secoli XIII e XIV* (Florence, 1876), pp. 382–3; *Cronaca fiorentina di Marchionne di Coppo Stafani*, ed. N. Rodolico, *Rerum italicarum scriptores*, 2nd edn, vol. 30, pt 1 (Città di Castello, 1903 – Bologna, 1955), section 834, pp. 357–8.

37. 'Diario d'anonimo fiorentino', pp. 400, 525–6.

38. L-T. Maes, 'La peine de mort dans le droit criminel de Malines', *RHDF* 28 (1950), p. 382–4; M.K. Schüssler, 'German crime in the later Middle Ages: A statistical analysis of the Nuremberg Outlawry Books, 1285–1400', *Criminal Justice History* 13 (1992), p. 30; Gonthier, *Cris de haine*, p. 191.

39. A. Zorzi, 'The judicial system in Florence in the fourteenth and fifteenth centuries', in *Crime, Society and the Law in Renaissance Italy*, p. 54; G.S. Pene Vidari, 'Sulla criminalià e sui banni del comune di Ivrea nei primi anni della dominazione sabauda (1313–1347)', *Bollettino storico-bibliografico subalpino* 68 (1970), pp. 204–5.

40. Muchembled, *Le temps des supplices*, p. 57.

41. Schüssler, 'Nuremberg Outlawry Books', p. 31.

42. *Najstarsze Ksiegii i rachunki miasta Krakowa od r. 1300 do 1400*, ed. F. Piekosinski and J. Szujski (Cracow, 1878), pp. 3–46, 55; *Early Records of the Burgh of Aberdeen, 1317, 1398–1407*, ed. W.C. Dickinson (Edinburgh, 1957). See also the extended discussion of the Cracow exile registers in H. Zaremska, *Les bannis au Moyen Age* (Paris, 1996), pp. 125–60.

43. Gonthier, *Châtiment du crime*, pp. 135–6.

44. Zaremska, *Les bannis au Moyen Age*, pp. 163–71.

45. *ORF*, vol. 8, pp. 54, 96; vol. 20, p. 135; Gonthier, *Châtiment du crime*, pp. 130–1.

46. *Early Records of the Burgh of Aberdeen*, p. 217.
47. *ORF*, VIII, p. 130.
48. Muchembled, *Le temps des supplices*, pp. 28, 39, 48, 82.
49. *ORF*, vol. 20, pp. 129–36, 142–51.
50. *Statuti della città di Roma del secolo XIV*, ed. C. Re (Rome, 1883), pp. 106–17.
51. Lavoie, 'Les statistiques criminelles et le visage du justicier', pp. 6–9; Zorzi, 'La politique criminelle en Italie', p. 93.
52. P. Roqué Ferrer, 'L'infrazione della legge a Cagliari dal 1340 al 1380', *Quaderni sardi di storia* 5 (1985–6).
53. P. Schuster, 'Il funzionamento quotidiano della giustizia nel tardo Medioevo: I registri contabili come fonte di storia criminale', *Quaderni storici* 102 (1999), pp. 768–9; and see T. Dean, 'Criminal justice in mid-fifteenth-century Bologna' in *Crime, Society and the Law in Renaissance Italy*, ed. T. Dean and K.J.P. Lowe (Cambridge, 1994), p. 26.
54. Schuster, 'Il funzionamento quotidiano della giustizia nel tardo Medioevo', pp. 750–7; Dean, 'Criminal justice in mid-fifteenth-century Bologna', pp. 28–9.
55. Zaremska, *Les bannis au Moyen Age*, pp. 111–14.
56. M.I. Rodriguez Flores, *El perdono real en Castilla (siglos XIII–XVIII)* (Salamanca, 1971), pp. 47, 66–70.
57. Spierenburg, *Spectacle of Suffering*, pp. 46–52, 61–3.
58. E. Cohen, '"To die a criminal for the public good": the execution ritual in late medieval Paris', in *Law, Custom and the Social Fabric in Medieval Europe*, ed. B.S. Bachrach and D. Nicholas (Kalamazoo, 1990).
59. P. Braun, 'Variations sur la potence et le bourreau: A propos d'un adversaire de la peine de mort en 1361', in *Histoire du droit social: Mélanges en hommage à Jean Imbert*, ed. J-L. Harouel (Paris, 1989), p. 107.
60. *Documents inédits concernant la ville et le siège du bailliage d'Amiens*, ed. E. Maugis (2 vols, Amiens and Paris, 1914), II, p. 168; Heers, *Gilles de Rais*, pp. 193–4; P. Lemercier, 'Une curiosité judiciaire au Moyen Age: la grâce par marriage subséquent', *RHDF* 34 (1956); P. Texier, 'Les fonctions du pèlerinage imposé dans les lettres de rémission du XIVe siècle', *Mémoires de la Société pour l'histoire du droit et des institutions des anciens pays bourguignons, comtois et romands* 45 (1988), p. 428.
61. D. Balestracci, 'Il gioco dell'esecuzione capitale: note e proposte interpretative', in *Gioco e giustizia nell'Italia di commune*, ed. G. Ortalli (Treviso and Rome, 1993).
62. *Costituto di Siena*, II, p. 264.
63. G. Cozzi, *Repubblica di Venezia e stati italiani: politica e giustizia dal secolo XVI al secolo XVIII* (Turin, 1982), pp. 84–5.
64. *Select Cases in the Court of King's Bench under Richard II, Henry IV and Henry V*, ed. G.O. Sayles (London, 1971), pp. 91–2.
65. G. Brucker, *The Society of Renaissance Florence* (New York, 1971), pp. 111–13.
66. Braun, 'Variations sur la potence et le bourreau', pp. 105–6.
67. *Statuti di Perugia*, II, p. 60.
68. *Matthaei Parisiensis monachi Sancti Albani chronica majora*, ed. H. Richards Luard (London, 1880), V, pp. 34–5. Note, however, that the chronicler has the king adding a qualification – *nisi pro conjuge* – that would seem to vitiate the main clause of this law.

69. *Fabliaux* with this theme include *Le prêtre teint* and *Le prêtre crucifié*. For the illustration: Gonthier, *Cris de haine*, p. 188.
70. *Constitutions y altres drets de Cathalunya*, vol. I, p. 177.
71. C. Gauvard, *'De grace especial': Crime, état et société en France à la fin du Moyen Age* (Paris, 1991), p. 818; Vespasiano da Bisticci, *Le Vite*, ed. A. Greco (2 vols, Florence, 1970–6), I, pp. 94–5.
72. *Deux chroniques de Rouen*, ed. A. Heron (Rouen and Paris, 1900), pp. 102–3.
73. Chambers and Dean, *Clean Hands and Rough Justice*.

chapter 7

CRIME IN LITERATURE

Two tales about robbers and abbots open this chapter on crime and literature. The first comes from Giovanni Boccaccio's fourteenth-century collection of short stories, the *Decameron*, and the second from the fifteenth-century *Gest of Robin Hood*.[1] These are, of course, very different types of literature: prose and verse, Italian and English, authored and anonymous; however, I wish to use their convergent representations of bandits to explore the various ways that literature and history may come together.

Boccaccio's *Decameron* is organised as a series of one hundred tales told over a period of ten days by a group of ten young Florentines. Each day a fresh theme for the stories is chosen. On Day Ten the theme is liberality, and the character Elissa tells the following story of Ghino di Tacco, a noble Sienese bandit of the late thirteenth century (see above, p. 33–4). The Abbot of Cluny was travelling from Rome to Siena in order to take a cure at the baths for a stomach complaint. Passing too close to Ghino's band of brigands, the abbot was captured, along with all his servants, horses and belongings, and taken to Ghino's castle. There he was questioned regarding his destination and the purpose of his journey. When Ghino heard of the abbot's illness, he decided to cure him himself, putting him alone in a small, dark room and feeding him with nothing more than bread and wine. Within a few days, the abbot recovered. Ghino then reunited him with his servants and laid on a lavish banquet for them all. He explained to the abbot that he had been forced into brigandage not through love of evil, but through the need to defend himself against his political enemies. He said that the abbot was free to go, but invited him to take or leave as many of his possessions as he wished. Impressed by this generosity, the abbot took only the bare necessities, leaving all his other goods to Ghino, and returned to Rome. There he praised Ghino as a fine physician and, using Ghino's own argument that his actions were political, not criminal, persuaded the pope to forgive him.

The earliest of the surviving Robin Hood ballads, called the 'Gest', combines three distinct stories. The opening story, of Robin Hood and the poor knight, is intercut with two others: in one, Little John steals all the sheriff's money and silver plate, and when the sheriff pursues him into the forest, he is captured by Robin Hood; in the other, the king, disguised as an abbot, seeks out Robin Hood in the forest in order to halt the outlaws' plundering of his deer, and ends up taking Robin into his service. The first story also involves an abbot. Robin instructs his men to go out and bring in some captive to 'dine' with him, memorably telling them to target only abbots, bishops, earls and haughty knights, and to spare women and peasant farmers. From their look-out point, Robin Hood's men spy a knight riding through Barnesdale, Yorkshire. They 'invite' him to dinner. Robin is curious about this knight, on account of his disconsolate and unkempt appearance. He questions the knight about his wealth. The knight claims to be penniless, having mortgaged his lands to the abbot of St Mary's, York. He needed the money, he says, in order to release his son from the consequences of killing a knight at a tournament. Robin orders Little John to unpack the knight's baggage to see if he is telling the truth. When it turns out that he is, Robin lends him £400 to redeem his mortgage. One of Robin's men challenges this act of charity, and is told that 'it is alms to help a gentle knight, that is fallen in poverty'. The loan is also seen by Robin as a service to the Virgin Mary, and the knight, re-clothed and re-equipped by Robin, is called 'Our Lady's messenger'. Although the knight is now able to repay the mortgage on his lands, the abbot refuses to discharge it, arguing that the deadline had expired; but the knight insists on making the repayment, pouring the coins onto a table.

Despite the differences in genre, we have here two tales that share a common plot: high-status travellers are captured by a notorious bandit, but when he discovers their actual plights, he assists them, the one to recover physical health, the other to recover financial well-being. The aim of this chapter is to offer an explanation for this common plot. Doing this will involve first an examination of historians' uses of medieval crime literature, and then a survey, drawing more heavily on literary theory, of other possible approaches.

Historians and literature: verification

What medieval historians have usually done with medieval crime literature is to look for the correspondences with history, as if historical and literary evidence were mutually reinforcing, each confirming the veracity or verisimilitude of the other. For example, court records have been used to verify the plot and details of *The Tale of Gamelyn*, a story from mid-fourteenth-century England.[2] This is the story of an aggressive inheritance dispute between two brothers. The elder, wicked brother disinherits his younger brother, the eponymous hero of the tale, and uses against him all the corrupted might of the judicial system: the sheriff and his posse, the corrupt judge, the bribed jury. Gamelyn retreats into the forest, the greenwood, and joins a band of outlaws; and it is through using these forces that he eventually overcomes the corrupt court in a violent show-down which ends in the hanging of the judge, the sheriff and the twelve jurors. The violence in the poem is notable for being 'graphically and even gleefully told', the plot being 'punctuated by the sound of oaken staves thwacking ribs and cracking bones'.[3] Kaeuper confirms from legal records the likelihood of the various elements of this tale: the form and level of violence, the outlaw band, the bribed and browbeaten jurors, the oppressive sheriff and corrupt judge, even the unofficial trial and execution of judge and jury. All these could and did happen, though not together. Where historical and literary sources differ, Kaeuper harmonises them. For example, the *Tale* clearly approves of its hero's use of violence and expects no help from the law, whereas legal records condemn or complain of similar self-help and expect injustices to be set right by the law. These, he says, are simply two sides of the same coin: the same disputants who use violence and threats are likely to take their adversaries to court, as complementary means of pursuing a dispute.

This desire to use historical records to verify features of contemporary literature has found its most fertile ground in the Robin Hood ballads. In this case, it should be acknowledged, the purpose of such an approach has been to establish a date of composition and an original audience for ballads that appear for the first time in printed versions in the late fifteenth and early sixteenth centuries. However, the fifteenth-century audience was not the original audience for these tales. Almost certainly the original stories were later adapted or re-interpreted for new audiences, so historians have sought to find the original audience through archaic elements preserved in the texts.

For over thirty years, the belief in a real Robin Hood was sustained by two arguments, one from within the text of the ballads, and one from outside it. First it was argued that the topographical precision of the *Gest*, its accurate knowledge of places and place names in this corner of Yorkshire, was an authentication for the ballad as a whole. Second, it was pointed out that a number of other literary outlaws, both medieval and modern, were based on real, historical persons: by induction, this could be true of Robin Hood too. These two props supported a long endeavour to align various internal elements of the story with external elements of social or political history in order to solve the puzzle of the *Gest*'s origins. This puzzle is thus cast as one of transfer from reality to liter- ature: a real Robin Hood gave rise to the literary character, 'posthumously transformed', in the words of Dobson and Taylor, 'into the stereotyped role of the "social bandit"'. Thus the issues in the poem of freedom and resistance to Church landowners, together with the bandits' attitude to the king (a saviour, not an oppressor), have been seen as indicating authorship in the later fourteenth century, a period of peasant unrest and confrontation with the judicial and political authorities (seen as corrupt, not legitimate, delegates of royal power). However, other alignments have also been discovered. Maddicott has found in an earlier decade of the century, the 1330s, a real abbot of St Mary's, York, who lent money to knights, and a real, corrupt sheriff of Nottingham. This was also the period, he reminds us, of real gangs active in the Midlands, one of which left a posthumous reputation for righting the wrongs perpetrated by royal justice ('Folville's laws').[4] It was also the period of 'songs' or poems of protest at other aspects of royal government, for example taxation. Both of these fourteenth-century 'solutions' have been challenged in turn by the proponents of an origin even further back in time: the power of the sheriff, monastic lending, distraint of knighthood, all suggest, it is argued, that the *Gest* originated in the thirteenth century, not later. This argument is supported by the fact that a Yorkshire outlaw called Robert Hood is recorded in 1230.

Objections can be made to each of these hypotheses. It can be argued in each case that the alignment of internal and external elements is unconvincing: thus, the absence in the poem of any reference to the prob- lems of serfdom is used to break the supposed link to late fourteenth- century unrest. Alternatively, it can be argued that a given internal element does not refer to any specific period: for example, it is claimed that sheriffs were unpopular throughout the later Middle Ages and so cannot 'prove' an origin in the thirteenth century.[5]

Much of the discussion of the early ballads of Robin Hood has concen- trated on attempts to determine the social character of the 'original' audience. Again, in order to solve this problem, certain elements of the ballads are aligned with the interests or activities of social groups. Thus, in one reading, the fact that the outlaws poach with bows and arrows, not dogs, suggests that the ballads voice the interests of the peasantry. Conversely, in another reading, the topics of the *Gest* – the redemption of a mortgage, hospitality, and so forth – are taken as 'knightly'. In a third reading, the urban elements of the ballads are used to argue for an audience among the mobile urban population of wage-labourers and servants.[6] However, as has recently been argued, we do not have to choose between these interpretations. Once we understand the composite nature of the text of the *Gest*, it is suggested, we can see that its constituent tales addressed different audiences. There was no single, original audience. Robin Hood, as he first appears to us, was already a hero for all classes.[7]

A variant of this approach has been to compare elements of the bandit group in literature and legal records. Here the supposition is that the author/s of the ballads would have drawn on knowledge of real outlaws and incorporated 'something of the organisation, tactics, patrons and personnel of bands', while changing the character of the leader, in order 'to make him more liked than feared'.[8] Hanawalt claims that there are close resemblances between real and fictional gangs of outlaws in their personnel, rewards and techniques. Thus Robin Hood sends his followers out in twos and threes to prey on travellers, as real bandits did; his band included middling peasants and rural artisans, as real bands did; and he divided the spoils and used the castle of a friendly knight, as real bandit leaders did. Unfortunately, the evidence points rather more strongly to the differences. Robin Hood's band contains no woman (Maid Marian was a sixteenth-century addition), no cleric (likewise Friar Tuck) and no kinsmen. Medieval gangs would have contained all of these. Robin's robberies also netted far larger sums than real gangs': 'Robin Hood confines his thefts to high-value, glamour items, whereas real bandits focused more on low-value household goods and food.' Finally, real gangs attacked precisely those social groups whom Robin exempted, namely peasants and women.

For many years, the debate seemed to have stuck in this condition: those looking for historical confirmation of the ballads had plenty of options to choose from. More recent developments have offered a different solution. First, the name 'Robehood' was found being applied in government records to an outlaw in Berkshire in 1262, either as an alias or as a common legal name for an outlaw. The probability grows that Robin Hood was always a fiction. Second, Dobson and Taylor have come to approach the *Gest* as an archaeological excavation, not as a text with a single author at a single moment in time. 'We should expect to find a confused series of different chronological layers', they insist. In effect, they apply reception theory to this text, reminding us that the existing version is a reworking of earlier tales, adapted for a fifteenth-century audience. Some of these earlier tales were not originally about Robin Hood at all: it has long been known that the story of Robin Hood and the Potter derives from a tale told of an earlier outlaw, Eustace the Monk, and it is possible that some elements of the *Gest* also derive from other outlaw tales. Peter Coss, for example, has attempted to dismantle the composite *Gest* into its constituent tales.[9] In the reworking of these tales, however, some archaic or displaced elements have remained, perhaps including the location of Robin's gang in Barnesdale. It is these displacements and reworkings that may be held responsible for the major anomaly of the whole Robin Hood series: that a sheriff of Nottingham should concern himself with an outlaw in Yorkshire. The search for a real Robin Hood has thus been brought to an end.[10] One literary scholar has dismissed historians' 'oversimple view that literature offers a straightforward reflection of the society that produced it', reminding us that poets 'select, distort and magnify', and are influenced by literary conventions.[11] Fittingly, however, it was a historian who first condemned the 'recurring effort to manufacture an authentic, documented individual called Robin Hood'.[12]

History and literature: some theory

This 'oversimple' approach to the study of history and literature has provided an easy target for literary historians. Using literature as a form of supplementary evidence is a common method: this, after all, is what I have done in previous chapters, where, for example, I have used literary descriptions of prison to confirm the unhealthiness of conditions in medieval gaols (above, p. 123) or stories centring on sodomy to confirm the unmentionable nature of this sin and crime (above, p. 58). However, this seems an insufficient response to both the fictionality and the literary qualities of these texts. Given the richness and complexity of theoretical discussions in the twentieth century of the relation of literary text to context, it is possible in this bandit-focused chapter to explore only some of these approaches, at various points on the critical spectrum. At one end, we find structuralist analyses which deny the role of social context or authorial biography in explicating meaning from literary texts. The author's life is irrelevant to the meaning of his text. The death of the author is pronounced. Mirroring this, at the other end, are poststructuralist theories, which collapse the distinction between literary text and socio-historical context. In this view, there are only texts and intertexts, and no 'reality' outside them to stabilise their meanings. There is an incompatibility here with traditional historical discourse, with its grounding in authorial intention and social context in its handling of aesthetic objects. As one literary historian has said, 'For historians the text exists as a function or articulation of context. In this sense, historians work at the juncture of the symbiosis between text and context.'[13] Other literary approaches are more compatible, for example, reception theory, with its stress on the parts played equally by author, reader and text, in the production of meaning; or some forms of intertextuality, in which meaning is established only through explicit or implicit reference to other texts. The rest of this chapter attempts to explore the new understanding of our bandit stories that use of these techniques allows us to achieve. In doing so, it will offer an explanation to the puzzle stated at the beginning of this chapter: why do the Robin Hood ballads share a plot with Boccaccio's tale of Ghino di Tacco?

Intertextuality

Now compare both the tales with which this chapter began with the following story.[14]

A bandit of the worst sort, a prince of thieves, preyed on the region where he lived, robbing and killing many people. One day a devout abbot got on his horse and rode out to where this robber and his companions lived. Spying him from afar, they rode out to seize his horse and clothes. The abbot asked their leader what he wanted.

'I want that horse and all your clothes.'

'I have ridden this horse and worn these clothes for some time,' the abbot conceded. 'It isn't right that only I should enjoy God's goods, so I would like to give them to you, if you need them.'

'We'll sell them today so that we can buy bread and wine.'

'Why do you expose yourself to such danger? Come with me to my monastery, and whatever you want I shall get for you.'

'I can't eat your beans and kale, or drink your rotten wine and beer.'

'I shall give you white bread, the best wine, and as many dishes of meat and fish as you desire.'

The robber was won over and agreed to do what the abbot wanted, for a while. The abbot put him in a fine room in the monastery, with a large fire, a beautiful bed and smooth coverings, and assigned a monk to prepare everything he wanted. But the monk was under orders that, after the robber had eaten splendidly, he was to eat in his presence only bread and water. After some days, the robber, seeing the monk's diet, began to think that he must have committed many sins to be doing such harsh penance, and asked him if he had killed men, given that he afflicted himself every day. 'No,' came the reply. Had he committed adultery or fornication?

'No, I've never touched a woman.'

'So what have you done?'

'I do these things, fasting, praying and other works of penance, so as to earn God's favour.'

The robber was struck by this reply, and began to wonder: 'What an unhappy wretch I am. I've done so many crimes – thefts, homicides, adulteries, sacrilege – and never fasted for a day. Yet this innocent monk does such penance.' And he called the abbot, fell at his feet, and asked to be received into the monastery as a brother. And he came to outdo all the others in his abstinence and devotion. Such is the power of good example.

This comes from the 'exemplary tales' (*exempla*) of a great thirteenth-century preacher, Jacques de Vitry. There were many collections of *exempla* made in later medieval Europe. They were intended for the use of preachers, to enable them to adapt the style and content of their sermons to their audiences. The *exempla* in Jacques de Vitry's sermons served as early and influential models: this tale of a bandit was copied and adapted by many later compilers.

The argument here starts from the observation that both Boccaccio's novella and the anonymous Robin Hood ballad have the *exemplum* as their intertext. Their meaning is to be grasped through the creative tension between literary text and *exemplum*. This is more easily demonstrated for Boccaccio's bandit tale. In writing *The Decameron*, Boccaccio utilised, often in a parodic way, many existing forms of narrative, and it has been said that 'no form of medieval short story-telling is as constantly present in *The Decameron* as exemplary literature'.[15] The Boccaccio story is quite clearly a simple inversion of Jacques de Vitry's exemplary tale. In the latter, the abbot seeks out the bandit, willingly surrenders his belongings, and persuades him to undergo a spiritual cure. Boccaccio reverses these elements. The abbot falls into the bandits' hands, refuses to give up his property, and undergoes enforced physical healing. The result is an indictment of contemporary prelates for having abandoned Christ's message of evangelical charity. The abbot has to learn charity from the most unlikely source. As in Boccaccio's other parodies of exemplary literature, motivations and rewards are secularised: the abbot is cured of a physical, not a spiritual, ailment, and Ghino di Tacco earns his reward in this life, not the next. It is on account of this secularisation of the *exemplum* that Boccaccio's tales have been called 'anti-*exempla*'. From this argument, we can proceed in two directions: towards the connections between religious literature and crime, and towards those between secular literature and crime.

Religious literature and crime

To grasp how the Robin Hood ballad also alludes to *exempla*, we have to place Jacques de Vitry's tale in the broader context of other *exempla* about bandits and robbers. These fall into four different types of story:

The conversion or salvation of robbers
This can come about through the intervention of a holy figure, such as an abbot or hermit, but usually happens through the robber's devotion to

the Virgin Mary. The most elaborate version of this story comes from another early thirteenth-century collection of *exempla*, that of Caesarius of Heisterbach.[16] Caesarius locates the story near the north Italian city of Trent. A robber, who had been plaguing the area, captures a monk, believing him to be carrying money. As he is led to the bandit's lair, the monk questions the bandit about his past and his religious beliefs. 'Your hair's already going white. Don't you fear for your soul?' asks the monk. 'No more than a beast,' comes the brusque reply. 'I have no hope for the salvation of my soul, as I know it is lost,' the bandit declares. 'What if I showed you a path to salvation? Would you let me?' The robber accepts, and is taught by the monk that on Saturdays he should fast and refrain from evil. He follows this teaching for some time, but as a consequence is captured one Saturday, offering no resistance. But quickly the Virgin Mary starts to work in his favour. The judges offer to banish him, but the bandit chooses to die, saying 'It's better that I pay for my sins now than later'; in other words, to pay by punishment of the body on earth rather than punishment of the soul in hell. He confesses his sins, is beheaded and buried. But that very night, five female figures – phantoms, the civic guards thought – dig up the body, cover it with a purple cloth and carry it to the city gate. One of the ladies, whose name was Mary, says to the guards, 'Tell your bishop that he is to bury my chaplain, whom you have beheaded, with honour, in the place I shall indicate.' The bishop does as he is told, in admiration and fear, burying the corpse not as that of a robber, but of a Christian martyr.

Numerous other *exempla* contain this essential element of the robber saved either from the gallows or from hell. The salvific agent is often his devotion to the Virgin Mary, combined with confession of sins and contrition. In one story the saint takes the weight of the robber's body as it hangs from the gallows, and thus preserves his life (see Illustration 11). In another, the robber is beheaded, but his head carries on talking, crying out to the Virgin Mary to be allowed confession, until a priest arrives to receive it. In a third, a hermit is seduced by the devil to leave his cell and join a bandit gang; during five years of robbing and killing he nevertheless maintains his devotion to the Virgin Mary, and she eventually appears to him and shocks him into confessing his sins and returning in great contrition to the religious life.[17] Such stories are to be understood as allegories, and some of them spell out the religious significance of each character and action. The thief stands for the devil; the robber's victim stands for the Christian believer who is assailed by temptation to sin. But even minimal devotion to the Virgin Mary can overcome the devil. That this caused some perplexity among sermon audiences is suggested by those *exempla* that address directly the issue of the excessive clemency of allowing robbers into heaven. This problematic redemption of the apparently unredeemable was a feature of Marian 'rescue stories'.[18] Why should anyone lead a virtuous life if they can behave like these thieves but ensure their salvation through minimal devotion and a scaffold confession? The authors of *exempla* provide two answers: first, that God wishes to damn none of his Christians, no matter how great a sinner, if he dies in great repentance; second, that God prefers sinners to be punished on earth as penitents than in hell as unrepentant.[19]

This discussion has clear connections to Robin Hood. The most obvious clue is provided by the role of the Virgin Mary. We have seen how *exempla* stress devotion to this saint as the one practice able to save the irredeemable sinner. It is this context that therefore explains one of the puzzling elements of the *Gest of Robin Hood*: Robin's devotion to the Virgin Mary.

> Robin loved Our dear Lady:
> For doubt of deadly sin
> Would he never company harm
> That any woman was in.[20]

Literary and social historians have tended to minimise this element of the ballads. Some treat it merely as evidence of the popularity of the cult of the Virgin Mary.[21] Though Robin's devotion is presented as sincere, Gray sees it as mixing seriousness with parody and irony. He points out that Robin's expression of devotion is followed by Little John's 'enthusiastic words on the outlaw life', and that when Robin's men rob a monk of St Mary's they call him 'Our Lady's messenger'.[22] What neither has recognised is the intertextual meaning: despite the irony, Robin is being presented as a redeemable bandit. His devotion is, to use a poststructuralist concept, 'already written' in the *exemplum* and is to be understood by reference to the 'good' bandits of the *exempla*.

The other elements of the exemplary bandit tales also have meaning for Robin Hood, as we shall see.

Tricks used by thieves and robbers

Exempla present us with a veritable catalogue of *modus operandi*. Thus, we find thieves who pass themselves off as the victims of theft and accuse the real owners of stealing; who pretend to be messengers from husbands and persuade wives to entrust them with valuable property; who dress up as monks so as to approach wary travellers without arousing suspicion; who dress up as women and play on popular superstitions regarding sorcery; who act in concert to distract the attention of people in a market so as to make off with their goods; and who, when pursued, know how to trick their pursuers.[23]

Protection against thieves

Divine intervention or miraculous events are the only protection. This is shown in such stories as those of the thief struck down half-dead as he tried to steal part of a silver image of the Virgin and child from a church, of the angels who protect a monk from robbers in the forest, of the priest who uses a crucifix to expel robbers from his church, or of the church robbers who made off with a crucifix but got caught in marshland and were captured by their pursuers.[24]

Thieves quarrel among themselves

A prime example here is a story that another collector of *exempla*, Etienne de Bourbon, tells from his own experience as a confessor. Like the abbot in Jacques de Vitry's story, he actively sought out a feared, inveterate robber in order to encourage him to confess his sins. Through an intermediary, the robber arranged a secret meeting with this friar in the forest. When they met, the robber admitted that he hardly slept a wink out of fear of his companions: he did not let them approach him or lie near him, he always went about clothed and armed, and lived in constant fear.[25]

Secular literature

The purpose of conducting this survey of religious tales about crime is that secular literature echoes and reflects many of the same plots and concerns. For example, fear of thieves and their pilfering skills is also suggested in a thirteenth-century fabliau, 'Haimet and Barat', in which a pair of thieves is able to steal eggs from under a nesting magpie, the clothes from a man's back without him noticing, or a ham cooking in a pot by spearing it from the roof with a dart. Nothing can be hidden from such accomplished operators. The same theme is used by Eustache Deschamps in a dialogue poem between two thieves. One of them claims to know three or four 'games' and lists them as cutting purses and belts; stealing coins, cups, goblets and silver spoons; horse rustling; and using a knife to slit open a bag and instantly lift its contents. 'But what do you do if you're caught by a *sergent*?' asks his partner. 'I run, I flee, I go straight to a church,' says the other, and states his confidence in always being able to evade capture and to carry on thieving.[26] Again the church is implicated in the continued activity of a criminal.

The motif of the robber's treacherous accomplices also transferred into secular literature. The best example comes in 'The Pardoner's Tale', in Chaucer's *Canterbury Tales*. Three debauchees ('riotours') observe from the tavern the funeral of an old companion of theirs, killed while drunk by a thief. They swear an oath of brotherhood, to seek out and slay the killer. They set off and by chance they find a treasure of gold florins under a tree. They decide to stand watch over it until night-fall, and one of the three goes into town to fetch some food and drink. The two who remain plot to kill him on his return, so as to have his share of the hoard too; but their companion, hoping to kill them and have all the treasure for himself, brings back poisoned drinks. On his return, he is killed by his partners; and they, drinking unsuspectingly the poisoned wine, die in turn. The tale preserves unadulterated its clear religious content: the tavern and drink are the sources of evil and treachery; selfish individual greed prevents such men from honouring their oaths.

Finally, we can also see further ironic treatment of religious themes in the Robin Hood ballads. Each of the motifs that we have examined in the *exempla* are parodied. Religion does *not* protect its servants from robbery at Robin Hood's hands: a monk of St Mary's is beaten and robbed in the *Gest*. When Robin Hood dons a disguise, it is as a potter incompetently selling his wares at a loss (in *Robin Hood and the Potter*). A quarrel between Robin and Little John breaks out but is soon repaired as Little John, trusting again in the Virgin Mary to keep Robin safe, rescues him from prison (in *Robin Hood and the Monk*). Like Boccaccio's tales that invert *exempla*, the early Robin Hood ballads reflect and ironically comment on an influential literature that had used the figure of the bandit as a representation of sin and of God's power to forgive.

Narratology

The intertextual approach, in some versions at least, can give historians a handle on literature. At the other extreme, structuralist and narratological analysis denies the significance of context in understanding literary texts. At the outset of his ground-breaking *Grammar of the Decameron*, Todorov proclaimed that looking for significance in fields 'as distant [from the text] as the biography of the author or contemporary society' was an error, and insisted that analysis of structural elements was the only proper method for literary studies.[27] As both the *Decameron* and late medieval *exempla* have been subjected to narratological analysis, it is worth surveying these approaches here with a view to gauging their usefulness to historians.

The aim of this sort of structural analysis is to reveal the basic elements of narrative and to show how different stories combine those elements in different ways. This analysis operates at two levels: decomposition and combination.

Todorov *decomposes* Boccaccio's *novelle* into basic narratological elements:

1. He first distinguishes propositions (for example, Ghino di Tacco cures the ailing abbot) and sequences of propositions.
2. He dissolves propositions in turn into proper names (Ghino) and predicates (that is, adjectives and verbs, such as 'to cure').
3. Next, he classifies verbs into three groups: those that modify a situation, those that transgress a law and those that punish a transgression. In the case of Ghino di Tacco, the cure modifies the situation, but the abduction is also a transgression that deserves punishment.

Todorov then notes the *combinations*: the varieties of verb and predicate can be combined in different ways, which Todorov calls 'modes'. He classifies four types of mode: obligatory (something that has to happen), optional (something chosen or desired), conditional (something that can happen only when a condition has been met) and predictive (something that one character predicts will happen). Thus, Ghino opts to cure the abbot, and by doing so to endow him with generosity; while the pope has an obligation to punish Ghino for his detention of the abbot and for his other crimes.

Among the many possible permutations of sequences, Todorov sees those in the *Decameron* falling into two broad groups: attributive sequences, in which a character lacks a specific attribute but gains it through the development of the tale, and law sequences, in which the main character commits an offence or a sin, but manages to escape the due punishment. All of this analysis Todorov then reduces to the level of abstract formulae, using abbreviations (opt, obl) for the various combinations of verb and predicate. To take the story of Ghino di Tacco, it could be expressed simply as an attribute sequence in which the abbot lacks, but then gains, generosity:

$$X - A + YA + (XA)optY \Rightarrow Ya \Rightarrow XA$$

in which   X = the abbot
                Y = Ghino di Tacco
                A = generous
                a = cure
                − = negation
                + = successive action
                ⇒ = implied action

However, the story of Ghino is also a law sequence, as it starts in an ambush and ends in a pardon, so we would need to add the elements of obligation and avoidance of punishment, perhaps in the following way:

$$X - A + YbX + (ZcY)obl + (XA)optY \Rightarrow Ya \Rightarrow XA \Rightarrow ZA(Y - c)$$

in which   Z = the pope
               b = capture
               c = punish

Conventional historians are likely to reject this approach as so abstract as to be unusable. Historians prefer prose. It is perhaps wrong to use Todorov to characterise narratology, as it has many more, less abstract, varieties. However, Todorov's analysis does capture the strongly formalist, non-contextual nature of narratology. This approach is not unusable by historians: if applied to historical rather than literary material, to chronicle accounts of crimes, let us say, its utility would become more apparent. Structural analysis of this kind is simply a way of finding the basic building blocks of a large and varied collection of narratives. However, its rejection of social or biographical context makes it difficult for historians to handle: just as narratology resists history, so historians resist narratology. As Greenblatt puts it, we should not 'decisively separate works of art from the minds and lives of their creators and audiences'.[28]

Brémond's narratological analysis of Jacques de Vitry's *exempla* perhaps offers more to the historian.[29] Brémond follows a different path from Todorov. He starts from a fundamental difference: what distinguishes an *exemplum* from an anecdote is the provision of a lesson in the true path to salvation, in what should be done in order to be saved and what should not be done in order to avoid being damned. Meritorious actions bring rewards, demeritorious ones bring punishment. In Jacques de Vitry's *exempla* punishment or reward usually follows some kind of test. Brémond sees in a majority of these *exempla* a four-part sequence: an introductory setting, a test, then merit leading to reward or demerit leading to punishment. The example of the bandit leader clearly falls into this pattern: the bandit is given a challenge by the abbot – to live for a period in the monastery – and is rewarded first with physical comfort, then with conversion and salvation. It should be noted that this element of test is also present in both Boccacio's tale of Ghino and Robin Hood's initial reception of the poor knight.

What historians would seem to need in their attempts to use literary sources is an analytical tool that is more contextual than narratology allows, and more precise than historicist literary study. Something of this sort has been worked out by Dominick LaCapra who has proposed three main contexts of interpretation: the author, the reception of the text, and ideology.[30] For him the authorial context includes the biographical and social situation of the writer as well as the place of the text within a tradition or genre; the context of reception explores the way that literary texts were read and used by different social groups or in different settings; and the ideological context relates the text to the prevailing discourse/s of contemporary society and their role in supporting power structures. This places the text in relation to three historical contexts – author, readers, class – while also reminding us of the relation of text to its own literary antecedents. Focusing on these elements would certainly prevent historians treating literature as a mirror to the world or a window on it. As we have seen, genre, authorship and readership define the social meaning that we can take from these literary texts. The debate about the original audience for the Robin Hood ballads, for example, was essentially about trying to define the social meaning of these stories: were they addressed to peasants or the aristocratic household? Did they express peasant complaints, or parody courtly romance? We have also seen, to take another example, how the religious ideas of the *exemplum* are inverted and parodied in the secular tale and ballad. In the *exemplum* the whole tale is a metaphor for the evangelical mission of the friars to seek out and rescue even the worst sort of outcast; the tale and ballad invert this by making the bandit the agent for good.

Reception theory

The relationship between fiction and a period's systems of thought has also been examined at the theoretical level by Wolfgang Iser.[31] Fiction and reality are not opposites, he argues, but fiction tells us something *about* reality. It does this by incorporating much that is familiar to the reader – 'familiar territory', he calls it – and then modifying or transforming it in a new direction. This familiar territory can take the form either of social norms or of past literature. Different genres of text have different mixtures of these elements, but they all use elements from existing social systems or thought systems. Literature does not, however, simply copy or replicate those systems, but reacts to them, being triggered by their 'limited ability to cope with the multifariousness of reality'. For the literary historian, then, fiction draws attention to deficiencies and weaknesses in those systems of thought or society. In its period, literature has the function either of challenging a prevailing thought system or of bolstering it.

This theory would seem to fit the three pieces of fiction examined in this chapter. The 'familiar territory' in Boccaccio's tale and the Robin Hood ballad is made up of varying combinations of 'extratextual' reality and past literature. Boccaccio's tale has a higher element of reality: Ghino di Tacco is a documented robber-baron, whereas there was no original Robin Hood and English outlaw gangs had a different composition and a different *modus operandi.* The Robin Hood ballads incorporate more elements of past literature, from the outlaw legends of twelfth- and thirteenth-century England. Despite these different mixtures of elements, both tale and ballad could be said to respond to a deficiency in the prevailing thought system regarding the status of the bandit or outlaw. To evangelical, mendicant preachers, stories about bandits were used to stress the inclusiveness of God's love for all sinners and the ever-present possibility of redemption. Indeed it could be said that these principles stood at the origin of Christianity in the story of the good thief redeemed at Christ's crucifixion. But this redemptive figuration of the bandit raised problems and tensions with other attitudes. One problem was that it seemed to sanction the postponement of confession and repentance until the latest possible moment. Collections of *exempla*, by including stories that specifically take up this issue, signal that lay people (mis)understood bandit tales in this way. Second, this attitude to bandits contrasted with the attitude in *exempla* and other literature to thieves, who are seen as infinitely inventive, uncatchable pests who can be foiled only through their own quarrelsomeness and struck down only through divine intervention. A third problem was the evident tension between mendicant and secular attitudes to bandits and outlaws: governments sought to extirpate bandits, not redeem them, while local society possibly supported them in their wrong-doing through a sense of social solidarity (as once propounded by Eric Hobsbawm).[32]

It is one of the claims of the comparative method that it allows the discovery of new insights into old problems. A comparative study of bandit literature has enabled just such new insight. The eyes of English social and literary historians have been trained on two main issues in addressing the *Gest of Robin Hood*: the 'original' audience, and the correspondences between literary outlaws and their real counterparts. They have looked neither to religious literature, nor to modern literary theory to open up new paths of understanding. Narratology and intertextuality help us to perceive not only the shared narrative elements of the three stories we have examined, but also suggest the connections that the medieval audiences would have made between them.

Notes

1. Giovanni Boccaccio, *The Decameron*, trans. G.H. McWilliam (Harmondsworth, 1972), pp. 737–42; R.B. Dobson and J. Taylor, *The Rymes of Robin Hood: An Introduction to the English Outlaw*, 3rd edn (Stroud, 1997), pp. 79–88.
2. R. Kaeuper, 'An historian's reading of *The Tale of Gamelyn*', *Medium Aevum* 52 (1983). J. Scattergood, '*The Tale of Gamelyn*: the noble robber as provincial

hero', in *Readings in Medieval English Romance*, ed. C.M. Meale (Cambridge, 1994) adds little.

3. Kaeuper, 'An historian's reading of *The Tale of Gamelyn*', p. 52.

4. For the activities of the Folville gang, see E. Stones, 'The Folvilles of Ashby-Folville, Leics., and their associates in crime, 1326–47', *Transactions of the Royal Hist. Society* 7 (1957).

5. R.H. Hilton, 'The origins of Robin Hood', *Past and Present* 14 (1958); J.C. Holt, 'The origins and audience of the ballads of Robin Hood', *Past and Present* 18 (1960); M.H. Keen, 'Robin Hood, peasant or gentleman?', *Past and Present* 19 (1961); J. Bellamy, *Robin Hood: An Historical Enquiry* (London and Sydney, 1985), for which see the review by J.C. Holt in *Albion* 18 (1986), pp. 79–80; J.R. Maddicott, 'The birth and setting of the ballads of Robin Hood', *English Historical Review* 93 (1978).

6. Hilton, 'Origins of Robin Hood'; Holt, 'Origins and audience'; R. Tardif, 'The "mistery" of Robin Hood: a new social context for the texts', in *Robin Hood: An Anthology of Scholarship and Criticism*, ed. S. Knight (Cambridge, 1999).

7. R. Almond and A.J. Pollard, 'The yeomanry of Robin Hood and social terminology in fifteenth-century England', *Past and Present* 170 (2001).

8. B.A. Hanawalt, 'Ballads and bandits: fourteenth-century outlaws and the Robin Hood poems', in *Robin Hood: An Anthology of Scholarship and Criticism*, p. 265.

9. P.R. Coss, 'Aspects of cultural diffusion in medieval England: the early romances, local society and Robin Hood', *Past and Present* 108 (1985), pp. 70–2.

10. Dobson and Taylor, *Rymes of Robin Hood*, pp. xxi–ii, 11–15.

11. D. Gray, 'The Robin Hood poems', *Poetica* 18 (1984), and now in *Robin Hood: An Anthology of Scholarship and Criticism*, p. 34.

12. Hilton, 'Origins of Robin Hood', p. 31.

13. E. Fox-Genovese, 'Literary criticism and the politics of the New Historicists', in *The New Historicism*, ed. H.A. Veeser (New York and London, 1989), p. 217.

14. *The Exempla or Illustrative Stories from the Sermones Vulgares of Jacques de Vitry*, ed. T.F. Crane (London, 1890), pp. 29–30.

15. C. Delcorno, 'Metamorfosi boccacciane dell' "Exemplum"', in *Exemplum e letteratura tra Medioevo e Rinascimento* (Bologna, 1989), p. 284.

16. *Die Fragmente der Libri VIII Miraculorum des Caesarius von Heisterbach*, ed. A. Meister (Rome, 1901), pp. 191–3; F.C. Tubach, *Index exemplorum: A Handbook of Medieval Religious Tales* (Helsinki, 1969), no. 4781.

17. *Anecdotes historiques, légendes et apologues tirés du recueil inédit d'Etienne de Bourbon*, ed. A. Lecoy de la Marche (2 vols, Paris, 1877), no. 119, I, p. 103; J. Klapper, *Erzählungen des Mittelalters* (Breslau, 1914), nos 186, 196, pp. 384–7, 400–1.

18. For example: G.D. Guyon, 'La justice pénale dans le théâtre religieux du XIVe siècle: Les Miracles de Notre Dame par personnages', *RHDF* 69 (1991).

19. *Anecdotes . . . Etienne de Bourbon*, no. 26, I, pp. 33–4; Klapper, *Erzählungen*, p. 387; *Caesarii Heisterbacensis monachi ordinins Cisterciensis Dialogus miraculorum*, ed. J. Strange (2 vols, Cologne, 1851), vol. I, p. 135 (III.19).

20. 'A Gest of Robin Hood', I.10, in Dobson and Taylor, *Rymes of Robin Hood*, p. 79.

21. S.H. Rigby, *English Society in the Later Middle Ages: Class, Status and Gender* (Basingstoke, 1995), p. 251.

22. Gray, 'The Robin Hood poems', p. 27
23. *Caesarii Heisterbacensis... Dialogus miraculorum*, I, p. 377 (VI.24); *La scala coeli de Jean Gobi*, ed. M-A. Polo di Beaulieu (Paris, 1991), nos 545, 547, 548, pp. 401–2; *Les fabulistes latins*, ed. L. Hervieux (4 vols, Paris), IV, pp. 222–3, no. 51a; *Anecdotes... Etienne de Bourbon*, nos 205, 369, I, pp. 178–9, 324–5.
24. *Anecdotes... Etienne de Bourbon*, no. 429, I, p. 273; *Liber exemplorum ad usum praedicantium*, ed. A.G. Little (Aberdeen, 1908), p. 33, no. 55; *La Tabula exemplorum secundum ordinem alphabeti. Recueil d'exempla compilé en France à la fin du XIIIe siècle*, ed. J.T. Welter (Paris, 1926), p. 61, no. 225; *Caesarii Heisterbacensis... Dialogus miraculorum*, II, pp. 233–4 (X. 21).
25. *Anecdotes... Etienne de Bourbon*, nos 425, 515, I, pp. 369–70, 444–5.
26. *Oeuvres complètes de Eustache Deschamps*, V, pp. 291–2 (Ballade 1022).
27. T. Todorov, *Grammaire du Décaméron* (The Hague and Paris, 1969), pp. 9–10.
28. S. Greenblatt, *Renaissance Self-Fashioning: From More to Shakespeare* (Chicago and London, 1980), p. 5.
29. C. Brémond, J. Le Goff and J-C. Schmitt, *L' "Exemplum"* (Turnhout, 1982), pp. 111–143.
30. D. LaCapra, *History and Criticism* (Ithaca and London, 1985), pp. 125–31.
31. W. Iser, *The Act of Reading: A Theory of Aesthetic Response* (London, 1978), pp. 53–83.
32. E.J. Hobsbawm, *Bandits* (Harmondsworth, 1969).

CONCLUSION

A t the end of his book on crime in early modern England, Jim Sharpe drew up a sort of balance sheet of the continuities and changes in crime and the criminal law in his period. Among continuities he noted that the pattern of serious crime varied very little, either across time or between urban and rural areas; that England continued to rely on unpaid amateur local officials; that the system of law itself was an unbroken thread across the centuries; and that the selectivity of its application was, likewise, unchanging. Among differences, he listed the criminalisation of the poor and changes in the pattern of punishment: on the one hand, shaming punishments declined, hangings decreased in number, and there was a harder line against out-of-court settlements, while on the other the 'house of correction' was born, which incarcerated criminal convicts sentenced to hard labour.[1]

It is disconcerting to find some of the same elements of continuity and change evident in the period of this book too. Our period sees the creation of some of the very continuities that Sharpe observes: for example, in England, the reliance on unpaid judicial officers such as the Justice of the Peace. The selective application of punishment is also a clear feature, found in the treatment of rapists in Venice or in the hanging of a certain type of male offender. As for changes, vagabondage was, in the post-plague period, associated with crime and to some extent criminalised. Some shaming punishments, such as the 'race' for adulterers in southern France, declined. Public executions decreased in number in the fifteenth century. Kings and governments tried to curtail out-of-court action whether in the form of private revenge or composition. Imprisonment was a small but growing part of the repertoire of penalties.

This sharing of continuities and changes across the normal dividing line of late medieval and early modern to some extent deprives both periods of their distinctiveness. Other changes reinstate the boundaries, for example the transition in the late fifteenth or early sixteenth century to greater princely use of judicial 'terror' and the more elaborate staging of public execution as a spectacle of power. The fifteenth century also seems to witness a more impatient state attitude to sanctuary and clerical immunities, and a gradual fading of the imperative of revenge under the triple assault of the law, the Church and more civilised ideals of behaviour.

At the other end of our period, in the late twelfth and early thirteenth centuries, we see the emergence and application of new methods of trial that solved the withdrawal of the ordeal as a mode of proof. Obviously, not all of these changes apply to all of the geographical areas considered in this book, but together they constitute what is, at the same time, the beginnings of the modern penal system and a distinctive period of coexistence of the modern and the pre-modern: of public and private prosecution of crime; of trial and punishment by the state, and private revenge and composition; of salaried public officials and widespread gift-giving; of offences that were both crimes and sins and might be dealt with as either. It is perhaps this pattern of coexistences that give the late medieval period its peculiar character.

Note

1. J.A. Sharpe, *Crime in Early Modern England, 1550–1750* (London, 1984), pp. 170–82.

BIBLIOGRAPHICAL NOTE

$$\text{❦}$$

A s I have provided quite full notes to each chapter, I shall take the opportunity of this bibliographical note to give a *tour d'horizon* of recent contributions to the study of criminal law, justice and crime in the later medieval period, and to point readers to particular authors who are most rewarding.

This book was conceived with its own structure and argument, but in the writing it has in part become an English-language response to key researches and syntheses published in French in the 1990s. So the works of four French historians must be given pride of place. Only these works in French have even attempted the sort of coverage aimed at in this book, though they mostly fall short of this book's range. Nicole Gonthier has published two works of synthesis, one on punishment, the other on violence in towns in the Middle Ages: *Le châtiment du crime au Moyen Age* (Rennes, 1998) and *Cris de haine et rites d'unité: La violence dans les villes, XIIIe–XVIe siècle* (n.p., 1992). Both are valuable for their clear structures and for their combination of evidence from chronicles and archives. However, though they occasionally look outside France for material, they are both heavily dependent on the two cities where Gonthier has done archival research, namely Lyon and Dijon. Something of the same problem affects H. Zaremska's book on exiles, *Les bannis au Moyen Age* (Paris, 1996). This work was first published in Warsaw in 1994. Again, there is an attempt at European coverage, though the book's strength is its discussion of Polish material. The third author in this French catalogue is Claude Gauvard. Her two-volume study of royal pardons in the reign of Charles VI, *'De grace especial': Crime, état et société en France à la fin du Moyen Age* (Paris, 1991), is a masterpiece, and attentive readers of my footnotes will recognise how much I am endebted to her. This work is special because it is so much broader than its title: it is a history, informed by sociology and anthropology, of law, justice, crime and power in the French late medieval state; and it makes suggestive points of contact with France's neighbours. The work is not without faults, as some reviewers have pointed out,[1] but it remains essential and stimulating reading. Part of one chapter of this work has been translated in the collection of essays edited by B.A. Hanawalt and D. Wallace, *Medieval Crime and Social Control* (Minneapolis and London, 1999).

Lastly, Anne Porteau-Bitker, though she has produced no general book, has written numerous articles on a variety of aspects of criminal justice, for example, imprisonment, rape and women: 'L'emprisonnement dans le droit laïque du Moyen Age', *RHDF* 46 (1968); 'Criminalité et délinquance féminines dans le droit pénal des XIIIe et XIVe siècles', *RHDF* 58 (1980); 'La justice laïque et le viol au Moyen Age', *RHDF* 66 (1988). These articles are based solidly on surveys of law and custom and move from these to look at cases and individuals.

In English, the works of Andrew Finch, principally on Normandy, are very helpful, for example, 'Women and violence in the later Middle Ages: the evidence of the officiality of Cerisy', *Continuity and Change* 7 (1992); 'The nature of violence in the Middle Ages: an alternative perspective', *Historical Research* 70 (1997).

Among Italian historians, the one who has done most to advance the study of crime is Andrea Zorzi. In the interests of balance I have not been able to use as many of his publications as I might have liked. Although his work has focused on Florence in the fourteenth and fifteenth centuries, it also includes many comparative insights. A list of his main publications can be found in some of his recent studies, such as his survey of Italian penal policy in *Crime, histoire et sociétés* 2:2 (1998). It is worth singling out his historiographical survey ('Giustizia criminale e criminalità nell'Italia del tardo medioevo: studi e prospettive di ricerca', *Società e storia* 46 (1989)), and his pieces on, respectively, executions, corruption, judicial office and the judicial system: 'I fiorentini e gli uffici pubblici nel primo Quattrocento: concorrenza, abusi, illegalità', *Quaderni storici* 66 (1987); 'Giusdicenti e operatori di giustizia nello stato territoriale fiorentino del XV secolo', *Ricerche storiche* 19 (1989); *L'amministrazione della giustizia penale nella repubblica fiorentina: aspetti e problemi* (Florence, 1988). For English readers, a piece summarising many of his main arguments was translated in *Crime, Society and the Law in Renaissance Italy*, ed. T. Dean and K.J.P. Lowe (Cambridge, 1994). This latter volume serves as a good introduction to recent research, and should be read alongside *Violence and Civil Disorder in Italian Cities, 1200–1500*, ed. L. Martines (Berkeley, 1972). In English, several articles by American scholars are particularly useful for the cities of late medieval Tuscany: W.M. Bowsky, 'The medieval commune and internal violence: police power and public safety in Siena, 1287–1355', *American Historical Review* 73 (1967); M.B. Becker, 'Changing patterns of violence and justice in fourteenth and fifteenth-century Florence', *Comparative Studies in Society and History* 18 (1976); S. Cohn, 'Criminality and the state in Renaissance Florence', *Journal of Social History* 14 (1980). Sam Cohn's many other publications have many sections on violent crime, for example two chapters of his *Women in the Streets: Essays on Sex and Power in Renaissance Italy* (Baltimore, 1996). Zorzi's work on Florence may also be contrasted to work on Venice by Crouzet-Pavan, Ruggiero and Chojnacki: E. Crouzet-Pavan, 'Recherches sur la nuit vénitienne à la fin du moyen âge', *Journal of Medieval History* 7 (1981); *'Sopra le acque salse': Espaces, pouvoir et société à Venise à la fin du Moyen Age* (Rome, 1992), ch. 12; G. Ruggiero, *Violence in Early Renaissance Venice* (New Brunswick, 1980); *The Boundaries of Eros: Sex Crime and Sexuality in Renaissance Venice* (New York and Oxford, 1985); and S. Chojnacki, 'Crime, punishment and the Trecento Venetian state', in *Violence and Civil Disorder in Italian Cities, 1200–1500*, ed. L. Martines (Berkeley, 1972).

For England, an essential starting point remains F. Pollock and F.W. Maitland, *The History of English law before the Time of Edward I* (2nd edn, Cambridge, 1968), although Maitland's style is probably now indigestible to undergraduate students and some of his views have been superseded by modern research, for which see H. Summerson, 'Maitland and the criminal law in the age of *Bracton*', *Proceedings of the British Academy* 89 (1996). Among more modern authors, several have been especially prolific or inventive. J.G. Bellamy has written numerous wide-ranging surveys and monographs, starting with *The Law of Treason in England in the Later Middle Ages* (Cambridge, 1970), and continuing with *Crime and Public Order in England in the later Middle Ages* (London, 1973) and *Criminal Law and Society in Late medieval and Tudor England* (Gloucester and New York, 1984). His later book on Robin Hood, however (*Robin Hood: An Historical Enquiry* [London, 1985]), has been sharply criticised: see, for example, the review by J.C. Holt in *Albion* 18 (1986), pp. 79–80. B.A. Hanawalt, 'Violent death in fourteenth- and early fifteenth-century England', *Comparative Studies in Society and History* 18 (1976); 'Fur-collar crime: the pattern of crime among the fourteenth-century English nobility', *Journal of Social History* 8 (1975); 'The female felon in fourteenth-century England', *Viator* 5 (1974) and *Crime and Conflict in English Communities, 1300–1348* (Cambridge, Mass., 1979). But, reader beware, her use of sources has been criticised: see C. Smith, 'Medieval coroners' rolls: legal fiction or historical fact?', in *Courts, Counties and the Capital in the Later Middle Ages*, ed. D.E.S. Dunn (Stroud, 1996); and the reviews by A. Harding in *American Journal of Legal History* 25 (1981), pp. 69–70, and J. Given in *Speculum* 56 (1981), pp. 139–40. Another series of stimulating articles have come from Henry Summerson, 'The structure of law enforcement in thirteenth-century England', *American Journal of Legal History* 23 (1979); and 'Crime and society in medieval Cumberland', *Transactions of the Cumberland and Westmorland Anti-*

quarian and Archaeological Society 82 (1982); 'Enforcement of the Statute of Winchester, 1285–1327', *Journal of Legal History* 13 (1992) and 'The criminal underworld of medieval England, *Journal of Legal History* 17 (1996).

Journals: As is apparent from the references so far, a large number of journals are likely to carry articles in the area of criminal law, crime and punishment. As well as the *Journal of Social History* and *Comparative Studies in Society and History*, three journals are worth mentioning. The first is *Past and Present*, which has carried the important Robin Hood debate in the year around 1960 (see above, p. 160, for references) and Lawrence Stone's famous article 'Interpersonal violence in English society, 1300–1980' in vol. 101, 1983 (with a response from J. Sharpe in vol. 108, 1985). More recently it has published D. Smail, 'Common violence: vengeance and inquisition in fourteenth-century Marseille', 150 (1996), as well as my own 'Marriage and mutilation: vendetta in late-medieval Italy', 157 (1997). The *Journal of Legal History* has, since its inception in 1980, published a small group of useful articles on private justice (vol. 4, 1983), informers (vol. 5, 1984), rape (vol. 9, 1988) and execution (vol. 16, 1995), as well as the two articles by Summerson referred to above. The first three volumes of the *Law and History Review* contained a striking number of impressive pieces on the Middle Ages: Carpenter on English law and justice, Blanshei on Bologna and Perugia, Helmholz on the Church courts, Powell on the arbitration of disputes, Miller on bloodfeud in Iceland and England, and Post on 'approvers'. Unfortunately, but understandably, later volumes did not keep up this pace, as an interest in early modern and modern England and North America took over. Nevertheless, this journal does still occasionally carry interesting medieval pieces, for example Ikins Stern on Florentine inquisition procedure in vol. 8 (1990) and Musson on juries in vol. 15 (1997). Finally, *Criminal Justice History*, though its main focus too lies in later and American history, has published an article on Bologna by Blanshei (vol. 2, 1981), one on fourteenth-century England by Post (vol. 7, 1986) and a useful survey by Rousseau (vol. 14, 1993).

Note

1. See the reviews by Hanawalt, in *Speculum*, 69 (1994), pp. 776–7, and by Auzary, in *Revue historique*, 289 (1993), pp. 213–15.

INDEX